# DATE DUE

| | | | |
|---|---|---|---|
| | | | |
| | | | |
| | | | |
| | | | |
| | | | |
| | | | |
| | | | |
| | | | |
| | | | |
| | | | |
| | | | |
| | | | |
| | | | |
| | | | |
| | | | |
| | | | |
| | | | |
| | | | |

DEMCO 38-296

# UNDERSTANDING
# AMERICAN BUSINESS
# JARGON

# UNDERSTANDING AMERICAN BUSINESS JARGON

## A Dictionary

*W. Davis Folsom*

GREENWOOD PRESS
Westport, Connecticut • London

**Library of Congress Cataloging-in-Publication Data**

Folsom, W. Davis.
    Understanding American business jargon : a dictionary / W. Davis
Folsom.
       p.    cm.
    Includes bibliographical references.
    ISBN 0–313–29991–9 (alk. paper)
      1. Business—Dictionaries. I. Title.
    HF1001.F65  1997
    650′.03—dc21      96–50211

British Library Cataloguing in Publication Data is available.

Library of Congress Catalog Card Number: 96–50211
ISBN: 0–313–29991–9

First published in 1997

Greenwood Press, 88 Post Road West, Westport, CT 06881
An imprint of Greenwood Publishing Group, Inc.

Printed in the United States of America

The paper used in this book complies with the
Permanent Paper Standard issued by the National
Information Standards Organization (Z39.48–1984).

10 9 8 7 6 5 4 3 2 1

*To my wife and best friend, Kathy*

# CONTENTS

# PREFACE

This book is designed to assist business people and students with the confusing and continually changing realm of American business English. Regardless of how you feel about it, global business has become a reality, and American business presence can be observed throughout the world. A few years ago, U.S. troops entering Somalia were greeted by young people cheering "Michael Jackson!" During the Gulf War the Saudi Arabian government restricted movement and interaction of American soldiers so its society would not be "corrupted" by American ideas. The sixteenth-century royal palace in Kirktipur, a village in the Kathmandu Valley in Nepal, has a large Coca-Cola sign hanging from it. In his book *Video Night in Kathmandu*, Pico Ivy depressingly describes seeing the movie *Rambo* dubbed in five South Asian languages. Trade treaties like NAFTA try to protect "cultural industries," but American companies, celebrities, and brands are recognized everywhere.

With this influence in the global marketplace comes the use of American business jargon. The major business media journalists in the United States are generally careful either not to use jargon terms or to explain them when used. But the headline writers for print media and business people interviewed by journalists use an abundance of jargon.

My interest in business jargon began innocently enough. A few years ago I walked into a classroom about one minute late. In the back row sat a group of four young men I knew well from previous classes. Walking by, I read the lips of one student saying, "Oh ——! He *is* here!" To which I replied, "How is my Group W Bench today?" The students smiled, but their expressions told me they did not know what I meant. Reaching the front of the classroom I asked if anyone could explain the meaning of "Group W Bench." No one knew. I offered a little extra credit to the first student who could answer the question. The next day a student came to my office and correctly identified the origin of the phrase.* When I asked how he found it, he confessed that his friend had told him but that he had started by looking in the business and economics dictionaries in the library. This got me wondering how often I used phrases, terms, and analogies that are not familiar to my audience, and it stimulated my interest and research into business jargon.

From this story it should be clear that the author is not a lexicographer but instead a business professor with interest and experience in business communication. This dictionary is a compilation of business terms and expressions, and also of everyday American English phrases that are frequently used in the business environment. Native-born Americans use so much jargon that they are often not even aware that they are using it. Only when interacting with English-speaking foreigners do many Americans become conscious of their speech. Even then it is often difficult to limit the use of jargon. This can lead to many humorous experiences, but in a business setting, miscommunication can be costly. Take for example the two sayings *on the table* and *table an issue*. The first means something is open for discussion or debate, while the second means that discussion will be deferred to a later time. Imagine the misunderstandings that can be created by the use of jargon in business negotiations.

As any student of languages recognizes, languages constantly change. Sports, the military, government, science, and, today, technology are all sources of new words and phrases. It is difficult to keep up with changes in language and jargon. With the Internet providing global communication, the pace of change and the need for better understanding of English as used by American business people is greater than ever. Sample material from this book is available on the Internet at <http://www.usca.sc.edu/folsom/jargon.html>. Please send me your questions or suggestions for future editions.

---

*"Group W Bench" is a phrase from Arlo Guthrie's 1967 antiwar ballad *Alice's Restaurant Massacre*, referring to grouping of inductees who might be "unfit" for military service.

# ACKNOWLEDGMENTS

Many kind people contributed to this book. First, I would like to thank USCA students Kim Pressley, Pam Digesare, Jodi Redd, Thomas Fuss, John Dotson, Chris Walden, Tara Green, Audra Smith, and Joe Tucker, for their business jargon contributions. Second, I want to thank friends and colleagues who also contributed to this dictionary, including Julianne Morgan, Tom and Betty Pritchett, Jami and Leah Martin, Chet and Mary Grace Allenchey, Brendon Hanna, Brian and Gae Chilla, Robert Botsch, Murray Kaplan, Al Beyer, and Jerry and Faye Rosenthal.

I want especially to thank my mother Myrtle Folsom for proofreading this book, and my wife Kathy and son Bradley for tolerating with humor the many times I lapsed into jargonese instead of English while working on this book!

# STYLISTIC GUIDE

**Abbreviations**    Common business jargon abbreviations are included in the dictionary.

**Acronyms**    A separate list of acronyms is included at the end of the dictionary.

**Alphabetization**    Because so many business jargon terms are multi-word phrases, all terms are alphabetized by letter rather than word.

**Brackets**    Brackets indicate clarifying information provided by the author with quotations.

**Cross-references**    The reader is directed to synonyms and related terms in the dictionary. Terms that appear within an entry and are themselves main entries in the dictionary are designated in all capital letters. Those that are acronyms (which would ordinarily be capitalized) are specially designated with an asterisk.

**Examples**    A unique feature of this dictionary is the frequent use of business jargon as used in American media. The examples were selected to provide added understanding of the term and of the context within which business jargon is frequently encountered.

**Parentheses**          Parentheses are used for three purposes: to indicate
                         acronyms; to indicate the origin of a term or phrase; and
                         to include introductory or concluding words or phrases
                         that may accompany an entry.

**Semicolons**           Semicolons are used in definitions to indicate two or
                         more distinctly different meanings of a term or phrase.

# UNDERSTANDING AMERICAN BUSINESS JARGON

# A

**AAA.** American Automobile Association; top rating given by U.S. bond rating services.

**ABOVE AND BEYOND.** More than required.

**ABOVE BOARD.** Visible; honest.
"Wegerd president Leonard Greer insists everything is above board. The SEC* and state regulators are investigating." (*Forbes*, Oct. 10, 1994, p. 42)

**ACCELERATION PRINCIPLE.** Hypothesis that investment varies with the rate of change in aggregate demand. First introduced by John M. Clark in 1917, the principle was developed to explain the large variations in investment over the course of a business cycle. Keynes incorporated the acceleration principle into his General Theory.

**ACCOUNTABLE.** Responsible for.

**ACCOUNTING INFORMATION SYSTEMS (AIS).** Computerized information retrieval systems.

"While a convenience to experienced professionals, jargon can form a language barrier that is a formidable obstacle to newcomers. This is perhaps as much the case for accounting and information systems (AIS) professionals as it is for doctors, lawyers, or engineers." (*The CPA Journal*, Sept. 1993, p. 80)

**ACE.** Expert; to achieve a perfect score.

**ACE IN THE HOLE/UP YOUR SLEEVE.** Hidden advantage.
"Sears' strategic ace-in-the-hole with its Visa co-brand is one of research." (*Brandweek*, Nov. 6, 1995, p. 8)

**ACID TEST.** Final, decisive test; proof.
"Seven 'acid tests' of whether personnel was making an effective business contribution were discussed at the conference on restructuring business: The HR* contribution." (*People Management*, May 4, 1995, p. 18)

**ACID TEST RATIO/QUICK RATIO.** Financial test of solvency comparing a firm's liquid assets and liabilities.

**ACROSS THE BOARD.** Equal for everyone.
"Menu adoptions come as the industry tries to lift itself out of rampant value pricing, which has depressed margins across the board." (*Advertising Age*, Feb. 12, 1996, p. 12)

**ACT IN CONCERT (TO).** Work together.
"U.S. insurers and reinsurers also should act in concert with state and federal governments to prepare for catastrophes in the U.S." (*Business Insurance*, Jan. 17, 1994, p. 13)

**ACTION ITEMS.** To-do list.
"ACB [American Community Bankers] is actively seeking to implement a number of action items specified by the partnership to help families become homeowners." (*American Banker*, Oct. 25, 1995, p. 8A)

**AD INFINITUM.** Until infinity (Latin).

**ADJUSTED GROSS INCOME (AGI).** A measure of personal income used by the INTERNAL REVENUE SERVICE. AGI includes all sources of personal income minus allowances for contributions to INDIVIDUAL RETIREMENT ACCOUNTS, KEOGH PLANS, alimony payments, and other adjustments.

**AD-LIB   (TO).** Improvise.

"Dailey & Associates, which handles the Southern California Ford regional marketing effort and coordinated the campaign, encouraged the disc jockeys to ad-lib teaser spots talking about the event and to give their impressions to listeners." (*Advertising Age*, March 14, 1994, p. 12)

**ADMINISTERED PRICES.** Prices controlled by government.

**ADMINISTRIVIA.** All the trivial activities and reports required by administrators.

"As a project manager, I thoroughly enjoy the responsibility of coaching, supporting and managing people and projects but then there is the administrivia." (Mary Grace Allenchey, AT&T, 1996)

**AD NAUSEUM.** To the point of making people sick (Latin).

**ADOPTION PROCESS.** The steps consumers go through in accepting a new product, including awareness, interest, evaluation, trial, and rejection or adoption.

**AD VALOREM.** Value-added (Latin).

**AFFIRMATIVE ACTION.** Policies to address and redress employment discrimination.

"While the swirling debate over affirmative action focuses on getting minorities and women in the door, companies such as Polaroid Corp. are taking a longer view." (*Business Week*, Aug. 14, 1995, p. 60)

**AFFORDABILITY INDEX.** National Association of Realtors' index measuring housing costs in different regions of the United States.

**AFTER MARKET.** Market for stock after its initial offering; market for maintenance materials and parts.

**AGE THE ACCOUNTS (TO).** Arrange accounts in order of the dates they are due.

**AGING SCHEDULE/THE AGING.** A list of accounts receivable in order of how many days they are past due. The aging schedule is used by lenders when considering loans to businesses.

**AIR (TO).** Broadcast on television or radio.

**AIR IT OUT (TO).** Discuss openly (football).

**AIR ONE'S DIRTY LINEN/LAUNDRY.** Talk about one's problems.

**AIR TIME.** Broadcast time on television or radio.

"This year 30 seconds of air time on the Super Bowl will cost $1.2 million, a $300,000 increase over last year." (*Marketing News*, March 13, 1995, p. 15)

**ALL EARS.** Very eager; listening intently.

**ALL HELL BROKE LOOSE.** Things got out of control.

**ALL OR NONE (AON).** Stock market order prohibiting partial sales or purchases.

**ALL-OUT.** Full effort, holding nothing back.

**ALMA MATER.** Nourishing mother (Latin); school from which a person graduated.

**ALPHABET STOCK.** Categories of stock within a larger corporation. For example, General Motors has GM "E" shares, which represent ownership interest in GM's Electronic Data Systems division.

**ALPHA GEEK.** A firm's technology expert.

**ALSO-RAN.** Loser; a product or person who is not among the most successful.

**AMBULANCE CHASER.** Lawyer who specializes in personal injury claims; unethical lawyer.

"Frightened insureds are inviting prey for ambulance-chasers and industry-bashers. These rumor-mongers build on this distrust by citing horror stories about insurers who force weak, destitute insureds into quick claims settlements for amounts far less than what the insureds were rightfully due." (*American Agent and Broker*, July 1994, p. 6)

**AMERICAN DEPOSITORY RECEIPT (ADR).** Certificate backed by shares of a foreign company.

"ADRs are negotiable registered certificates issued by American depositories in the names of particular foreign entities, usually foreign corporations." (*CPA Journal*, July 1995, p. 70)

**AMERICAN DREAM.** Widely held perception that each generation of Americans will be better off than the previous generation.

**AMERICANS WITH DISABILITIES ACT (ADA).** 1992 federal legislation requiring businesses to provide greater access for customers and also accommodation for employees with special needs.

**AMPED.** Excited; high-energy.
"We're amped, we're pumped, we're ready." (John Wannemacher, Irwin Publishing, 1996)

**ANCHOR (TO)/ANCHOR TENANT.** The largest, best known tenant in a shopping mall; to hold in place.
"A recent modernization and lobby make over were instrumental in attracting an anchor tenant, the Topps Company, an entertainment and sweets company." (*Buildings*, April 1995, p. 46)

**ANGELS.** Investors in start-up companies who contribute a small amount of capital and provide advice to the new entrepreneur.
"The increasing role of friends and acquaintances—dubbed 'angels' in SILICON VALLEY—provides a new funding spigot and means that some ideas that traditional venture capitalists would have spurned can now get off the ground." (*Wall Street Journal*, May 20, 1996, p. B1)

**ANOINTED.** Chosen by top company executives (biblical).
"An era is coming to a close as Helen Gurley Brown begins a farewell tour as editor in chief of Hearst Corp.'s *Cosmopolitan*, but the 18-month transition to the anointed Bonnie Fuller may not end up being that long." (*Advertising Age*, Jan. 22, 1996, p. 4)

**ANTE BELLUM.** Before the war (Latin).

**ANTE UP (TO)** Pay up.
"After seeing declining prices and flat demand for half a year, polyvinyl chloride (PVC) producers are betting that market conditions have changed enough that their customers will ante up another 4 cents per pound." (*Chemical Marketing Reporter*, Jan. 15, 1996, p. 5)

**ANTI-NUKE.** Someone opposed to nuclear weapons or energy.

**A-OK.** Operating smoothly (the early NASA program).

**A 180.** An about-face, a complete reversal.
"Assistant Attorney General Anne Bingaman will reveal an enforcement agenda that represents a 180-degree turn from the anti-trust policy that has reigned for the past 15 years." (*Business Week*, March 7, 1994, p. 64)

**APPLE POLISH (TO).** Flatter; BROWN-NOSE.

**ARCHIE BUNKER.** A bigoted lower-class American; REDNECK. Archie (played by Carroll O'Connor) was a character in the *All in the Family* television series.

**ARM AND A LEG.** Expensive.

**ARMCHAIR GENERAL/QUARTERBACK.** Critic who does not have experience in the area he or she is critizing; know-it-all.

**ARMPIT.** A very undesirable place.

**ARMS-LENGTH TRANSACTION.** Transaction that complies with the legal requirements to avoid any conflict of interests. See CHINESE WALL.

**AS IS.** Sold with no warranty. Most used products are sold as is.

**ASLEEP AT THE SWITCH.** Not awake; not focused on one's duties (early U.S. railroad era).
    "The company's current troubles date back to the 1980s, when it fell asleep at the switch, letting upstart rivals cut into lucrative parts of the business." (*Barron's*, Aug. 7, 1995, p. 23)

**ASSET PLAY.** Takeover of a company whose assets are undervalued on the balance sheet.

**ASSET STRIPPER.** A CORPORATE RAIDER who buys a company intending to sell all or most of the company's prized assets to pay off the debt incurred in purchasing the company. An asset stripper calculates that the remaining parts of the company will be valuable.

**ASS-KISSER.** One who flatters superiors. See also BROWN-NOSE.

**ATTENTION, INTEREST, DESIRE, AND ACTION (AIDA).** Marketer's concept of consumer's mental buying process, including the stages of Attention, Interest, Desire, and Action.

**AT THE MARKET.** At the current market price.

**AT THE OPEN.** Stock market order to buy or sell at the first traded price.

**ATTRIT.** Abbreviation for "attrition." To attrit is to cut back the number of employees slowly by not replacing people who leave the company.

**AUDIT TRAIL.** Accounting method to document the source of a data entry.

**AUNT MILLIE.** Derogatory term for an unsophisticated investor. See also BLUE-HAIRS.

**AX OR AXE (TO).** Terminate from a job; eliminate. See also GIVE THE BOOT.

**AXE TO GRIND (HE/SHE HAS AN).** Something a person is angry or upset about; a personal agenda.

# B

**BABY BELLS.** Nickname for the seven regional telephone companies created with the breakup of AT&T (MA BELL) in 1984.

**BABY BOOMERS.** The first generation of people born in the United States after World War II (1945–1964).

**BABY-BUST GENERATION.** The low-birth-rate generation after BABY BOOMERS.
"Limited expansion is expected over the next 10 years in the U.S. apartment market, primarily due to the middle aging of the population and the modest size of the baby-bust generation." (*National Real Estate Investor*, May 1995, p. 26)

**BACK (TO).** Support financially.

**BACK AGAINST THE WALL.** No place to go; a difficult situation.
"Its [GM's] global sourcing strategy—to buy low-cost, quality components from anywhere in the world—alone puts the union's back against the wall." (*Ward's Auto World*, May 1995, p. 14)

**BACK AT SQUARE ONE.** Starting over.

"Following the Association of Petrochemical Producers in Europe (APPE) steering committee's decision in December 1993 not to proceed with plans to create a $136-million fund that would subsidize the closure of uncompetitive steam crackers, the European petrochemical industry's desperately needed restructuring process is back at square one." (*Chemical Week*, Jan. 5, 1995, p. 6)

**BACK BURNER (ON THE).** Kept in reserve; delay, hold back.

**BACK-DOOR.** Of questionable ethics; dishonest.

"Despite conceding some back-door deals, Delta Air Lines—and 6 other U.S. airlines—have made their $50 cap on travel agent commissions for domestic flights stick." (*Fortune*, May 15, 1995, p. 32)

**BACKFIRE (TO).** Produce results opposite of those expected.

"The chairman-to-be shows signs of carrying on USX's tradition of hard-nosed litigation that sometimes backfires." (*Business Week*, May 15, 1995, p. 47)

**BACKFIRED.** A plan that did not work and hurt the originator.

**BACK IN THE SADDLE AGAIN.** In control again.

**BACKLASH.** A negative reaction.

"Carriers who fail to invest in the proper network technology will face a customer backlash in today's competitive environment." (*America's Network*, Feb. 1, 1996, p. 2)

**BACK OFF (TO).** Slow down; moderate.

"During the U.S. budget negotiations, religious leaders intervened with press conferences and studies to pressure Congress to back off welfare reform." (*Forbes*, Feb. 26, 1996, p. 52)

**BACK OUT OF (TO).** Cancel a deal previously agreed upon.

**BACKSEAT DRIVER.** Constant critic; person giving unwanted advice.

"In creating a testimonial, engineers first need to rid themselves of the current American work ethic of doing the minimum level of service necessary to satisfy the employer. Second, they need to stop being backseat drivers and let the boss know that they support him." (*Broadcast Engineering*, Aug. 1995, p. 16)

**BACK TO THE SALT MINES.** Back to work.

**BAD DEAL.** Poor business transaction.

**BAD-MOUTH (TO).** Be critical of someone who is not present.
"When you get upstairs, continue to frame your efforts as a search for advice, and resist the temptation to bad-mouth your boss." (*Working Woman*, March 1995, p. 66)

**BAD PAPER.** Worthless money or checks.

**BAG OF SNAKES.** A business situation or segment which has been full of unfavorable surprises.

**BAIL OUT (TO).** Sell an investment without regard to the price.
"Many people think of contingency as the plan to bail out or divert the blame." (*Systems Management*, Feb. 1996, p. 47)

**BAILOUT.** Financial support or rescue.
"The timing of last week's bailout offers was hardly coincidental. Rockefeller Group, the borrower, has until September 12 to present a reorganization plan to the bankruptcy court." (*Barron's*, Aug. 21, 1995, p. 35)

**BAIT AND SWITCH.** An unethical sales technique wherein low-priced goods are advertised but not available when customers come to the store.
"Sellers sometimes practice a form of false advertising known as bait and switch. A low-priced good is advertised but replaced by a different good at the showroom." (*Journal of Political Economy*, Aug. 1995, p. 813)

**BAKER'S DOZEN.** Thirteen instead of twelve.

**BALDRIDGE AWARD.** 1988 federal government–sponsored award to companies which excel at improving the quality of their products; named after former Secretary of Commerce Malcolm Baldridge. Corporations sometimes promote the fact that they have won a Baldridge Award in their marketing efforts.

**BALL OF FIRE.** Highly energetic.

**BALLISTIC (TO GO).** Become very angry.
"An executive 'goes ballistic' when he/she explodes and turns irrational in unguided mode." (*Management Today*, March 1993, p. 84)

**BALLOON NOTE.** Loan with a large final payment.

**BALL-PARK ESTIMATE/FIGURE.** A quickly calculated estimate of costs.

"Thus, the result obtained with a specific heuristic can be considered 'good' (i.e., close to optimal) if that result is in the ball park of the result obtained through a maximally different method." (*Decision Support Systems*, Aug. 1995, p. 313)

**BALLS.** Nerve, courage.

**BALONEY.** Nonsense; boastful language.

**BANG FOR THE BUCK.** The most impact or results for one's money.

"Brown tries to get a lot of bang for the buck by not paying too much more than the market for a stock while finding companies with dramatically superior earnings growth and return on equity." (*Fortune*, Aug. 21, 1995, p. 127)

**BANG-UP JOB.** Very good luck.

**BANKROLL (TO).** Finance a business deal; a sum of money.

**BANNER YEAR.** Best year ever.

"Hollywood is having a banner year abroad, while foreign billings for U.S. engineering companies fell 31% from the previous year." (*Business Week*, Sept. 18, 1995, p. 45)

**BAR CODE.** Computerized electronic-scanning label on products.

**BARE-BONE.** Lean; without any extras.

"Cut to the bare-bone in the late 1980s and the early 1990s, corporate/institutional advertising programs that promote the name, image and reputation of the company rather than specific products or services, are undergoing a fundamental rethinking that appears to be positioning the programs for a strong rebound." (*Business Marketing*, Aug. 1994, p. 20)

**BARGAIN-BASEMENT.** Cheap, inexpensive. Macy's department store in New York City was famous for bargains that could be found in its basement store area.

"Considering the demographics of its users and the minimal costs involved in establishing a presence, the Net represents a bargain-basement sales/advertising/public relations medium that distributors should not ignore." (*Industrial Distribution*, Feb. 1996, p. 68)

**BARGAINING CHIP.** Something to be offered.

"Last week, Senate Majority Leader Bob Dole offered auctions of digital spectrum as a billion-dollar bargaining chip in the ongoing budget negotiations with the White House." (*Broadcasting & Cable*, Jan. 8, 1996, p. 4)

**BARKING UP THE WRONG TREE.** Asking or speaking with the wrong person or with someone who has already made his or her decision.

**BARNBURNER.** Exciting contest.

**BAROMETER STOCK.** A stock whose price movements are representative of general market conditions.

**BASELINE.** Parameter against which a project can be evaluated.

**BASH.** Big party. See also SHINDIG.
"At a November 1995 cable TV bash, Barry Diller told the audience that Ted Turner would not get the top job if the Time Warner/Turner Broadcasting deal went through." (*Forbes*, Jan. 1, 1996, p. 18)

**BASIS POINTS.** Fractions of 1 percent. One hundred basis points equals 1 percent.

**BASKET CASE.** A hopeless situation/person.
"By downsizing government, privatizing state-owned industry and pegging its currency to the dollar, Argentina has gone from economic basket case to miracle in just 3 years." (*Financial World*, Feb. 1, 1994, p. 54)

**BAT A THOUSAND (TO).** Be successful every time; in baseball to bat a thousand means to get a hit every time at bat.

**BAT AROUND (TO).** Discuss.

**BATH (TO TAKE A).** Lose a lot of money.

**BATTING AVERAGE.** Percentage of the time one is successful (baseball).
"The U.S.' largest pension funds have accumulated major-league batting averages in selecting top-performing domestic equity and fixed-income money managers during the last 5 years." (*Pensions & Investments*, May 2, 1994, p. 1)

**BE FLAT (TO).** Have sold all. See also WORK-OUT.

**BEAMER.** Nickname for a BMW car.

**BEAN COUNTER.** A low-level clerk; negative reference to an accountant.
"In response to *Management Accounting*'s January 1995 fax survey, readers responded that they were most interested in the articles titled 'What Corporate America wants in Entry-Level Accountants, and 'Shedding the Bean Counter Image.' " (*Management Accounting*, March 1995, p. 18)

**BEAN TOWN.** Boston, Massachusetts.

**BEAR.** Investor who thinks the stock market will decline.
"BULLS and bears make money. Pigs get slaughtered." (Jim Reilly, Robinson-Humphrey Co., 1996)

**BEAR HUG.** The rescue of a company from a hostile takeover by a WHITE KNIGHT.
"The GE bid is what WALL STREET calls a 'bear hug,' an unsolicited takeover offer which the buyer makes public to put pressure on the target company's board of directors." (*Corporate Growth Report*, March 21, 1994, p. 7148)

**BEAT A DEAD HORSE.** Continue to argue/discuss an issue after recognizing that it cannot be resolved.

**BEAT AROUND THE BUSH.** Avoid getting to the point.

**BEATS ME!** I do not know.

**BEAT THE LITTLE GUY.** Take advantage of a smaller competitor.

**BEAT THE BUSHES (TO).** Search everywhere; aggressively market even in rural or unlikely places.
"These discounts invariably attract classic, value-oriented investors who beat the bushes for dollars they can pick up for 80 cents." (*Barron's*, Oct. 23, 1995, p. 35)

**BEEF UP.** Expand, make stronger.
"In a major strategic shift, Prudential Insurance Co. of America is beefing up its money-management business to play an equal role with its huge insurance operations." (*Wall Street Journal*, Nov. 16, 1995, p. A1)

**BEHIND THE EIGHT-BALL.** Under pressure (billiards).

"Companies that do not know what their clients want are starting out behind the eight ball." (*Management Review*, Sept. 1994, p. 10)

**BELL-RINGER.** Exciting, new high; door-to-door salesperson.

**BELLS AND WHISTLES.** Features, details.
"However, everything in the BOX amounts to very little without the applications. Too much time and energy are spent on bells and whistles." (*Journal of Systems Management*, July/Aug. 1995, p. 12)

**BELLWETHER INDUSTRY.** An industry whose performances serve as a leading indicator for the overall economy.
"Minneapolis and St. Paul are often looked to as the bellwether for the managed-care industry." (*Managed Healthcare*, Aug. 1995, p. 37)

**BELLY UP (TO GO).** Bankrupt.
"When an offshore fund goes belly up however, investors can forget about finding recourse on the islands because consumer protection regulations are virtually unknown, except for the most basic anti-fraud rules." (*Futures: The Magazine of Commodities and Options*, Jan. 1994, p. 22)

**BELOW BOOK.** Less than list price; less than the value of a company's assets.
"Corporations selling below book value also make interesting investment prospects." (*Business Week*, Dec. 20, 1994, p. 163)

**BELOW THE BELT.** Nasty; unfair. In boxing, a punch below the belt is illegal and can lead to disqualification.

**BELT-TIGHTENING.** Cost-cutting. See also DOWNSIZING.
"And U.S. companies keep strengthening profits through belt-tightening. Weyerhauser Co. is surging on sky high paper prices, yet it has just asked managers to find $600 million in operating savings over three years." (*Wall Street Journal*, Nov. 22, 1995, p. A1)

**BELTWAY BANDITS.** Consultants working in the Washington, DC area, technically with offices inside the Beltway (Interstate 495 and a section of I-95).

**BENCHMARKING.** Measuring performance by comparing to industry leaders.
"Benchmarking, the continuous process of measuring products, services and practices against those of recognized industry leaders, is without a doubt making a notable contribution to emptyheadedness. In

a word, playing follow the leader in business is the best way to come in second, third or not at all." (*Supervision*, Jan. 1994, p. 3)

**BENCH STRENGTH.** Other personnel available to assist or take over from current leaders (baseball).

"In newly restructured companies, he explains, 'there's no bench strength.'" (*Wall Street Journal*, Sept. 9, 1996, p. A1)

**BENCH WARMER.** A person who is not among the top performers (baseball).

**BETA FACTOR/COEFFICIENT.** Stock market measure of price variability. A statistical measure of the relative risk of a common stock compared with the market for all stocks.

"The conventional wisdom has been that portfolio betas are more stable than those for individual securities." (*Journal of Business Finance and Accounting*, Sept. 1994, p. 909)

**BET THE FARM/RANCH (TO).** Risk everything.

"Derivatives are designed to help companies reduce or hedge market risk exposure. Nonetheless, these financial instruments also offer companies enticing opportunities to bet the farm on which way the market winds will blow interest rates, currency exchange rates, stock prices or commodity prices." (*Oil & Gas Investor*, April, 1995, p. 26)

**BETTING ON THE OUTCOME.** Not knowing the end result but wagering on what one believes it will be.

**BETWEEN A ROCK AND A HARD PLACE.** A difficult situation.

"U.S. prison and prison food services are between a rock and a hard place with overcrowding, and the prevailing tough-on-crime political sentiment." (*Restaurants & Institutions*, March 1, 1995, p. 121)

**BETWEEN JOBS (TO BE).** Unemployed.

**BIBLE BELT.** People of conservative, religious-oriented values. Geographically, the area bounded by Virginia, Florida, and Texas is generally considered the Bible Belt in the United States.

**BIG APPLE.** New York City.

**BIG BITE.** Large amount.

"The legislation is designed to prevent 15 income-tax states from relentlessly pursuing retired citizens into no-tax states and taking a big bite out of tax-deferred retirement accounts." (*Barron*'s, July 3, 1995, p. 32)

**BIG BLUE.** International Business Machines, IBM.

"Just who is 'Big Blue'? For years, it had been the nickname of International Business Machines Corp. But last week IBM legally ceded the name to a Long Island, N.Y. entrepreneur." (*Wall Street Journal*, Nov. 13, 1995, p. B1)

**BIG BOARD.** New York Stock Exchange.

"He believes the BULL MARKET will end in panic-selling so severe that the Big Board will have to temporarily halt trading under a rule enacted after the 1987 crash." (*Business Week*, Aug. 21, 1995, p. 62)

**BIG BROTHER.** Powerful opposing force, usually the government. The term is derived from George Orwell's classic book, *1984*.

" 'The little town of Stillwell is up against big brother,' Mr. Langley says." (*Wall Street Journal*, June 3, 1996, p. A1)

**BIG BUCKS.** Lots of money.

**BIG CHEESE.** Important person.

**BIG D.** Dallas, Texas.

**BIG ENCHILADA.** Significant person.

**BIG FISH/CHEESE.** Important person or company.

"In those days, few people owned stocks. those who did watched the big fish, including Mr. Raskob." (*Wall Street Journal*, Sept. 9, 1996, p. C1)

**BIB LEAGUES.** Important people; large, dominant organizations (baseball).

"During the American Society of Travel Agents international conference in Manila, the Philippines demonstrated to the 500 travel agents in attendance the country's desire to enter the travel-and-tourism big leagues." (*Hotel-Motel Management*, April 3, 1995, p. 4)

**BIG PICTURE.** The overall view of things.

"Beware of executives who feel they have their eye on what they enjoy calling 'the big picture.' . . . It's the boss's view of reality and you can't understand it." (*Supervision*, Jan. 1994, p. 3)

**BIG SIX.** Six largest U.S. accounting firms.

"Leading accountants Ernst & Young have called for an independent regulator of auditors, breaking rank with the remainder of the Big Six which would rather continue with the existing system of self-regulation." (*Management Today*, Aug. 1995, p. 12)

**BIG THREE.** The three largest U.S. automobile manufacturing firms: Ford, General Motors, and Chrysler.

"Despite the effort by Big Three automobile makers to FLESH OUT QS 9000 requirements and make them more understandable, the February 1995 revision falls short." (*Quality*, Aug. 1995, p. 10)

**BIG-TICKET ITEMS.** High-priced goods.

**BIG-TIME SPENDER.** Extravagant consumer.

**BIG WHEEL/SHOT.** Manager; important person; a person who just thinks he or she is important.

**BILLED AS.** Advertised as.

**BIMBO.** An attractive woman not known for her intellect.

"A bimbo is a woman of little brains but possessing other attributes." (Murray Kaplan, Kaplan & Associates, 1996)

**BINGO CARD.** Reader's enquiry card in a magazine.

"A simmering controversy is bubbling to the surface on the roll of bonus leads derived from bingo cards." (*Advertising Age's Business Marketing*, April 1995, p. 1)

**BIRD DOG (TO).** Track down; stay focused on a project.

**BIRDYBACK.** Transportation system using both airplanes and trucks.

**BITCH SESSION.** Meeting where employees express their complaints. Management rarely encourages bitch sessions, but sometimes meetings turn into them.

**BITE THE BULLET (TO).** Go ahead with a difficult task even though it might be expensive.

"And unless providers realize that the old environment has in no way prepared them for the competition ahead—and unless they bite the bullet and do whatever it takes to correct that deficiency—they are not going to succeed." (*Executive Speeches*, Sept. 10, 1994, p. 8)

**BITE THE DUST (TO).** Fail; die.

**BITE YOUR TONGUE (TO).** Be quiet, say nothing.

**BLACKBALL/BLACKLIST (TO).** Refuse to allow someone to work, join, or gain access to a group.

"Broadcasters and studios say they will fight Senator Byron Dorgan's revised TV-violence report card because it would create a violence 'blacklist' for advertisers." (*Mediaweek*, May 15, 1995, p. 8)

**BLACK BOX.** Unknown, complex technology or a situation where decisions are made without full information.

"Technobabble which perpetuates the black box syndrome will not get things done." (*Journal of Systems Management*, July/Aug. 1995, p. 12)

**BLACK HOLE.** A project with significant cost overruns (astronomy).

**BLACK KNIGHT.** Bad guy; initiator of a hostile takeover.

**BLACK MARKET.** Illegal buying and selling of products. See also PARALLEL ECONOMY.

**BLACK MONDAY.** October 19, 1987, when the DOW JONES INDUS-TRIAL AVERAGE fell 508 points, or over 20 percent.

"Hybrid funds suffered the least on Black Monday. It was mostly a stock market crash." (*Financial World*, March 1, 1994, p. 60)

**BLACK TUESDAY.** The October 29, 1929, stock market crash. The stock market crash symbolized the beginning of the Great Depression, though a downturn in the economy had already started.

**BLANK CHECK.** Total freedom of action; money provided without restrictions.

"I doubt that the editors of the Journal make their consumption/savings decisions by handing blank checks to businesses. Yet in exempting defense spending from market forces you would leave sacrosanct the most flagrant violator of the scrutiny of the marketplace." (*Wall Street Journal*, March 10, 1986, p. C22)

**BLANKET (TO).** Cover an area thoroughly and in detail.

"However, with 21 area managers and more than 100 distributors blanketing 54 countries, growth overseas just does not seem as difficult." (*International Business*, Dec. 1994, p. 76).

**BLEED (TO).** Extract large amounts of money from someone.

**BLIND AUCTION.** Sealed-bid auction.

**BLINDSIDE (TO).** Surprise an opponent.

"Some reckon he [President Clinton] might blindside Congress and unilaterally let national banks move into the huge, well-rewarded, and perhaps not-so-risky business of underwriting corporate debt and equities. (*Financial World*, April 25, 1995, p. 48)

**BLIND TRUST.** Financial management agreement wherein the trustee has complete control over investment of funds. Politicians in the United States frequently put their assets in a blind trust in order to avoid a conflict of interest when making government policies that affect business.

**BLISTER THE COMPETITION.** Outsell the other firms in a market.

"This is the way we can blister the competition." (Jami Martin, USC Corp. Nov. 23, 1995)

**BLOCKBUSTER.** A huge success.

"Walt Disney Co. . . . is marketing *Toy Story* as its year-end blockbuster, with licensing deals for spinoff toys and a promotional campaign at Burger King." (*Fortune*, Sept. 18, 1995, p. 154)

**BLOW BY BLOW**. In complete detail (boxing).

**BLOW HOT AND COLD.** Waver, change one's opinion back and forth.

"The official attitude toward foreigners blows hot and cold with the economy." (*Economist*, Dec. 12, 1994, p. 32)

**BLOW-IN.** An advertising piece inserted in but not bound into a magazine.

**BLOW THE WHISTLE (TO).** Attempt to stop something by reporting it to authorities. See also WHISTLE-BLOWER.

**BLUE-BOOK VALUE.** Market value of automobiles. Refers to Kelley's "Blue Book" of automobile prices.

**BLUE-CHIP.** Top quality, highest. In poker, the blue chip is the highest-valued chip.

"With $60 million in annual sales, New York-based Competitive Media Reporting (CMR) is a blue-chip player in advertising research." (*DM News*, June 10, 1996, p. 17)

**BLUE-COLLAR WORKER.** Non-professional employee; laborer. See WHITE-COLLAR.

**BLUE-HAIRS.** Elderly women consumers.

**BLUE LAWS.** Local or state regulations restricting some types of business activities on Sunday. Foreign visitors to the BIBLE BELT are often bemused to find they cannot buy liquor on Sunday in some parts of the region. The term is derived from the nineteenth-century, when "blue" meant drunk or lewd.

**BLUE RIBBON PROGRAM/COMMISSION.** Top quality; highly regarded.

**BLUESHIRTS.** IBM employees. See also BIG BLUE.
   "The blueshirts from Armonk (N.Y.) descended on the personal-computer division in Boca Raton (Fla.), crushing its autonomy and, by default, turning the market over to a multitude of competitors." (*Wall Street Journal*, May 30, 1996, p. A11)

**BLUE-SKY LAWS.** State securities laws requiring sellers of new stock issues to register and provide financial information about the company.

**BLUE STREAK.** Very rapid.

**BLURB.** A brief announcement about a product.

**BODY LANGUAGE.** Nonverbal communication.

**BOGUS.** False, fraudulent.
   "An official's vow to eliminate bogus advertising from the Cannes ad Festival raised a controversy." (*Adweek*, July 10, 1995, p. 25)

**BOHICA.** Bend over, here it comes again.
   "Bohica stands for something that, as a proper Bostonian, I am loath to spell out in this newspaper. I prefer to define it as 'bow out, here it comes again.' It refers to an increasingly common employee coping strategy for dealing with the steady stream of 'new and improved' programs and slogans in corporations today." (*Wall Street Journal*, Feb. 26, 1996, p. A12)

**BOILS DOWN TO.** Essence; most important considerations.
   "It essentially boils down to the company's size and financial strength, embodied in its triple-A rating—a coveted designation that grows rarer almost by the month." (*Investment Dealers Digest*, May 29, 1995, p. 14)

**BOILERPLATE.** Standard legal language used in contracts.

**BOILER ROOM.** A questionable sales organization, usually in telephone marketing.

**BOMB (TO).** Fail horrendously.

**BOMBSHELL.** Big surprise.
"Wendy Liebmann of WSL Marketing agreed that the fundamental changes in the way consumers buy apparel is a potential bombshell in what looks an otherwise promising year." (*Marketing News*, May 22, 1995, p. 1)

**BONA FIDE.** In good faith (Latin).
"In Parker versus U.S. (1995), a federal district court in Georgia ruled that there was not a bona fide sale, so property transferred to an investment fund in exchange for an income interest in the fund for life was includable." (*Banking Law Journal*, Feb. 1996, p. 205)

**BOOK THE GOODS (TO).** Place an order.

**BOOKS.** Financial records.

**BOOK VALUE.** The value at which an asset is carried on the firm's balance sheet.

**BOOMERS.** See BABY BOOMERS.
"BABY BOOMERS do not want to refer to themselves as babies so they call themselves boomers." (Professor Al Beyer, USC-Aiken, 1996)

**BOONDOGGLE.** A special deal; questionable public spending.
"To most of Los Angeles County's 9 million residents, the subway increasingly has the look of a boondoggle. Started a decade ago by then mayor Tom Bradley, the $5.8 billion project is plagued by $240 million in cost overruns." (*Business Week*, July 10, 1955, p. 39)

**BOOT (TO GIVE SOMEONE THE).** Terminate, fire someone.

**BOOT CAMP.** Training facility or program (military).
"Erlene Mikels . . . attended the group's boot camp a year ago to RUB ELBOWS WITH experts in the field and to polish up rusty marketing techniques." (*Wall Street Journal*, Jan. 16, 1996, p. B1)

**BOOT STRAP BUSINESS.** A venture started with very little capital.

**BOOT UP (TO).** Start a computer.

"This new networked-mirroring technology automatically senses server activity and boots up a standby machine when a primary server is down." (*Computer Reseller News*, March 6, 1995, p. 72)

**BORROWED UP.** Having taken out loans up to the lender's limit.

**BOTTLENECK.** Something that slows the production process.

"The same statistical tools that Deming developed to detect anomalies and bottlenecks on the assembly line have been used by TQM\* educators to isolate and resolve educational issues." (*Management Review*, Sept. 1995, p. 13)

**BOTTOM FISHING.** Buying stocks that have significantly declined in value.

"The bullish school . . . figures that the Mexican markets have passed their darkest hours and that it is time to start bottom-fishing for bargains." (*Barron's*, April 24, 1995, p. MW7)

**BOTTOM LINE.** An accounting profit or loss; the main idea.

"The bottom line for many of the interviewees was that very few companies embodied values consistent with those they hoped to live by." (*California Management Review*, Winter 1995, p. 8)

**BOTTOM OF THE BARREL.** Last resort, last option available.

"As inventories continue to scrape the bottom of the barrel, producers say prices may rise even more in the coming months." (*Chemical Marketing Reporter*, April 24, 1995, p. 31)

**BOTTOM OF THE LINE.** Least expensive; lowest quality.

**BOTTOM OUT (TO).** Reach lowest point or price.

"The RN Office-Market Index was slow to register price declines when the markets first weakened and then overstated the rate of decline once the market began to bottom out." (*Real Estate Economics*, Summer 1995, p. 101)

**BOUNCE IDEAS.** Share new ideas with others.

**BOUTIQUE.** A visible, specialized subdivision of a business.

**BOXED IN.** Having few or no choices; to narrow the possibilities.

"By using several methods, the consultant is able to 'box in' the value with a high degree of confidence." (*Rough Notes*, Feb. 1995, p. 30)

**BOXING PEOPLE.** Placing people in categories, stereotyping.

**BRACKET CREEP.** The tendency of inflation to push people into higher tax brackets.

"There was a huge but unlegislated hike in effective marginal tax rates in 1970–1980. This was because of bracket creep—the collision of inflation with a steeply progressive tax code." (*Forbes*, April 11, 1994, p. 45)

**BRADY BONDS.** Dollar-denominated bonds issued during the Bush administration, and used to assist Latin American countries in debt restructuring. The securities are named after Bush's Secretary of Treasury, Nicholas Brady.

**BREAK ALL THE RULES (TO).** Go against tradition.

**BRAINPOWER.** Knowledge, creativity.

"Knowledge comes the old-fashioned way—from working old-fashioned human brainpower, which has yet to be replaced by any series of electronic impulses." (*Vital Speeches of the Day*, Aug. 15, 1995, p. 661)

**BRAINSTORMING.** Group creative thinking; sharing wild ideas.

"The initial design concepts for a product are commonly developed during a brainstorming session where the initial thoughts of the design team members are merged to produce a unified concept." (*Plastics World*, March 1996, p. 29)

**BRASS.** Management. See also TOP BRASS.

**BREAD AND BUTTER.** Basic; main component.

"TRW cannot afford to ignore the Japanese market because auto parts are its bread and butter." (*Forbes*, July 31, 1995, p. 45)

**BREADWINNER.** Family member who brings home cash income. See also BRING HOME THE BACON.

"In many cases, the breadwinner wife still does the LION'S SHARE of child care." (*Working Women*, Feb. 1995, p. 6)

**BREAK DOWN (TO).** Stop suddenly or unexpectedly.

"When negotiations between nations break down, it might be time for a compromise." (*Management Today*, Aug. 1995, p. 71)

**BREAKING IT DOWN.** Separating into smaller parts; explaining in detail.

**BREAK THE ICE (TO).** Initiate conversation; make the first sale of the day.

"Twinning with North American cities helps to break the ice between Chinese and Canadian business executives." (*Canadian Business*, Aug. 1994, p. 83)

**BREAKTHROUGH.** Dramatically new product or idea.

**BRETTON WOODS.** Site of the major international finance conference held in 1944 (New Hampshire). At the Bretton Woods conference, a fixed exchange rate system was agreed upon, and the WORLD BANK and INTERNATIONAL MONETARY FUND were established.

**BRIDGE LOAN.** A short-term loan to facilitate a deal until permanent financing can be arranged.

**BRING HOME THE BACON (TO).** Earn income to support one's family.

**BRING UP TO SPEED.** Inform someone of the most recent events.

**BRINK OF.** The edge of.
   "Perhaps the most effective use of a stock ownership plan is when a company is teetering on the brink of bankruptcy and new managers are brought in to rescue it."(*Compensation and Benefits Management*, Winter 1995, p. 10)

**BROKEN RECORD.** Annoying, constant repetition.

**BRONX CHEER.** Boo. The Bronx is a borough in New York City, whose residents have become famous for voicing their disapproval.
   "NationsBank's merger with Boatmen's Bancshares . . . got a Bronx cheer. Why? By swapping two-thirds of a share of NationsBank for a share of Boatmen's, the eager suitor is giving up $30.13 in book value and getting $22.26 in return." (*Wall Street Journal*, Sept. 19, 1996, p. C1)

**BROWN-BAG (TO).** Bring one's lunch to the office.
   "Various methods for collecting customer feedback include surveys and 'brown bag' lunch seminars." (*Managing Office Technology*, May 1995, p. 44)

**BROWN FIELD.** An industrial site that is abandoned and unlikely to be redeveloped due to environmental contamination. In 1996, the Clinton administration introduced legislation to clean up brown fields and stimulate redevelopment of former industrial sites in urban areas.

**BROWN-NOSE (TO).** Flatter, kiss up to. See also ASS-KISSER.

**BROWNIE POINTS.** Positive marks or recognition an employee receives for his or her actions from superiors.
   "Today, they are reemerging as development assignments which can add valuable 'brownie points' to the CV of mid-career HIGH FLYERS." (*Industrial & Commercial Training*, 1995, p. 7)

**BUBBA.** Uneducated Southerner; among Southerners it is a term of endearment (corruption of "brother"). See also REDNECK. The author once played in a softball game in Charleston, South Carolina, where five of the players were nicknamed Bubba, and four Junior!
   "Alabama Governor Fob James says he wants legal jargon on torts simplified to 'Bubba language.' " (*Wall Street Journal*, April 3, 1996, p. S4)

**BUBBLE BURST.** Sudden decline in stock prices after a rapid increase.
   "Japan's financial markets are in turmoil more than 5 years after the Tokyo stock market bubble burst in 1990." (*Financial World*, Aug. 1, 1995, p. 10)

**BUCK.** Dollar; to ignore or oppose authority.
   "Older people want different things from work than younger ones. Most care more about personal satisfaction and making a contribution than earning big bucks and becoming CEO*." (*Fortune*, July 24, 1995, p. 102)

**BUCK STOPS HERE (THE).** Take responsibility. A sign on President Harry Truman's desk read "The buck stops here."
   "[GM CEO* John F.] Smith has also streamlined decision-making and improved coordination by creating a buck-stops-here strategy board, which he chairs." (*Fortune*, Oct. 17, 1994, p. 54)

**BUCKET SHOP.** A place where dubious business transactions take place; international travel consolidator.
   "Hibbard and a related bucket shop, F. N. Wolf, were effectively banned from retailing penny stocks in the summer of 1994 by the NASD for excessive markups similar to First Jersey's," (*Forbes*, Oct. 10, 1994, p. 42)

**BUCK THE TREND.** Act contrary to what others are doing.
   "The performance of consumer public relations overall proved to be rather indifferent in 1994 compared with 1993, although some consultantcies managed to buck the trend." (*Marketing*, May 25, 1995, p. xiii)

**BUCKLE DOWN (TO).** Get to work.

**BUDDHIST ECONOMICS.** Economic philosophy that challenges Western assumptions of materialism and motivation. The term and ideas were popularized among Westerners by E. F. Schumacher in his book *Small is Beautiful: Economics As if People Mattered*.

**BUG.** A weakness or problem in a system; to bother or pester; a secret listening device.

**BUILD A FENCE AROUND (TO).** Protect.

**BUILD/MAKE A BETTER MOUSETRAP.** Create a new or better product. Marketers use this phrase to represent firms with a production mentality, who focus on their product rather than the needs of their customers.

"If a man can write a better book, preach a better sermon, or make a better mouse-trap than his neighbor, though he builds his house in the woods the world will make a beaten path to his door." (Attributed to Ralph Waldo Emerson.)

**BULL.** Investor who thinks the stock market will rise; questionable advice.

"Besides the small fact that the bulls have been absolutely on the money and the BEARS dead wrong all year, what has fed investor complacency has been the supposed lack of feverish speculation, that universally perceived telltale sign that trouble is brewing." (*Barron's*, Aug. 18, 1995, p. 3)

**BULL'S EYE.** A perfect score, match, or outcome.

"Make your organization a bull's eye for HEADHUNTERS. Managers can no longer promise lifetime employment, but they can promise to make their employees very employable." (*Wall Street Journal*, Nov. 13, 1995, p. B1)

**BULLPEN.** People available to assist or relieve existing workers (baseball).

**BUMP (TO).** Use seniority to take the job of a younger employee. Bumping is allowed by the NATIONAL LABOR RELATIONS BOARD and the EQUAL EMPLOYMENT OPPORTUNITY BOARD.

**BUREAUCRATIC DELAYS.** Problems with government.

**BURNED OUT/BURNOUT.** Exhausted, tired; exhaustion.

"Results . . . showed that employees in a high-stressor job were rated as more effective, committed, and burned out than employees in a low-stressor job." (*Journal of Organizational Behavior*, July 1995, p. 353)

**BURROWING.** The practice of getting one's appointment status with the federal government switched from a political to career Civil Service position, thus protecting one from being terminated when one's party loses control in Washington.

**BUSH LEAGUE.** Insignificant; of minor importance (baseball).

**BUTT HEADS (TO).** Strongly disagree, compete.
  "Autodesk Inc. and Parametric Technology Corp. have begun to battle over the emerging middle market for CAD/CAM software. . . . Now they will butt heads as Autodesk moves up and Parametric moves down." (*Upside*, June 1995, p. 36)

**BUTTON DOWN (TO).** Seriously address; reach agreement on.
  "Many adults approach this segment with enthusiasm, grateful for a 2nd chance to button down the rules that competent writers employ." (*Training & Development*, April 1995, p. 13)

**BUTTON-DOWN & PINSTRIPES.** Corporate dress, suit and tie.

**BUTT OUT.** Mind your own business (considered rude or impolite).
  "Two weeks ago, in response to the trade talks, the chairman of Nissan Motor told both Japan and the U.S. to butt out of the private sector." (*Barron*'s, Sept. 26, 1994, p. 13)

**BUY DOWN.** A cash payment made to a lender in return for a lower interest rate.

**BUYING POWER.** Income, ability to purchase.
  "Local private and state-owned companies in Mexico are now on sale at discounted prices due to the dollar's enhanced buying power. The outlook for Mexico's economy in the coming year is good." (*International Business*, Aug. 1995, p. 34)

**BUY ON BAD NEWS (TO).** Stock market strategy of purchasing stock after unfavorable news.

**BUY THE FARM (TO).** Die.

**BUZZ WORDS.** Terms or phrases used by people within a specific group or industry.

**BY HOOK OR BY CROOK.** Any way it can get done.
  "By hook or by crook: Exploring the legality of an INS sting operation." (*San Diego Law Review*, Fall 1994, p. 813).

**BY THE BOOK/NUMBERS.** Following the rules.

# C

**CAFETERIA PLAN.** Benefit package that allows employee choice.

"Since image is everything these days, someone came up with the idea of using the term 'cafeteria plan' to describe a new way to sell employees on a substantially reduced benefits program." (*Supervision*, Jan. 1994, p. 4)

**CAKEWALK.** Something easy.

"No cakewalk for banks on Capitol Hill. Banks are having a harder time on Capitol Hill than they thought they would." (*American Agent & Broker*, May 1955, p. 20).

**CALIFORNIA PUBLIC EMPLOYEES' RETIREMENT SYSTEM (CALPERS).** Large, public retirement fund.

"The California Public Employees' Retirement System (CALPERS) has expanded its feared yet respected corporate governance programs. Now, it will examine the quality of individual company directors and monitor 6 times as many companies." (*Pensions & Investments*, Aug. 21, 1995, p. 2)

**CALL.** To challenge someone to justify their actions; a stock market option to buy a stock at a specific price for a period of time.

**CALL IN SICK (TO).** Take a day off from work.

"According to a survey conducted by the Gallup Organization, 24% of employed adults say that they call in sick at least once a year when they are not really sick." (*HR Magazine*, May 1995, p. 20)

**CALL ON THE CARPET (TO).** Reprimand.

**CALL THE SHOTS (TO).** Make the decisions.

"The North American staff of Deutsche Bank is finally about to learn who will call the shots in their U.S. operations—Morgan Grenfell." (*Investment Dealers Digest*, July 3, 1995, p. 3)

**CAN (TO).** Dismiss someone from employment; to terminate.

"What's more, once a company cans its plan, workers can no longer pile up credits toward their future benefits." (*Wall Street Journal*, Aug. 13, 1996, p. C1)

**CANNIBALIZE (TO).** Offer a new product that takes sales from another offering in the same product line.

**CAN OF WORMS.** A complex problem.

"One area that was targeted for cuts was federal food insurance; the premiums charged are considered artificially low by some people. Congress is reluctant to open a can of worms with so many potential voters." (*Barron's*, July 31, 1995, p. 41)

**CAPITAL FLIGHT.** The removal of funds from a country by investors during periods of political and economic turmoil.

"The cost was monetary and financial stability, with rising inflation and over valuation of the peso adding to capital flight and increased foreign long-term debt." (*Understanding NAFTA and Its International Business Implications*, 1996, p. 26.)

**CARDS ARE STACKED.** Situation where one has little chance of success.

**CAREER-LIMITING MOVE (CLM).** An action that will adversely affect one's future.

"If at a party you commented that the CEO's* spouse had put on a few pounds it would likely be a CLM." (Brian Chilla, Rock-Tenn Company, 1996)

**CARPE DIEM.** Seize the day (Latin). The saying, *carpe diem*, was made famous to Americans by actor Robin Williams in the film *Dead Poets Society*.

**CARROTS AND STICKS.** Positive incentives and negative consequences.

**CARRY (TO).** Take someone (Southern).

**CARRYING CHARGE.** Fee for purchasing something on credit.

**CARRY MUCH WEIGHT (TO).** Have significant meaning.
"A clinical pathway by itself may not carry much weight in defending a medical malpractice claim. A pathway should be integral to the medical record and should include outcome criteria and a variance record." (*Hospitals & Health Networks*, July 5, 1995, p. 58)

**CARRYOVER.** Inventory.

**CARRY THE BALL (TO).** Take charge of a project or situation (football).
"Most important, you have to persuade your top executives to carry the ball, balancing between candor and prudence, because reporters never want to quote the PR* guy." (*Wall Street Journal*, June 17, 1996, p. A14)

**CARTE BLANCHE.** Full authority to make decisions or commitments (French).
"Real estate advisors accustomed to having carte blanche in making investment decisions on behalf of their pension fund clients are in for a rude awakening because more and more plan sponsors as well as other institutional investors are availing themselves of new software programs to scrutinize their advisor's activities." (*Institutional Investor*, July 1995, p. 171)

**CASH COW.** Business in a slow growth market that generates surplus revenue.
"Amgen's cash cow drugs Epogen and Neupogen are maturing so annual revenue growth are expected to slow to 16%." (*Financial World*, July 18, 1995, p. 20)

**CASHIER'S CHECK.** A check issued by a bank with funds provided by the customer. Many businesses require payment in cash or by cashier's check, especially when doing business the first time.

**CASH IN ON (TO).** Profit from an opportunity.
"Atlanta-based Norrell Corp. has figured out how to cash in on the current out sourcing trend in businesses." (*Forbes*, Sept. 11, 1995, p. 42)

**CASH ON DELIVERY (COD).** A business transaction requiring payment when the goods are delivered.

**CASH SURRENDER VALUE (CSV).** The value of an insurance policy if canceled by the insured.

**CATCH-22 SITUATION.** An unresolvable contradiction or logic trap. The phrase comes from Joseph Heller's bestselling 1970s novel.

"It's a Catch-22 for employers and employees alike: In theory, work-family programs, including flexible schedules aim to LEVEL THE PLAYING FIELD for people with family duties. . . . But in practice, many women . . . who need to use them resist for fear of being relegated to the MOMMY TRACK." (*Wall Street Journal*, Dec. 13, 1995, p. B1)

**CAVEAT EMPTOR.** Let the buyer beware (Latin). The seller makes no guarantees.

"Invoking the principle of 'caveat emptor' (buyer, beware) the judge said the onus was on the purchaser to conduct a proper inspection of the property and to ask the vendor pertinent questions about the land before agreeing to buy it." (*Canadian Insurance*, July 1995, p. 22)

**CERTIFICATE OF ACCRUAL ON TREASURY SECURITIES (CATS).** U.S. Department of Treasury securities that pay no interest and are sold at a deep discount to face value (ZERO COUPON). Holders of CATS are paid full value of the security upon maturity.

**CERTIFIED CHECK.** A check guaranteed by a bank.

**CHANGE AGENT.** Consultant brought in to restructure a company.

"US corporations have been leaders in developing work-family programs, but Asian and European companies can teach the benefits of additional change agents such as unions, agencies, and the government." (*Personnel Journal*, April 1995, p. 85)

**CHANGE HANDS (TO).** Sell; get a new owner.

"Business activity on the Internet—as measured by interest in the World Wide Web—is growing by leaps and bounds. However, all of this activity means little if no cash changes hands." (*Communications Week*, March 13, 1995, p. S23)

**CHANNEL MANAGEMENT.** Managing distribution channels. Channel management involves placing greater emphasis on communicating with retailers and distributors in markets where end-users rely on the opinions and advice of these people.

"In addition, both Compaq and IBM now let major corporate customers buy directly from them, further adding to the unrest. . . . 'We're just giving customers the opportunity to be better satisfied,' insists Ronald Schneider, Compaq's director of channel management." (*Wall Street Journal*, Aug. 26, 1994, p. B4)

**CHANNEL BACK (TO).** Return.

**CHAPTER ELEVEN.** Bankruptcy laws allowing the debtor to maintain control of the business and to have latitude in negotiating new payment terms.

**CHAPTER SEVEN**. Bankruptcy proceeding where a court-appointed trustee oversees company activities, protects a company from creditors, and usually manages liquidation of the company's assets.

**CHARM SCHOOL.** A mocking term for training courses for newly appointed managers and other employees who now are in the PUBLIC EYE.
    "Charm school is a derisive or mocking term applied by cynics to military-instructor training courses and civilian train-the-trainer programs." (*Across the Board*, Nov./Dec. 1994, p. 51)

**CHARM THE PANTS OFF (TO).** Flatter.

**CHARTISTS.** Stock market analysts who graph movements of market statistics. See ELVES.
    "You can teach school on this chart, he asserts, pointing out a price formation known as a 'reverse head and shoulders'—a very BULLISH omen to the chartists." (*Wall Street Journal*, July 16, 1994, p. T2)

**CHASING DOWN SMOKESTACKS.** Making sales calls to industrial customers. See also COLD CALLS.

**CHECK IS IN THE MAIL.** A stalling tactic when confronted for payment.

**CHECK THE PULSE (TO).** Evaluate the current condition.

**CHECKOFF.** System where the employer withholds union dues from workers' paychecks.

**CHECKOUT.** Sales desk; to pay for one's purchases.

**CHEW OUT (TO).** Verbally reprimand; harshly criticize.

**CHICAGO BOYS.** Monetary economists; University of Chicago economists.

**CHINESE WALL.** Rules and safeguards to prevent improper disclosure of information within an organization.

**CHITCHAT.** Casual conversation.
"Well-intentioned remarks and innocent chitchat during the more informal parts of employment interviews can lead to legal difficulties." (*Law Practice Management*, March 1994, p. 50)

**CHICKENFEED.** Small sums of money.

**CHURN (TO)/CHURNER.** Turn over; improper stockbroker action of generating commissions by unauthorized buying and selling; deceptive insurance practice.
"If you bite, the extra cost will be subtracted from the savings (known as cash value) that you build up in your policy over the years. You are actually taking a hidden loan against those savings—which churners, by the way, call juice." (*Newsweek*, March 6, 1995, p. 46)

**CIRCUIT BREAKERS.** Rules created by the major stock exchanges and the SEC* to halt trading temporarily during periods of severe price fluctuations. These rules were created in response to BLACK MONDAY (1987), when the DJIA* fell over five hundred points in one day.
"The halts were among a package of so-called circuit breakers that were implemented to slow panic-driven stampedes out of stocks after the 1987 market crash." (*Wall Street Journal*, July 22, 1996, p. C1)

**CLASS ACTION.** A legal action filed by a group of people all with the same complaint against an individual or group. Class action lawsuits have become frequent and expensive for businesses in the United States.

**CLEAN SHEET/SLATE.** Fresh start; putting aside past errors.
"In return for Infinity's 'voluntary contribution' to the U.S. Treasury, the FCC will wipe clean a slate of indecency proceedings." (*Broadcasting & Cable*, Sept. 4, 1995, p. 6)

**CLEANING HIS/HER CLOCK.** A total victory over an opponent (boxing).

**CLEAR-CUT.** Obvious, well-defined.
"While this newfound interest is encouraging to entrepreneurs, it may not be profitable for banks with no clear-cut marketing plan. The successful small business banks are those whose managers understand

their market and evaluate their risks accordingly." (*U.S. Banker*, Aug. 1995, p. 63)

**CLEARING HOUSE.** An organization that provides for settlement of bank or stock market transactions; centralized source of services.

"The association will also serve as a clearing house of information on the subject of security." (*Electronic Business Buyer*, July 1995, p. 18)

**CLEAR SAILING.** No obstacles.

"Economic reform is never clear sailing, and the tax reform in China is no exception." (*International Tax Journal*, Winter 1995, p. 39)

**CLEAR THE AIR (TO).** Put aside past differences.

"Understandably, the doctors whose income dropped became resentful. Instead of fighting, though, they agreed to talk things out. That helped clear the air, and the physicians are exploring ways to share income." (*Medical Economics*, July 24, 1995, p. 107)

**CLIMB TO THE TOP (TO).** Become successful.

"To campaign for a director position, it is important to understand the forces that will aid in the climb to the top." (*Management Review*, March 1995, p. 49)

**CLINCH (TO).** Come to an agreement, close a deal.

"A landmark deal in Asia is the Hub River power plant project in Pakistan, which took 7 years to clinch the deal." (*Banker*, Jan. 1995, p. 55)

**CLINCHER.** Deciding element.

**CLIP JOINT.** A business that regularly overcharges customers.

**CLONE (TO).** Make copies of; a very close imitation.

"Chip maker Cyrix plans to start making personal computers, partly in a strategy to boost the brand recognition of its Intel-clone semiconductors." (*Wall Street Journal*, March 16, 1996, p. A1)

**CLOSE.** The end of the business day.

**CLOSE A POSITION (TO).** Eliminate a security from one's portfolio.

**CLOSE, BUT NO CIGAR.** Not quite correct.

**CLOSED-END INVESTMENT COMPANY.** A mutual fund which issues a limited and fixed number of shares and does not redeem the shares. Once issued, the closed-end shares trade like common stock with share values varying with the value of the price of the stocks held in the fund.

**CLOSED SHOP.** A firm in which union membership is a precondition for employment. The Taft-Hartley Act (1947) outlawed closed shops, but de facto closed shops exist in situations where union halls are used to match employer needs with worker qualifications.

**CLOSELY HELD.** A company with only a few stockholders.

**CLOSER.** Salesperson whose job is to finish the deal (baseball).

**CLOSE THE LOOP (TO).** Come full circle with a deal or transaction.

**CLOSE TO ONE'S VEST (TO KEEP).** Guard against others finding something out. In the card game of poker, players keep their cards close to their vest to prevent anyone from seeing them.

**CLOSING COSTS.** The variety of ancillary expenses involved in purchasing real estate.

**CLOSING TICK.** The number of stocks whose last trading price of the day was higher than the previous trade, minus the number of stocks whose last selling price was lower. A closing tick which is positive is considered BULLISH, while a negative closing tick is BEARISH.

**CLOUD ON A TITLE.** Any legal issue that questions or makes unclear the ownership of property. Clouds on a title usually must be removed before a business transaction takes place.

**CLOUT.** Influence.
    "The study includes cases in which companies already are using their purchasing clout to influence how paper is made." (*Wall Street Journal*, Dec. 20, 1995, p. C13)

**COALS TO NEWCASTLE (TO BRING).** Not needed; to do something unnecessary. Newcastle is a seaport in the coal-producing region of Great Britain.

**COFFEE BREAK.** Rest time in a workday.

**COIN A PHRASE (TO).** Make up words to describe something.

**COLD CALL.** Sales call to new potential customers without prior communication.

"Many life insurance agents and brokers are putting a new spin on the old industry standby, the 'cold call.' Bill Truax, president of Trufield Enterprises, suggests memorizing an all-purpose pitch to recite to prospects—preferably in person, but just as good over the telephone and in voice mail." (*National Underwriter*, July 3, 1995, p. 7)

**COLD CASH.** Currency, not a check.

**COLD WAR.** Post–World War II political and diplomatic conflict between the United States and the Soviet Union.
"This isn't a new problem for the GOP, but it has been aggravated by two losses. . . . The other was the fall of communism; the Cold War and anticommunism were a glue that united Republican factions." (*Wall Street Journal*, March 8, 1996, p. A1)

**COLLECTIVE BARGAINING.** Negotiations between management and representatives from employees' unions.

**COME IN LOW (TO).** Make a low bid on a contract.

**COME-ON.** A deceptive act; seduction.

**COME OUT OF LEFT FIELD (TO).** Surprise; suddenly become visible or important (baseball).

**COMER.** Someone or something with recognized potential.
"Last year's comer was clearly the ready-to-drink tea segment, which boosted its share of the New Age market to 22.6% from 15.3% in 1993." (*Supermarket Business*, Sept. 1995, p. 91)

**COMMERCIAL PAPER.** Short-term borrowing instruments used by U.S. businesses.
"Medium-term notes (MTN) issuers have sold everything from $1 million worth of one-year bonds to $300 million worth of 100-year bonds. In most securities firms, it is still linked with its bland cousin, commercial paper (CP)." (*Investment Dealers Digest*, May 22, 1995, p. 45)

**COMMUNITY PROPERTY.** Assets of a married couple belonging to both people. Divorce laws vary in the United States, with some states being community property states.

**COMP.** Free or complimentary.

**COMPARABLE WORTH.** Antidiscrimination argument that people doing the same job or having the same level of responsibility should be paid the same regardless of race or gender.

**COMPARISON SHOPPER.** Researcher used to investigate marketing practices of competitors. See also SECRET SHOPPER.

**COMPETITIVE EDGE.** Advantage.

**COMP TIME.** Compensatory time; time off for past extra work.
   "According to a recent opinion letter from the US DEPARTMENT OF LABOR (DOL), nonexempt employees who work overtime, must be paid for the extra hours rather than receiving compensatory time off. Before the opinion was issued, the DOL allowed an hour and a half of comp time for the overtime hours." (*Small Business Reports*, June 1994, p. 35)

**CONFIDENCE GAME.** Conspiracy where criminals gain the trust of an individual (PIGEON) and then cheat the person out of money.

**CONTINGENCY ALLOWANCE.** Allowance made for unforeseen delays or costs.

**CONTRACT MOD.** Contract modification; change order.

**CONTRARIAN.** Investor whose ideas are often opposite those of the majority of investors.
   "The Dogs of the Dow, which are the 10 stocks with the highest dividend yields in the DOW JONES INDUSTRIAL AVERAGE as of December 31, 1994, have returned a collective 19.3% over the past 6 months. The Dow Dogs amount to a contrarian investment strategy because the 10 high-yielding Dow stocks often are out of favor." (*Barron's*, July 3, 1995, p. 12)

**CONSTANT DOLLARS.** Dollars of a base year, used in adjusting prices for changes in inflation.

**CONSUMER CONFIDENCE.** Consumers' feelings about the future of the economy and their economic well-being. The University of Michigan Survey of Consumer Confidence is the most widely reported and respected measure of consumer confidence.

**CONSUMER DURABLES.** Consumer goods that have a use-life of more than one year, including automobiles, appliances, and furniture. "Consumer durables" is a category in GDP accounting. Changes in consumer durables expenditures are an indicator of consumer confidence.

**CONVENIENCE GOODS.** Goods consumers routinely purchase without comparison. These goods are usually brand-name, low-priced items and can be divided into three subcategories: staples, impulse items, and emergency items. Widespread distribution is critical to success in marketing convenience goods.

**CONVERTIBLES.** Corporate debt securities that can be exchanged for shares of stock.

**COOK THE BOOKS (TO).** Falsify records.
"In the same way a company can use 'CREATIVE ACCOUNTING' to make its financials look the way it wants them to, the federal government can cook its books, too." (*Secured Lender*, May/June 1995, p. 44)

**COOLING-OFF PERIOD.** Government-imposed period, usually sixty days, during which a union is restricted from striking and employers from locking-out employees.
"Piedmont, USAir Group, and National Mediation Board officials are scheduled to resume contract talks before a 30-day cooling off period ends March 25." (*Aviation Week & Space Technology*, March 14, 1994, p. 38)

**COPY.** Words in an advertisement.

**COPYCAT.** Anyone in the copy industry; a product made to resemble an existing popular product.

**CORE BUSINESS.** Basic activities.
"This term almost always includes an announcement by the straight-faced president, CEO* or chairman of the board, 'We are pleased to announce that the company is returning to its core business.' . . . Actually, core business means that the company is bordering on insolvency as a result of ego-driven forays into a series of unrelated enterprises for which it had no knowledge or expertise then failed." (*Supervision*, Jan. 1994, p. 3)

**CORE COMPETENCIES.** The things a company does best.
"It all depends on core competencies. If your function is considered a core competency, you will be retained by the company." (Mary Grace Allenchey, AT&T, 1996)

**CORNER THE MARKET (TO).** Gain controlling interest in a company or product.

**CORNERSTONE.** Foundation; indispensable part.

"Optimism concerning small stocks rests on 2 cornerstones: Small stocks look cheap, and their potential to generate outstanding earnings in the face of an interest rate cut and renewed economic growth is great." (*Fortune*, Sept. 18, 1995, p. 237)

**CORPORATE ELITE.** Top executives.
"Black executives such as Robert Holland of Ben & Jerry's Homemade Inc. have emerged as titans among the corporate elite." (*Black Enterprise*, April 1995, p. 9)

**CORPORATE LADDER.** Business hierarchy. Managers are encouraged to try to climb the corporate ladder.
"The 3-day Ketchum exercise drew employees from all of its divisions and most rungs of the corporate ladder." (*Adweek*, July 31, 1995, p. 21)

**CORPORATE PILOT FISH.** Former employees who start a new business based primarily on contacts and contracts with their old company.
"Now consider the corporate pilot fish, a departed employee of a giant corporation who still swims with his former employer for sustenance and protection." (*Wall Street Journal*, April 9, 1996, p. B1)

**CORPORATE RAIDER.** Individual or group trying to take control of another company.
"Dreaded 1980s corporate raiders Carl R. Pohlad and Irwin L. Jacobs have joined forces once again. On March 14, 1994, they launched a $178 million hostile bid for Fibreboard Corp." (*Business Week*, April 4, 1994, p. 42)

**CORPORATE TAKEOVER.** One company buying another.

**CORRECTION.** Downward movement of stock market prices.

**COST AN ARM AND A LEG.** Very expensive.

**COST-PLUS CONTRACT.** Contract with payment based on costs plus a fee.
"Airplane manufacturers increasingly ask suppliers to fund development costs from overhead, although there is a powerful trend in the commercial aircraft industry ranging from cost-plus contracts to fixed-price contracts." (*Industrial Marketing Management*, July 1994, p. 235)

**COST-PUSH INFLATION.** Inflation caused by rising labor and material costs.

"Increases in productivity also reduce unit labor costs and thereby slash cost-push inflation pressures and enhance profits." (*Barron's*, July 4, 1994, p. 33)

**COUCH POTATO.** Lazy person; inveterate television watcher.

"Systems Integrators Inc. (SII) recently hosted a couch potato suite at the Las Vegas Hilton for Expo '94 conventioneers interested in electronic media." (*Editor & Publisher*, Aug. 27, 1994, p. 28)

**COULD NOT HACK IT.** Quit; could not take the pressure.

**COUNTER (TO).** Make a competing offer.

**COUNTERTRADE.** International barter. Countertrade is often used by developing countries lacking sufficient foreign currency to obtain goods and services from industrialized countries.

"By the year 2000, an estimated 1/2 or more of all international trade will be conducted as countertrade, a reciprocal exchange involving limited or no transfer of funds." (*Management Accounting*, April 1995, p. 47)

**COUNTERVAILING DUTY.** Import tax intended to protect a domestic industry.

"Anti dumping and countervailing duty laws (jointly referred to as Title VII laws), for example, are used to counter the alleged practices of dumping and government subsidization, respectively" (*World Economy*, March 1995, p. 295)

**COUNTERVAILING POWER.** Union power to counterbalance the power of major companies.

**COVER FOR SOMEONE (TO).** Temporarily take on another worker's responsibilities.

**COVER LETTER.** Letter sent with a document or resume introducing it or adding further explanation to the reader.

**COVER-UP.** An act to conceal a wrongdoing.

"Courts are now, however, showing signs of impatience with a system that encourages cover-up of unsavory facts about ex-employees." (*HR Focus*, May 1995, p. 15)

**COVER YOUR ASS (CYA).** Protect yourself from criticism or blame should a project fail.

**COWBOY.** An unmanageable person.

"Under the pressure of bad publicity and unhappy state insurance commissioners, many companies say they're starting to hogtie the very cowboys they used to love." (*Newsweek*, March 6, 1995, p. 38)

**CRACKPOT.** Someone with unorthodox ideas; crazy person.

"In their early days, entrepreneurs are labeled crackpots, dreamers, and unhireables. Only later do they earn respect." (*Inc.*, March 1994, p. 23)

**CRADLE TO GRAVE.** From birth to death; socialism.

"Yet, few companies have done anything to help employees break through disempowering attitudes that are firmly grounded in a cradle-to-grave employment mentality." (*HR Magazine*, Aug. 1995, p. 95)

**CRASH.** Dramatic drop or fall.

"Semiconductors have been the engine of the 1995 rally, and most of the lecturing about how technology stocks are due for a crash confuses the whole technology stock group with this one sector." (*Forbes*, Sept. 11, 1995, p. 264)

**CREATIVE ACCOUNTING.** Falsification of business records.

"Ex-Phar-Mor chief financial officer Patrick Finn testified to a federal jury that former President Michael Monus ordered him to COVER UP an intricate fraud scheme at the deep discount drug chain by using creative accounting." (*Discount Store News*, June 20, 1994, p. 104)

**CREDIT SCORING.** Computerized method of rating a consumer's credit worthiness based on income, past credit experience, and debt.

"Credit scoring attempts to quantify in a single number, the likelihood a potential borrower will repay his loan." (*Forbes*, Dec. 18, 1995, p. 96)

**CREDIT SQUEEZE.** Government anti-inflation policy where raising interest rates reduces consumer and business borrowing.

**CREDIT WATCH.** Announcement by credit rating agencies that a company is under review, usually indicating a possible lowering of the company's credit rating.

**CRITICAL-PATH ANALYSIS.** Management analysis of the most important sequence of an operation.

**CRONYISM.** Favoritism to people one knows. See also OLD-BOY NETWORK.

**CROSS-FERTILIZATION.** Mixing of ideas.

"Collaborative R&D* provides a forum for technical exchange and the cross-fertilization of ideas among member companies." (*Mechanical Engineering*, Sept. 1994, p. 85)

**CROSS-SABERS (TO).** Disagree or have a conflict with.

"Because pricing decisions are made by the sales service division, we often cross sabers with them." (Brian Chilla, Rock-Tenn Company, 1995)

**CROWDING OUT.** Economic theory that government borrowing in financial markets increases interest rates and reduces private-sector borrowing and investment.

**CROWN JEWELS.** Most successful products or divisions of a company.

"*Cosmo* remains one of the crown jewels of the Hearst magazine empire, but has been stagnant on the ad front recently." (*Advertising Age*, Aug. 28, 1995, p. 13)

**CRUNCH THE NUMBERS.** Calculate the cost, price, value.

"Besides being easy to use, the applications have to be able to crunch the numbers quickly and accurately and present data graphically." (*InfoWorld*, Sept. 24, 1994, p. 89)

**CULL (TO).** Reject the lowest-quality items.

"Pringle's decision to return to core values and cull wasteful diversification is the right one." (*Marketing*, April 6, 1995, p. 13)

**CULTURAL DIVERSITY.** Recognizing various ethnic groups and their contribution to the workplace.

"Before implementing a cultural diversity training program, managers should ensure that the CEO* supports the initiative and the diversity training is perceived positively by employees." (*Security Management*, July 1995, p. 25)

**CUSH-JOB.** Easy job.

**CUT AND RUN (TO).** Stop and leave, often without finishing a job (nautical).

**CUT ONE'S LOSSES (TO).** Concede defeat. See also BAILOUT.

**CUT THE CAKE (TO).** Complete a business deal.

**CUT THE MUSTARD.** Able to meet the standard, effective.

**CUTTHROAT COMPETITION.** Tough competition.

"Meanwhile, the pharmaceutical industry, squeezed by health plan payers, their allies, and cutthroat competition into giving discounts on an unprecedented scale." (*Drug Topics*, July 24, 1995, p. 54)

**CUTTING EDGE.** Newest, most advanced technology.

"The void in corporate loyalty can be filled with individual honor, the excitement of working on the cutting edge and the fulfillment of contributing to the common good." (*Wall Street Journal*, Jan. 5, 1996, p. B1)

**CYBERNATE (TO).** Control by computer.

**CYCLE BILLING.** System distributing billing activities over a time period.

# D

**DAISY CHAIN.** Collusion among buyers who bid up the price of a stock and then sell to unsuspecting investors.

**DARWINISM.** See ECONOMIC DARWINISM.

**DATING.** Extending credit beyond the usual agreement.

**DAY ORDER.** A stock market order directing execution that day or otherwise canceling the order.

**DEAD CATS BOUNCE.** See EVEN DEAD CATS BOUNCE.

**DEAD IN THE WATER.** Unable to move, stuck (nautical).
   "With national health care reform literally dead in the water, it falls to the states and local communities to provide leadership in improving health care for children." (*Business & Economic Review*, Jan.–March, 1995, p. 11)

**DEAD ON ARRIVAL (DOA).** Not viable. Frequently, the president's budget plan is declared "dead on arrival" by the opposition party in

Congress. In medicine, "dead on arrival" refers to the patient's condition when reaching the hospital.

**DEAD TIME.** Time not working. When an assembly line is temporarily halted, workers have dead time.

**DEAD WOOD.** People who are part of an organization but no longer contribute to the firm's output. Before DOWNSIZING in corporate America, people who were considered dead wood were often PUSHED UPSTAIRS.

"Get rid of dead wood, advises *Economic Notes*, a monthly newsletter for unions, in a piece on how to revitalize union locals." (*Wall Street Journal*, Feb. 20, 1996, p. A1)

**DECERTIFICATION.** Cancellation of union representation by employees.

**DECISION TREE.** Flow chart to facilitate analysis of a complex problem.

"Quality cost reporting provides a clear picture of the improvement opportunities that have always been accepted as legitimate operating costs. The decision tree helps with not only defining the major costs, but also with refining the details of the quality costs report." (*Quality Progress*, Aug. 1995, p. 168)

**DEEP-DISCOUNT BOND.** A bond sold at a price well below face value.

**DEEP IN/OUT OF THE MONEY.** A call option with an exercise price significantly higher than the current market price is considered deep out of the money.

**DEEP POCKETS.** Companies or investors with lots of money.

"Speaking at the annual Public Risk Management Association conference, attorney Cheryl L. Duryea . . . said that public official's liability is a growing area of the law. She attributed the growth not just to the public's perception of such entitles as having deep pockets but also to increasing anti-government sentiment. (*Business Insurance*, June 19, 1995, p. 24)

**DEEP SIX (TO).** Dispose of. A military term referring to discarding something at sea, where it will not be found.

**DE FACTO.** In fact (Latin). A situation where customary practices have become the accepted standard without rules or regulation.

"Secure Hypertext Transport Protocol and Netscape Communications Corp.'s Secure Sockets Layer (SSL) have quickly become the de facto standards and are making their way into the majority of World Wide Web browsers and servers shipping." (*Communications Week*, Jan. 29, 1996, p. 41)

**DE JURE.** By law (Latin).

**DELI.** Delicatessen; meat, cheese, and sandwich store.

**DELINQUENCY.** When loan payments are overdue.

**DELIVER THE GOODS (TO).** Perform, come through, succeed.
"From the beginning, there were endless tasks to be done, but the only real problem was finding committed, intelligent, creative people who could become a powerful team and deliver the goods even though du Preez could pay them." (*People Management*, May 18, 1995, p. 26)

**DEMAND-PULL INFLATION.** Inflation caused by excessive demand, usually brought on by overly stimulative fiscal or monetary policies.

**DEMAND WENT SOFT.** People no longer wanted the product.

**DE-MARKETING.** Rationing limited quantities of a good, thereby restricting demand.

**DE NOVO.** Anew (Latin). Ignoring past problems or performance.
"Banks can establish branches in states where they do not own a deposit-taking institution but only if the state authorizes de novo branching." (*Credit Union Magazine*, June 1995, p. 14)

**DEPARTMENT OF HOUSING AND URBAN DEVELOPMENT (HUD).** Federal agency that provides incentives and financing for housing programs in the U.S.

**DEPARTMENT OF LABOR (DOL).** Federal agency that oversees labor laws and programs. Usually considered a lesser White House Cabinet appointment, first-term Clinton administration Secretary of Labor, Robert Reich, became a leading spokesperson of social policy.

**DEPOSITORY INSTITUTIONS DEREGULATION AND MONETARY CONTROL ACT (DIDMCA).** 1980 federal legislation that drastically changed banking rules, including gradual elimination of interest-rate ceilings and restrictions on stock brokerage firms offering checking accounts. Among bankers it is referred to as the "1980 Act" or DIDMCA.

**DERAIL (TO).** Wreck, throw off course.

"In an effort to derail Bell Atlantic's strategy for early entry into the video-delivery business, Comcast asked the FCC to block the telco's plans to own both wireless and wired video systems in the same area." (*Broadcasting & Cable*, June 5, 1994, p. 14)

**DESK JOCKEY.** Office worker.

"An editorial notes that the one-dimensional desk-jockey who has spent little time outside of corporate walls will have a difficult time making it in the restaurant industry." (*Nation's Restaurant News*, Aug. 29, 1994, p. 21)

**DEUTSCHE MARK (DM).** The unit of German currency.

**DEVIL'S ADVOCATE (LET ME PLAY).** Ponder or predict criticism of a project as a means to improve the quality of the proposal.

"In addition to being an effective role model, the new strategic leader needs at least one good alter ego, devil's advocate, or contrarian to avoid getting into a rut." (*Planning Review*, Sept. 10, 1994, p. 6)

**DEVOLUTION.** Delegation of power by a central government to local governments. Often power and responsibility is transferred without sufficient funds to maintain the programs.

"An editorial discusses devolution. It is a creative way of using the innovation and flexibility available at the state level to achieve national objectives." (*Business Week*, Aug. 7, 1995, p. 84)

**DIALING AND SMILING.** Telephone solicitation of new customers. See also COLD CALL.

**DIALOGUE MARKETING.** Marketing programs designed to build a relationship with the customer. See also RELATIONSHIP MARKETING.

**DICKER (TO).** Negotiate.

**DIE OR MOVE AWAY (TO) (DOMA).** A customer-oriented company wants to lose customers only if they DOMA.

**DIFFERENT BREED.** Different type; unusual.

"Today's employers, however, are looking for a different breed of job candidates—those with a wide range of knowledge and skills." (*World Wastes*, July 1995, p. 20)

**DIFFERENTIALLY ABLED.** POLITICALLY CORRECT manner of describing a person with handicaps.

**DIGERATI.** Computer experts; a pun on the word "literati" (lovers of literature).

**DILBERT/DILBERT PRINCIPLE.** Referring to a popular 1990s cartoon by Scott Adams which finds humor in corporate absurdities.

"The Dilbert Principle is adapted from the PETER PRINCIPLE, a popular management aphorism of a few years ago. Mr. Adams observes that the most ineffective workers are systematically moved to the place where they can do the least damage: management." (*Wall Street Journal*, May 30, 1996, p. A11)

**DIME A DOZEN.** Very cheap.

**DIME STORE.** Business selling low-priced goods.

"In 1994, the Federal Reserve Board hiked interest rates as astonishing 6 times in 10 months, rocking stock and bond funds. Derivatives issues unraveled like dime-store stocks, steeping losses." (*Money*, Feb. 1994, p. 72)

**DINGBAT.** A dumb person. The term was frequently used by ARCHIE BUNKER to describe his wife on the 1970s situation comedy *All in the Family*. It is considered crude and sexist language.

**DINOSAURS.** Large companies that have not changed with the times.

"Such company ploys as divide-and-conquer were one driving force behind the stunning July 27 merger announcement by 3 of the US' largest industrial unions the United Auto Workers, the International Association of Machinists, and the United Steelworkers. . . . Critics see the merger as the last gasp of 3 dinosaurs, but it could help labor fend off extinction." (*Business Week*, Aug. 14, 1995, p. 42)

**DIRTY LAUNDRY.** Questionable or scandalous past activities. See also SKELETONS IN THE CLOSET.

"Mary Shapiro says she is leaning toward airing a bigger chunk of brokers' dirty laundry on the Internet and plans to increase penalties on brokerage-firm supervisors who fail to rein in brokers with bad disciplinary histories." (*Wall Street Journal*, March 25, 1996, p. C1)

**DIRTY TRICKS/POOL.** Dishonest or underhanded practices (referring to the game of billiards).

"Market share obsession easily leads to price wars, product proliferation, and dirty tricks." (*Management Today*, Dec. 1994, p. 29)

**DISCONNECT.** A conflict or inconsistency.

"The trendy word for the mid-1990s may be 'disconnect,' used as a noun. . . . Skip Beebe, . . . spoke at an association meeting about an apparent disparity between what corporate tenants want and the type of office product available in the market. 'There are some disconnects,' Beebe said." (*Atlanta Business Chronicle*, Jan. 26, 1996, p. 12)

**DISCONTINUOUS CHANGE.** Completely rethinking the way things are done in an organization.

"Discontinuous change threatens authority because it's the idea that the best way to go about doing something may not be the way it's currently done. . . . " (*Across the Board*, Nov./Dec. 1993, p. 51)

**DISCOUNT (TO).** Lower the price.

**DISCOUNT WINDOW.** Term referring to Federal Reserve short-term loans to banks.

"Large banks must make greater efforts than others to obtain funding in national money markets before turning to the discount window; these banks usually turn to the window only late in the reserve maintenance period, which is when reserve pressures tend to appear." (*Federal Reserve Bulletin*, Nov. 1994, p. 968)

**DISINTERMEDIATION.** The removal of financial intermediaries from the saving-investment process.

"This movement to cut out the middleman is part of a massive socioeconomic phenomenon known as disintermediation." (*Futurist*, May/June 1995, p. 12)

**DIVERSIFICATION.** Increasing the variety of investments or products, usually as a way to reduce risk.

**DIVERSITY.** With reference to minorities, ethnic groups.

**DOCTOR (TO)/DOCTORING.** Reference to altering records (implies illegal or unethical activity).

The San Francisco FED is investigating its Los Angeles branch for doctoring numbers in the cash-handling reports it compiles for Washington." (*Wall Street Journal*, June 3, 1996, p. A1)

**DODGE REPORTS.** F. W. Dodge monthly report of new construction activity in the United States.

**DOG.** Unsuccessful product; a low-growth product with a low market-share.
"Of course, he says with a smile, 'a company may be debt-free for two reasons. If it's a dog, it's because no one will lend them money.' " (*Wall Street Journal*, May 28, 1996, p. R18)

**DOG-AND-PONY SHOW.** Simple, planned presentation; too often dog-and-pony shows insult the intelligence of their audience. See also MUSHROOM JOB.
"However, after a dog-and-pony show purporting to consider new missions, Clinton and O'Leary have joined two factions in Congress—unreconstituted Cold Warriors [see COLD WAR] and delegates seeking to preserve weapons spending in their districts—to endorse continuing the same costly, and ecologically disastrous mission despite the lack of a significant nuclear threat." (*Positive Alternatives*, Fall 1995, p. 5)

**DOG-EAT-DOG.** Highly competitive.
"Many employers and employees are happy with their medical savings account (MSA) programs, but not everyone has positive feelings about MSAs. Jack Burry, chairman and CEO* of Blue Cross & Blue Shield of Ohio, says that MSAs threaten to turn health insurance into a dog-eat-dog market." (*Business Insurance*, March 6, 1995, p. 13)

**DOLLAR DRAIN.** The impact on the United States of continually running a trade deficit, causing dollars to leave the country.

**DO LUNCH (TO).** Arrange to have lunch together.

**DOMINO EFFECT.** One action causing a series of impacts.
"The battle in California is expected to have a domino effect, eventually reaching all Americans." (*Black Enterprise*, Nov. 1995, p. 133)

**DONE DEAL.** An agreement even though a contract has not been signed; FAIT ACCOMPLI; a certainty.
"May 1995's job report reveals 2 consecutive months of declining payroll employment. Except for recession-related periods, this has not occurred since the 1950's. If this further depresses consumer spending, the recession is a done deal." (*Forbes*, July 17, 1995, p. 327)

**DON'T FIGHT THE TAPE.** Do not try to go against the direction of the market.

**DON'T HOLD YOUR BREATH.** Do not expect anything to happen quickly.

**DON'T STEP ON MY AIRHOSE.** Do not interfere with what I am doing. Employees often fear managers will step on their airhose, making it more difficult to do their job.

**DON'T TAKE ANY WOODEN NICKELS.** Be careful, take care of yourself. The phrase was a fad in the 1920s.

**DO ONE'S HOMEWORK (TO).** Prepare.
   "The 2 secrets of a successful practice management system are: 1. do one's homework and select a system that is applicable and do-able, and 2. determine the practice management policies early on and enforce them fairly and consistently." (*Practical Accounting*, 1995, p. 101)

**DOTTED LINE.** Place for signature on a form or contract.
   "Any reliable real estate agent will quickly—and rightly—point out that he or she performs far more services than merely getting someone to sign on the dotted line of an offer to buy." (*American Salesman*, Feb. 1995, p. 7)

**DOUBLE BOTTOM.** Stock market chart with two declines followed by a recovery.

**DOUBLE-DIPPING.** Practice of retiring, collecting a pension, and then starting a second career.

**DOUBLE INCOME, NO KID (DINK).** Working couples who do not have children.
   "A recent *American Demographics* article noted the growing numbers of childless couples as one of the most significant demographic trends of the past 15 years. Since then, the acronym DINK (double income, no kids) has been attached to such couples. (*D&B Reports*, May/June 1987, p. 10)

**DOUBLE-TIME.** Quickly (military).

**DOVETAILS.** Links together.
   "Only large firms with large volumes of accounts receivable may be able to justify the cost of an in-house, technology-based solution that dovetails with its business patterns and staff resources." (*Corporate Cash Flow*, Sept. 1994, p. 30)

**DOW JONES INDUSTRIAL AVERAGE (DJIA).** Weighted average of the prices of thirty stocks considered representative of the U.S. economy. The DJIA is the most frequently quoted measure of the U.S. stock market. As the economy has moved away from manufacturing to service industries, the DJIA has been reconfigured to reflect the changing economy.

**DOWN AND DIRTY.** Hastily written first draft.

**DOWN AND OUT.** Broke (having no money).

**DOWNLINE.** Sellers in a MULTILEVEL MARKETING chain whose sales generate commissions.

**DOWNSIZE (TO)/DOWNSIZING.** Reduce the size of a company.

**DOWN THE DRAIN/TUBE.** Lost, wasted.
"When the Interstate Commerce Commission decided against allowing a Southern Pacific (SP)–Santa Fe merger, SP was close to going down the drain." (*Railway Age*, Nov. 1994, p. 22)

**DOWN THE ROAD.** In the future.

**DOWN TIME.** Any period when workers or machines are idle.
"Many industrial plants are sold on total productive maintenance (TPM) programs. TPM uses cross-functional team concepts to maintain equipment in a predictive manner, using preventive maintenance to prevent costly down time." (*Plant Engineering*, Aug. 7, 1995, p. 102)

**DOWN TO BRASS TACKS.** Dealing with essentials.

**DOWN TO THE WIRE.** Last-minute, completed just before the deadline (horse racing).
"The battle between Viacom and WALL STREET arbitrageurs over a huge amount of derivative securities is going down the wire." (*Barron's*, Aug. 21, 1995, p. MW10)

**DOWNSIDE.** Negative.
"The key to these savings is the recognition that the plan sponsor bears almost all of the downside risk, but only receives part of the upside reward." (*Pensions & Investments*, Sept. 4, 1995, p. 52)

**DOWNWARDLY MOBILE (DOMO).** A young person who gives up a high-paying, high-pressure job to pursue a more satisfying lifestyle is sometimes labeled a DOMO.

**DRAG YOUR FEET (TO).** Delay, deliberately complete a task slowly.

**DRAW A PICTURE (TO).** Explain in detail.

"In several other assignments, Price Waterhouse has worked with executives who have elected to first draw a picture of both the long-term outlook for the company and the impact that efficiency initiatives might have, before reengineering." (*Planning Review*, Nov. 12, 1994, p. 18)

**DRAWBACK.** Repayment of a customs duty when goods are exported again.

**DRAWBACKS.** Problems.

"By drawing on the literatures of cognitive psychology, marketing, and existing statutory information disclosure, the drawbacks of relying on health care report cards as a quality assurance system are explored." (*Yale Journal on Regulation*, Winter 1995, p. 207)

**DRAW DOWN (TO)/DRAWDOWN.** Reduce; amount that has been borrowed under a loan agreement.

"In boom times, business adds to inventories at an increasing rate, which aids gross domestic product growth. But in recession, inventories start looking menacing. They are the overhang that business must draw down before resuming normal production." (*Barron's*, March 27, 1995, p. 40)

**DRESSING UP A PORTFOLIO.** Practice by mutual fund managers of selling stocks about which there has been bad news, or buying stocks that have received positive news, so that the quarterly report will look good.

**DRIVE HOME (TO).** Emphasize.

"Martin Direct will drive home its message of purchasing Geico car insurance to public transportation commuters in New York and Chicago." (*Adweek*, Aug. 28, 1995, p. 8)

**DROP A BUNDLE (TO).** Lose or spend a lot of money.

"Attracted at least partly by the promise of globalization, a lot of wealthy organizations want to get into the action and are willing and able to drop a bundle to get in." (*Forbes*, Nov. 21, 1994, p. 244)

**DROP THE BALL (TO).** Fail to do what one said one would.

**DUAL BANKING.** Regulatory system in the United States whereby some banks, called national banks, are chartered and regulated by federal agencies while others are regulated by state banking authorities.

The rules differ, which creates incentives for new banks to do regulatory shopping.

**DUAL-CAREER MARRIAGE.** Husband and wife both work (especially, both professionally).

**DUCKS IN A ROW (TO GET ONE'S).** Organized.
"It's mindboggling that the developers wouldn't push the launch back until the fall so we could get all of our ducks in a row." (*Wall Street Journal*, Aug. 7, 1996, p. B1)

**DUB (TO).** Copy; label; a copy of an audio or video recording.
"Job sharing is the alternative work arrangement that some people dub the most complicated, problematic flexible work option." (*Personnel Journal*, Sept. 1994, p. 88)

**DUE DILIGENCE.** Thoroughly investigated (legal).
"Mr. Rowan and Mr. Gstalder negotiated for nearly ten months before making a deal. 'We did serious due diligence on each other,' says Mr. Gstalder." (*Wall Street Journal*, Jan. 17, 1996, p. A1)

**DUMP (TO).** Sell in foreign markets at prices below domestic market prices.

**DUN (TO).** Exert pressure for payment of past-due accounts.

**DUN & BRADSTREET (D&B).** Established credit evaluation company. Creditors and potential investors will often ask for a company's D&B report.

**DUPE (TO).** Duplicate; deceive.

**DUTCH AUCTION.** Pricing method used in the U.S. government securities market, where the lowest price bid necessary to sell the entire amount of securities offered becomes the price at which all are sold.

**DYNAMIC SCORING.** Political/economic forecasting technique that assumes that budget reductions stimulate economic activity thereby further reducing budget deficits.
"The Republicans are embracing dynamic scoring, the theorem that one can have his cake and eat it, too. The theorem postulates that one can cut taxes and accurately forecast the economic stimulus and additional revenues that the cut will produce." (*Barron's*, Dec. 19, 1994, p. 3)

# E

**EAGER-BEAVER.** Very energetic.

"He [Mr. Buchanan] had complained to the president that eager-beaver trustbusters were causing damage [to] party contributions. . . . There is a way we can trust-bust without doing in some of our best friends." (*Wall Street Journal,* March 14, 1996, p. A1)

**EAR CANDY.** Flattery. Compliments designed for a specific audience.

**EARL SCHEIB.** A quick and cheap job (reference to well-known car-painting firm).

**EARLY BIRD.** Person or object which arrives before the regular time.

"A glimmer of a silver lining is beginning to form around some of the 2nd quarter's darkest data. Several early-bird readings for June 1995 suggest that much of the economy's weakness will prove to be temporary." (*Business Week*, July 3, 1995, p. 23)

**EARMARK FOR (TO).** Set aside for.

"Precisely how much investors earmark for index funds and for active management depends on their investment horizon and risk tolerance." (*Money*, Aug. 1995, p. 68)

**EARNEST MONEY.** Deposit made when entering into a contract.

**EARNINGS PER SHARE (EPS).** Total profit for a period divided by the number of shares of stock outstanding.

**EARN ONE'S STRIPES (TO).** Put in time with an organization, thereby earning one's position or promotion (military).

**EASY AS A, B, C.** Very simple.

**EASYGOING.** Mild-mannered.

**EASY MARK.** Someone or something easily cheated.
"The company had acquired a reputation as an easy mark in the claims business." (*Business Marketing*, Feb. 1994, p. 34)

**EAT SOMEONE'S LUNCH (TO).** Overwhelm the competition. to eat the lunch of a competitor implies that one is taking bread (sales) from it right under its nose.

**ECONOMIC DARWINISM.** Survival of the strongest in the marketplace.
"Competition yields efficiency and efficiency benefits society. However, competitive societies live in fear; deadlines, sales quotas, profit margins, making the cut, or getting the job are all part of competitive market pressures. Competitive markets have been called 'economic Darwinism.'" (*Understanding NAFTA and Its International Business Implications*, 1996, p. 244)

**ECONOMIC GIANT.** Corporate or business leader.

**ECONOMIC MELTDOWN.** A severe downturn in the economy (nuclear reactors).
"An editorial discusses the US trade policy with Mexico. Today, Mexico is in economic meltdown, plunging toward a recession after a calamitous peso devaluation." (*Business Week*, March 6, 1995, p. 128)

**ECONOMIC TIDES.** Shifts in economic conditions.

**E.G. (EXEMPLI GRATIA).** For example (Latin).

**EGGS IN ONE BASKET.** All one's money in one investment.

" 'You don't want to have all your eggs in one basket, which is bad for any investment,' says Harry Markowitz, who won the Nobel in 1990 for his work on the theory of portfolio diversification." (*Wall Street Journal*, July 15, 1996, p. C1)

**EGO TRIP.** Self-centeredness.

**EIGHT-HUNDRED POUND GORILLA.** Powerful, important person or group.

"Fidelity, the 800-pound gorilla of brokerage-house clients, wants electronic access to the models used by the firms' analysts to estimate earnings of the companies they follow." (*Wall Street Journal*, Aug. 30, 1996, p. C1)

**EIGHTY-SIX IT (TO).** Throw it away.

**EIGHTY-TWENTY RULE.** The concept that a few items or customers generate most of the company's sales.

**ELECTRONIC FUNDS TRANSFER SYSTEM (EFTS).** Bank processing system that allows payments to be made without having to write a check.

**ELEPHANT HUNT.** Trying to find a major corporation to move into one's community, stimulating economic development. When South Carolina "snared" BMW Corp. and Alabama "bagged" Mercedes Benz to their state, they had carried out successful elephant hunts.

**ELEPHANTS.** Large institutional investors who tend to have a herd instinct, moving together as a group.

**ELEVENTH HOUR (AT THE).** Very last minute.

"In Mexico, the government of President Carlos Salinas de Gortari is spending nearly $1 billion on high-tech gizmos that promise to deliver a clear vote in the August 1994 presidential elections. . . . However, political analysts and opposition party members believe this eleventh-hour conversion to fair elections is half-hearted." (*Business Week*, June 13, 1995, p. 55)

**EL JEFE.** The boss (Spanish), a term of respect.

**ELVES.** Stock market technical analysts. Elves chart the movement of statistical measures of the stock market including volume, short sales, ODD-LOT sales and others. Elves make financial recommendations

based on these statistics, as opposed to changes in the FUNDAMEN-
TALS of a company or industry. See also CHARTISTS.

**EMINENT DOMAIN.** The power of government to seize private property for a public purpose.

**EMPLOYEE STOCK OWNERSHIP PLAN (ESOP).** A company program fostering employee purchases of stock. ESOPs have sometimes
been used by management to divest a company of unwanted divisions,
selling them to the employees, using their retirement funds.

**EMPLOYER IDENTIFICATION NUMBER (EIN).** The Internal
Revenue Service requires all employers to have an EIN.

**EMPOWERMENT.** To allow greater employee decision-making.
     "Management's definition [of empowerment]: Work harder with fewer
people, don't rock the boat and don't complain." (*Supervision*, Jan. 1994,
p. 3)

**EMPTY NEST.** A family whose children have grown up and left home.

**EMPTY SUITS.** Robot-like middle management executives.

**ENDANGERED SPECIES.** Nearing extinction.

**END-USER.** Ultimate user of a product or service.

**ENERGIZING VISION.** New idea. See also PARADIGM SHIFT.
     "Inspiring leadership, of the heart, engages with people, giving them
an energizing vision. All managers must exercise strategic and supervisory leadership of the head and hands. However, good managers go
further and inspire people with the heart—rendering their leadership
transforming." (*Leadership Organizational Development Journal*, June
1994, p. 8)

**ENTREPRENEURIAL SPIRIT.** Eagerness to take business risks.

**ENVIRONMENTAL IMPACT STATEMENT (EIS).** Government
document evaluating the environmental impact of a proposed project
or policy. Environmentalists have often insisted that government agencies produce a full EIS as a way to stall a program or project that they
oppose.

**ENVIRONMENTAL MOVEMENT.** Groups that encourage the pres-
ervation and protection of the earth.

"In the environmental movement's early days, the roles of those involved were simple and clearly defined. Coalitions of environmental groups lined up on one side, accusing big business of fouling the environment for the sake of profits." (*ENR*, Aug. 21, 1995, p. 51)

**ENVIRONMENTAL PROTECTION AGENCY (EPA).** Government environmental policy and enforcement agency created in 1970.

**E PLURIBUS UNUM.** "One among many" (Latin). The motto found over the wings of the eagle on a U.S. dollar bill.

**EQUAL EMPLOYMENT OPPORTUNITY COMMISSION (EEOC).** Government-created commission (1964) empowered to enforce equal opportunity laws in the United States.

**EQUITIZE/EQUITIZATION.** To reduce corporate debt in favor of equity.
"Thundering stocks alone do not account for the impulse to 'equitize'—certainly not among most of the nation's 20 million businesses. they are undergoing a private equitization, plowing earnings back into operations." (*Wall Street Journal*, Jan. 5, 1996, p. B1)

**ERROR RATE.** Number of faulty products expressed as a percentage of total output.

**ESCALATOR CLAUSE.** Part a contract providing for future increases in payments, taxes, wages, etc.

**ESQUIRE (ESQ.).** Honorary title used by attorneys.

**ET AL.** And others (Latin, abbreviated).

**EUROBOND.** A bond sold outside the United States but denominated in U.S. dollars.

**EUROPEAN UNION (EU).** Agreement among Western European countries creating access to each other's markets and allowing a flow of workers within the Union.

**EVEN BREAK.** A fair and equal chance.

**EVEN DEAD CATS BOUNCE.** Even stocks or bonds that were once considered worthless can rise in price.

**EVEN KEEL.** Balanced, steady.

"Dunkin' Donuts was founded by Rosenberg's father, and the younger Rosenberg spent his summer vacations as a boy working in the business. Bob Rosenberg earns respect through his soft-spoken, even-keel manner, which is the center of his ability to help others grow." (*Nation's Restaurant News*, Nov. 1995, p. 177)

**EXECUTIVE SUITE.** Top management position.

**EXIT INTERVIEW.** Personnel office interview of someone who is leaving the company.

"According to Jeff Grout, managing director of the recruitment agency Robert Half, exit interviews can be an outstanding source of feedback about an organization." (*Management Today*, Jan. 1995, p. 10)

**EXPLODING OFFER.** Job offer that has a specific deadline, after which it is no longer available.

**EX POST FACTO.** From a thing done afterwards (Latin), subsequently.

**EXPONENTIAL SMOOTHING.** Market forecasting method weighting past results.

**EXPOSURE.** In finance, exposure is financial risk; in marketing, exposure refers to visibility.

**EXTERNALITIES.** Costs or benefits not included in market prices.

**EYE-TO-EYE.** In agreement.

"On GATT\*, the Clinton administration reportedly was seeing eye-to-eye with steelmakers. The administration accepted about 80% of the fine-tuning provisions that the Congressional Steel Caucus wanted to insert in implementing legislation." (*Iron Age New Steel*, July 1994, p. 46)

**EYEBALL (TO).** Check by casually viewing.

**EYEBALL-TO-EYEBALL.** Direct communication. See also FACE-TO-FACE.

"But top congressional Republicans expect—and most congressional Democrats fear—that when these eyeball-to-eyeball confrontations transpire, after one veto, it will be Bill Clinton who blinks, following short-term political considerations." (*Wall Street Journal*, July 20, 1995, p. A13)

# F

**FACE-OFF.** Confrontation, argument (hockey).

**FACE THE MUSIC (TO).** Take the consequences.
" 'We know that we're going to face the music on paying something for the digital licenses DOWN THE ROAD, but we were absolutely opposed to any changes in the legislation,' one industry lobbyist said." (*Wall Street Journal*, Jan. 9, 1996, p. A3)

**FACE TIME.** Visibility in the office.
"Face time: concept that equates time spent in the office with career success." (*Wall Street Journal*, July 25, 1995, p. B1)

**FACE-TO-FACE.** In person.
"An editorial notes that business is not always conducted in cyberspace; more than anything, it is done face-to-face at parties, over a beer, in elevators." (*Advertising Age*, June 19, 1995, p. 21)

**FACE VALUE.** On a bond, the amount originally borrowed and to be paid at maturity.

**FAIRNESS DOCTRINE/EQUAL TIME.** Principle that U.S. media must provide time for opposing views on important social issues.

"The Fairness Doctrine refers to a former policy of the Federal Communications Commission (FCC) wherein a broadcast station which presented one viewpoint on a controversial public issue had to afford the opposing viewpoint an opportunity to be heard." (*Federal Communications Law Journal*, Sept. 1994, p. 51)

**FAIT ACCOMPLI.** An accomplished fact (French); something already taken place.

"In fact, though, people familiar with the situation say Ms. Brown had little part in the decision. It was brought to her as a virtual fait accompli fewer than two weeks earlier." (*Wall Street Journal*, Feb. 1, 1996, p. A1)

**FALL BY THE WAYSIDE (TO).** Decide not to continue; fail.

"Economists can so dislike the conclusions of an article that they comb through the article with the sole hope of refuting its logic. . . . They focus on minor points in the hope that more major issues will fall by the wayside." (*Journal of Economic Issues*, March 1995, p. 175)

**FALL DOWN ON THE JOB (TO).** Fail at one's responsibilities.

**FALLEN ANGELS.** Stocks or bonds which were originally considered of high quality but subsequently have become risky.

"CA [Computer Associates] is going to do a wonderful job here. They've proven that they can take fallen angels and revitalize them, said Charlie Federman." (*Wall Street Journal*, May 26, 1995, p. A3)

**FALL GUY.** Person blamed for a bad decision.

"Until stability prevails, the current trading crisis will continue. The media buyers and those clients who have chosen centralization should not, however, tolerate being used as fall guys." (*Marketing*, March 17, 1994, p. 10)

**FALLOUT.** Repercussions, side effects of a decision (reference to nuclear weapons).

"Fallout from the scrapping of Enron Development Corp's $2.9-billion power project in Dabhol, India, is still settling on the countryside of Maharashtra state and the companies that were part of the project." (*ENR*, Aug. 28, 1995, p. 25)

**FAMILY LEAVE.** Time off from work to take care of family members.

"To be sure, government can create laws and regulations to assist American families, the Family Leave bill vetoed by President Bush being the most recent example." (*B & E Review*, June 1993, p. 13)

**FAMILY VALUES.** Values associated with traditional home life in America. See also OZZIE AND HARRIET. In the 1990s the term has become associated with anti-abortion and anti-homosexual political groups.

**FAM TOUR.** Familiarization tour offered by to travel agents and convention organizers by tourism industry operators.

**FANNIE MAE.** See FEDERAL NATIONAL MORTGAGE ASSOCIATION.

**FAQs.** Frequently Asked Questions, especially with reference to the Internet.
"A list of frequently asked questions (FAQ) regarding unions and union membership are answered." (*Occupational Outlook Quarterly*, Winter 1994–1995, p. 16)

**FAR OUT.** Weird, out-of-the-ordinary (1960s slang).
"*People* magazine has gone online, with an electronic version of CompuServe. The online edition is typical of the magazine itself—trendy, but not too far out." (*Information*, March 1995, p. 17)

**FARM OUT (TO).** Subcontract; delegate.
"As large corporations cut costs and focus on CORE BUSINESSES, they increasingly farm out data processing, software development and telecommunications." (*Forbes*, March 27, 1995, p. 138)

**FAST BUCK.** Quickly earned money.
"Independent sales organizations (ISO), once viewed as sleazy, fast-buck operations, have transformed themselves into legitimate, and formidable, competitors for merchant business." (*Credit Card Management*, Nov. 1994, p. 86)

**FAST AND LOOSE.** Irresponsible; deceitful.
"In Asia, there is the potentially explosive combination of investment-bank salesmen from the financial capitals of the West playing fast and loose and their inexperienced Asian counterparts. The financial fire they are playing with falls under the rubric of derivatives." (*Far Eastern Economic Review*, Dec. 8, 1994, p. 48)

**FAST-TRACK.** The way to rapid promotion or success.

"According to Trask, building an HR department FROM SCRATCH has required as much care as delivering the perfect pizza. Within 2 years, Trask and her team of 7 HR personnel have standardized Papa John's culture, benefits, recruitment and retention efforts to keep the company on the fast track." (*Personnel Journal*, Sept. 1995, p. 38)

**FAST-TALKING.** Persuading with deceitful statements.

**FAT CAT.** Tycoon; wealthy person.
"A measure from the Clinton Administration, which is intended to make sure expatriating fat cats pay their fair share of taxes, is rocketing through the Senate despite protests that it would violate treaties governing human rights." (*Barron's*, March 27, 1995, p. 39)

**FAUX PAS.** Mistake ("false step," French).

**FEATHERBEDDING.** The practice of retaining unnecessary union jobs.
"In addition, Britain, long the home of rigid unionism, is now more flexible than the US when it comes to eliminating union featherbedding." (*Forbes*, March 28, 1994, p. 74)

**FEATURE DUMP.** Salesperson or sales promotion which talks about the product features only.

**FED.** See FEDERAL RESERVE BOARD.

**FEDERAL DEPOSIT INSURANCE CORPORATION (FDIC).** A quasi-government organization created during the Depression to insure depositor's funds in commercial banks after nearly ten thousand banks failed in two years.

**FEDERAL FUNDS.** Deposits made by commercial banks in their Federal Reserve Banks to meet reserve requirements.

**FEDERAL HOME LOAN BANK (FHLB).** Government system created to provide credit to the savings and loan industry. In 1989 the FHLB was replaced by the Federal Housing Lending Board.

**FEDERAL HOME LOAN MORTGAGE CORPORATION (FHLMC), "FREDDIE MAC."** Publicly held corporation that packages and resells mortgages to institutional investors.

**FEDERAL INSURANCE CONTRIBUTION ACT (FICA).** Federal law requiring employers and employees to contribute a percentage of their wage income to Social Security and Medicare programs.

**FEDERAL NATIONAL MORTGAGE ASSOCIATION (FNMA), "FANNIE MAE."** Originally a government agency (1938), this mortgage market intermediary buys federally insured mortgages from lenders, thereby releasing funds so that lenders can make more loans, and then packages the loans for resale to investors.

**FEDERAL RESERVE BOARD (FRB), "FED."** Semi-autonomous group responsible for monetary policy in the United States. The Open Market Committee of the Fed meets monthly, in secrecy, to review the performance of the economy and consider changes in discount rates, reserve requirements, or funds available in the lending markets.

**FEDERAL SAVINGS AND LOAN INSURANCE CORPORATION (FSLIC).** FSLIC was a quasi-government organization created during the Depression to insure depositor's funds in Savings & Loans. FSLIC went bankrupt in the 1980s. Bankrupt S&Ls* were taken over by the RTC*, and solvent S&Ls became members of FDIC*.

**FEDERAL TRADE COMMISSION (FTC).** Created in 1914, the FTC's goal is to stop unfair trade practices, including monopolies, price discrimination, and false advertising.

**FEEDBACK.** Response; especially, evaluation of performance.

**FEEDER.** A source of materials or supplies for a manufacturer.

**FEEDING FRENZY.** Impulsive buyer activity.
   "One thing seems sure: a feeding frenzy of mergers will ensue as companies scramble to keep up with Disney." (*Money*, Sept. 1995, p. 66)

**FENCED IN.** Cannot get out.

**F2F.** FACE-TO-FACE.

**FIAT MONEY.** Currency that has no intrinsic value. Fiat money is money because government declares it to be "legal tender." The danger with fiat money is that a government may decide to create too much of it, the most famous case being in Germany between World War I and World War II.

**FIGHTING BRAND.** Branded product introduced to compete with a competitor's product and protect the company's leading brand.

"British Airways (BA) is jeopardizing long-standing relationships with travel agents by launching World Offer, its first ever price-fighting brand. World Offer is an umbrella brand for discounted economy class tickets to destinations identified as having spare capacity." (*Marketing*, March 31, 1994, p. 5)

**FILE THIRTEEN.** Trash basket.

**FILTER OUT (TO).** Remove.

**FINDER'S FEE.** Fee charged by an intermediary in a business transaction.

**FINE PRINT.** Details of a contract.

"Environmental laws and rules, now 17 volumes of fine print, often seem to MISS THE MARK or prove counterproductive." (*Across the Board*, May 1995, p. 40)

**FIRE (TO).** Dismiss from a job. See also CAN.

"Why do seemingly well-intentioned folks go to great lengths to avoid using the words 'fired' or 'SACKED' and instead blither about 'initiating a career-alternative enhancement program?' " (*Industry Week*, Sept. 19, 1994, p. 18)

**FIRE AWAY (TO).** Begin asking questions whenever ready.

**FIRST CLASS.** Best available.

**FIRST IN, FIRST OUT (FIFO).** Accounting method which assigns cost to the ending inventory by assuming that the cost of the units in the ending inventory is also that of the most recent units purchased.

**FIRST OUT OF THE GATE (TO BE).** Initial leader; fast starter.

"The Risk Assessment bill will be first out of the gate to relate directly to the 9 major environmental statutes." (*Environment Today*, Jan./Feb. 1995, p. 22)

**FIRST STRING.** Best individual(s) (sports).

**FIRSTHAND.** Directly.

**FISCAL DRAG.** The time between when a government spending policy is approved and when it affects the economy.

"But like Mr. Bush before him, Mr. Clinton has locked in the fiscal drag of a tax increase. (*Wall Street Journal*, April 5, 1994, p. A18)

**FISCAL YEAR.** Year for accounting purposes, not necessarily beginning in January. The U.S. government's fiscal year runs from October 1 through September 30.

**FISH OR CUT BAIT (TO).** Be forced to decide.

**FISHBOWL.** In the public eye.

**FISHING EXPEDITION.** An enquiry into an issue without a developed plan.
   "This type of unplanned search for interesting findings has been called many things, from data sifting to a systematic fishing expedition." (*Marketing News*, April 25, 1994, p. 4)

**FISHYBACK.** Transportation system using both trucks and ships.

**FIT AND FINISH (TO).** Quality of execution of details; to complete the final details.
   "Overall, the fit and finish of both interior and exterior features are outstanding in keeping with the Toyota touch." (*Machine Design*, March 9, 1995, p. 304)

**FIVE AND DIME/TEN.** A variety store selling cheap items; low-priced merchandise.
   "Farah's main challenge will be to transfer the merchandising power that made his reputation at chains such as Saks Fifth Avenue from high fashion to five and dime goods." (*Discount Store News*, Jan. 2, 1995, p. 4)

**FLAK.** Abuse or criticism (World War II, German; or "flack").
   "The company cannot seem to stop attracting attention—not all of it good. Much of the flack has been aimed at ads for Death cigarettes, an account BHO won in January 1994." (*Adweek*, Oct. 31, 1994, p. 27)

**FLAG (TO).** Call attention to; stop production of.

**FLAGSHIP BRAND.** Leading brand.
   "McCann Amster Yard has drawn on the glamour of the early 1960s for an advertising campaign to rebuild Bacardi Martini's flagship brand." (*Adweek*, June 26, 1995, p. 6)

**FLAME (TO).** Send nasty messages on the Internet.

**FLAT.** Empty; completely sold out. In bond trading, "flat" means without any accrued interest.

**FLAT CHARGE.** Fixed price.

**FLESH OUT (TO).** Fill in the details of an agreement or procedure. After business or political leaders reach an agreement, staff members are often directed to flesh out the details.

**FLEXTIME/FLEXITIME.** Policy allowing workers to define their own working hours.

**FLIGHT TO QUALITY/VALUE.** Movement of capital to the safest investments.

**FLIP (TO).** Buy and then quickly sell shares of stock purchased in an INITIAL PUBLIC OFFERING.

**FLIP-FLOP (TO).** Change back and forth.
     "Socially, the wired society is likely to bring flip-flops in behavior like the changes wrought by the telephone, which made it acceptable for a man to talk to a strange woman without introduction by a 3rd party." (*Fortune*, March 20, 1995, p. 94)

**FLYING CIRCUS.** A fly-in and inspect tour by corporate executives. Such executives are likely to receive TRAVEL DAZZLE.

**FLOAT (TO).** Initiate; the time between when a check is written and when an account is debited.
     "Still, a planned merger is not the only reason to float a debt issue." (*Chemical Week*, Sept. 13, 1995, p. 28)

**FLOAT A LOAN (TO).** Borrow money.

**FLOOD (TO).** Overwhelm with the details; supply large quantities.
     "The wine market is flooded with value wines—fine tasting varieties that sell for under $10 a bottle." (*Business Week*, Aug. 28, 1995, p. 86)

**FLOOD OF ORDERS.** A sudden increase in demand.
     "In anticipation of a flood of orders for the Alpha chip, DEC built semiconductor foundries." (*Computer Technology Review*, Spring/Summer 1994, p. 8)

**FLOOR.** A lower limit, usually imposed by government on prices or wages.

**FLOP.** Failure.

**FLUB (TO).** Miss.
"The move to new $200,000 computer system at Professional Salon Concepts precipitated a plunge in sales, one of the few in the company's 11-year history, and almost caused the company to flub hundreds of critical shipments to customers." (*Inc.*, Dec. 1994, p. 46)

**FLUFF IT AND FLY IT (TO).** Make it look good and then sell it.

**FLUNKY.** Low-level employee. See also GOFER.

**FLUSH.** Having plenty of money.

**FLY-BY-NIGHT (BUSINESS).** Temporary; firm of questionable ethics.
"Terry Alexander is well known in Canadian circles for promoting PENNY-STOCK companies on the Vancouver exchange, which itself is unfortunately infamous as a haven for fly-by-night outfits." (*Barron's*, Aug. 21, 1995, p. 23)

**FOCUS GROUP.** A small group of potential consumers brought together to discuss a product or idea. Focus groups are used to get in-depth information from a small, select groups of customers or potential consumers.
"The men gathered in a focus group to discuss midlife crises generally regard them as vaguely embarrassing things that other people—men and women—sometimes have." (*Fortune*, Sept. 18, 1995, p. 72)

**FOLD (TO).** Close, quit.
"Executives at Detroit Newspapers, the joint agency that operates Knight-Ridder's morning *Free Press* and Gannett's evening *News*, vigorously deny any intention to fold the *News*, despite the continuing shrinking of its circulation." (*Editor and Publisher*, July 22, 1995, p. 11)

**FOLLOW-UP (TO).** Response to an inquiry; to check on status.
"Indeed, studies have found that sales forces' follow-up rates on leads nearly quadruple—from 10% to 39%—when a structured lead-management system is put in place." (*Sales & Marketing Management*, Sept. 1994, p. 46)

**FOLLOW THROUGH (TO).** Finish, complete a task.

**FOOD AND DRUG ADMINISTRATION (FDA).** Federal agency responsible for food, drug, and medical safety in the United States. The FDA was created in 1906 by the (Teddy) Roosevelt administration, in part because of Roosevelt's experience with contaminated food during the Spanish-American War.

**FOOD FOR PEACE.** International food giveaway program (Public Law 480).

**FOOTHOLD.** A beginning, a start.

**FOOT IN THE DOOR (TO GET ONE'S).** Establish an initial contact.
"The Ad Store has gotten its foot in the door at Coca-Cola. The 15-month-old New York shop was given the go ahead to produce 8 to 12 spots for the clients's Coca-Cola Classic brand." (*Adweek*, Jan. 23, 1995, p. 22)

**FORCE IN NUMBERS.** Power resulting from the presence of a large group.

**FORCE MAJEURE.** External contingencies that unavoidably affect performance of a contract (French).
"Regarding the passed deadline, Mr. Salih cited 'force majeure,' which allows a company to depart from the terms of a contract when an unanticipated event arises." (*Wall Street Journal*, Sept. 20, 1995, p. B4)

**FORCE THE NUMBERS (TO).** Make up numbers; manipulate statistics.

**FOREIGN/FREE TRADE ZONE (FTZ).** A special government program or location where firms can import materials and not pay duties until products made from the materials leave the FTZ. Products that are exported are exempt from import duty.

**FORMICA PARACHUTE.** Unemployment compensation. When U.S. corporations DOWNSIZE, executives often receive GOLDEN PARACHUTES, while rank-and-file employees receive only minimal unemployment compensation.

**FORTRESS EUROPE.** Protectionist policies of European countries (World War II).
"U.S. companies worried about the barriers brought on by 'Fortress Europe' now face another barrier to trade—extending credit without getting burned. Until recently, most business between the U.S. and Europe was done on a letter of credit basis." (*Global Trade and Transportation*, April 1994, p. 41)

**FORTUNE 500.** *Fortune* magazine's list of the five hundred largest manufacturing companies in the United States. In 1995 *Fortune* developed a separate list of the five hundred largest service companies.

**FOR YOUR INFORMATION (FYI).** For your consideration, usually not requiring a response.

**FOULED UP BEYOND ALL RECOGNITION (FUBAR).** A mess. "With its myriad of programs the welfare system in the U.S. is FUBAR." (Professor Martin McMahon, University of Kentucky, 1996)

**FOUR-FIFTHS RULE.** Used by the EEOC*. If an employment practice results in minorities being hired at a rate less than 80 percent of white applicants, the EEOC may rule that the minority group has been adversely affected by the practice.

**FOUR Ps.** A firm's marketing mix: product, price, promotion, and place.

**FOUR TIGERS.** Taiwan, Singapore, Hong Kong, and Korea.
   "Most Americans know that Taiwan is one of Asia's 'Four Tigers,' but few are aware of the spectacular statistics behind the country's achievements." (*Forbes*, Jan. 16, 1995, p. 35)

**FREDDIE MAC.** See FEDERAL HOME LOAN MORTGAGE CORPORATION.

**FREEDOM OF INFORMATION ACT (FOIA).** Federal law requiring open access to government information.

**FREE-FLOWING.** Loose.

**FREE LUNCH.** Something for nothing—proverbially, what there is no such thing as. In business the saying "there's no such thing as a free lunch" means that everything has a cost.

**FREE ON BOARD (FOB).** Invoicing term meaning that the buyer pays shipping costs.

**FREE RIDERS.** Those who do not pay but enjoy the benefits.

**FREE-WHEELING.** Creative; ignoring rules or laws.
   "Machine-tool firms generally are not famous for free-wheeling management, but many are now among the nation's most progressive companies when it comes to management styles and technical innovation." (*Machine Design*, Sept. 26, 1994, p. 16)

**FRINGE BENEFITS.** Nonwage compensation that comes with a job. Fringe benefits may include health insurance, travel and clothing allowances, retirement plans, and other PERKS.

**FROBNICATE/FROB (TO).** Manipulate or adjust.

"If someone is turning a knob on an oscilloscope, then if he's carefully adjusting it he is probably tweaking; if he is just turning it but looking at the screen he is probably twiddling it; but if he is just doing it because turning a knob is fun, he's frobbing it." (Professor Julianne Morgan, USCA, 1996)

**FROM SCRATCH/THE GROUND UP/THE WORD "GO."** From the beginning.

"In these days of ownership CHURN and affiliation switches, many stations face having to start a newscast from the ground up." (*Broadcasting & Cable*, Sept. 4, 1995, p. 31)

**FRONT LOADING/FRONT-END LOAD.** Loan fee or sales commission paid from the initial funds borrowed.

**FRONT MONEY.** The initial amount needed to start a project.

**FRONT OFFICE.** The central office, office that deals with customers.

**FROWN UPON (TO).** Disapprove of.

**FROZEN ASSETS.** Assets that cannot be bought or sold because of a legal dispute.

**FRUITS OF ONE'S LABOR.** Money or assets one worked to acquire.

**FUBAR.** See FOULED UP BEYOND ALL RECOGNITION.

**FUDGE THE FIGURES (TO).** Cheat with numbers. See also CREATIVE ACCOUNTING.

"Some economists worry about how the public, especially investors, will greet the new GDP data. Making matters potentially worse, the BEA may fudge the dollar equivalents of the chain-weighted indexes to make everything add up." (*Business Week*, July 31, 1995, p. 74)

**FULFILLMENT.** Filling orders from mail-order marketing.

"Fulfillment houses and in-house departments are working in ways to bring customer service up to speed by implementing formal service programs and restructuring their management philosophies to emphasize customer retention." (*Folio*, Sept. 1, 1995, p. 50)

**FULL COURT PRESS.** Maximum pressure, all-out effort (basketball).

"The U.S. Department of Labor and scores of pension groups are making a full court press on the American public and Congress to get them into better shape on saving and retirement issues." (*Business Insurance*, Sept. 18, 1995, p. 48)

**FULL FAITH AND CREDIT.** The promise that accompanies government debt issues.

"Perhaps the most important new condition is that deals be backed with some full-faith credit guarantee." (*International Business*, May 1995, p. 20)

**FULL OF BULL/HOT AIR.** Meaningless talk, boastfulness.

**FULL-SERVICE AGENCY.** A large advertising agency that can provide anything a client wants.

"Jack Myers, president of Myers Communications, said that the trend away from independents is less a function of them losing the business than full-service agencies responding to these changes and winning it." (*Advertising Age*, April 10, 1995, p. 1)

**FUMBLE (TO).** Make a mistake, error (football).

"Katie Muldoon of Muldoon & Baer Inc. says people fumble the all-important selling of their business plan all the time. She says entrepreneurs have to know their audience, write to their audience, and present their plan in a well-organized format." (*Success*, May 1995, p. 14)

**FUNDAMENTALS.** Basic operations or activities of a business. In the 1990s many American businesses are returning to their fundamentals. See also CORE BUSINESS.

**FUZZWORD.** Business jargon.

"In effect, a fuzzword carries with it an aura of a new, more exciting reality, but one that has no basis in the real world." (*Marketing News*, May 10, 1993, p. 4)

# G

**GAINSHARING.** Management program where workers' pay is related to various performance goals.

"Gainsharing is tied to the achievement of specific goals, such as productivity, quality improvement and cost effectiveness." (*Wall Street Journal*, May 30, 1996, p. A11)

**GALLEY.** Preliminary layout for a print publication.

**GAME PLAN.** Marketing strategy (football).

"Increased growth and an enhanced focus on marketing technology will be the game plan for Westin Hotels & Resorts following its recent sale and naming of Juergen Bartels as chairman and CEO.*" (*Hotel & Motel Management*, June 19, 1995, p. 1)

**GAME THEORY.** Management planning technique based on anticipating competitors' actions and reactions.

**GARAGE SALE.** Sale of unwanted items at extremely low prices.

"Viewers must sort through an unlabeled mass of cooking implements, kerosene lamps, manual typewriters, wooden eagles, rusty bicycles, cut-glass decanters and antique chests—it's like being at a garage sale." (*Wall Street Journal*, May 12, 1995, p. A11)

**GARBAGE IN, GARBAGE OUT (GIGO).** Output can be no better than the quality of the inputs.

"Systems are no better than the quality of data received from users; reusing proven building blocks frees users to focus on the difference between what is already available and what they need. The smaller this crucial gap, the smaller the risk of 'design gigo' (garbage-in-garbage-out)." (*Software Magazine*, Nov. 1994, p. 96)

———— **GATE.** A scandal.

"Since Watergate, the 1970s political scandal that ended the Nixon presidency, visible unethical activities in the U.S. are commonly referred to as '———— gates.' " (Dr. Robert Botsch, professor of political science, USCA, 1996)

**GATEKEEPER.** Person who controls access to managers. Gatekeepers are important members of organizational buying centers. They control the flow of information to be reviewed by the group making purchase decisions.

**GAZUMP (TO).** Raise the price after initially agreeing to a lower one (real estate).

"Gazumping may sound like a polite response to a sneeze, or perhaps a sneeze itself. . . . 'It's become slang for when a seller disappoints an intended purchaser by raising the price after accepting his or her offer.' " (*Wall Street Journal*, June 6, 1996, p. B10)

**GEAR UP (TO).** Get ready.

"Marketing plans for the upcoming MCI/News Corp.'s Internet-based, online service will tap into Fox TV's allure with young audiences as the new $2 billion company gears up for an announcement on its programming and name by November." (*Brandweek*, Sept. 25, 1995, p. 5)

**GENERAL ACCOUNTING OFFICE (GAO).** Congressional accounting agency monitoring fiscal activities of the government. The GAO and its executive branch counterpart the OMB*, often differ in budget estimates and assumptions.

**GENERAL AGREEMENT ON TARIFFS AND TRADE (GATT).** 1940s United Nations'–sponsored agreement to reduce and eliminate trade barriers. The GATT was incorporated in the WORLD TRADE ORGANIZATION in 1994.

**GENERALLY ACCEPTED ACCOUNTING PRINCIPLES (GAAP).**
Accepted rules and procedures for accounting.

"Starting next year, all life insurers will need to comply with the same set of accounting standards if their financial statements are to be regarded as GAAP—the standard used by all publicly held companies." (*National Underwriter*, June 26, 1995, p. 37)

**GENERAL OBLIGATION BOND (GO BOND).** A municipal bond (tax-free for federal income) that is backed by the municipality issuing it. GO bonds are considered less risky than revenue bonds, which are issued by municipalities, tax-free, but are backed only by the revenue from the investment made with the funds from the sale of the bonds.

**GENERAL SERVICE (GS) RATING.** Most federal government service jobs in the United States have a GS rating which determines the payscale for the position.

**GENERATION X.** Young Americans in the 1990s searching for an identity.

"House of Seagram plans to reposition one of its trademark brands, 7 Crown, for the 21–29-year old market. The plan calls for restaging 7 Crown in the popular shooter category for the first time, as the company responds to the changing drinking habits of Generation X." (*Brandweek*, Jan. 30, 1995, p.14)

**GET A JUMP ON (TO).** A head start; to get started before your competitors.

"In other news, the best explanation for the stock market decline that began on Thursday and picked up steam in the final session is that mutual fund portfolio managers all decided to get a jump on the crowds and lit off for the hills or the beach or their backyard hammocks." (*Barron's*, May 29, 1995, p. 3)

**GET A KICK OUT OF (TO).** Enjoy.

"Some adult wearers opt for conspicuous styles. . . . The Grapevine, Texas, pediatric dentist, whose braces as a teenager didn't quite do the trick, says her patients get a kick out of it." (*Wall Street Journal*, Feb. 14, 1995, p. B1)

**GET AWAY WITH (TO).** Do something wrong without getting caught.

**GET BEHIND (TO).** Support.

**GET BOUNCED (TO).** Be forced out, fired.

**GET IT TOGETHER (TO).** Become organized.

"The era of cooperation-coordination is here, except in one area: rail management and rail labor still cannot get it together, working for mutual benefit." (*Railway Age*, Sept. 1993, p. 9)

**GET IT WHILE THE GETTING'S GOOD (TO).** Take the opportunity while it is there.

**GET LOST.** Go away (impolite command).

"Brand franchise mergers and acquisitions are on a roll, and will continue to be on a roll because consumers and retailers have forced marketers into that 'get out front or get lost' mentality that led to the Quaker, Grand Metropolitan and Campbell moves late last year and in early 1995." (*Brandweek*, June 26, 1995, p. 16)

**GET MILEAGE OUT OF (TO).** Exploit; to benefit from.

**GET ONE'S DUCKS IN A ROW (TO).** Get organized.

**GET RICH SCHEME.** Way to make money fast (often risky or fraudulent).

"Despite the potential of INFOMERCIALS, by 1994 this exciting, promising uniquely sales-intensive medium has remained a ghetto for gadgets, get-rich schemes and gaudy promises of fantasies fulfilled." (*Advertising Age*, April 11, 1995, p. S8)

**GET SIDETRACKED (TO).** Become distracted.

**GET THE AX (TO).** Be dismissed, eliminated.

"Americans want the government to reduce the federal deficit but do not want any cuts in entitlements—Medicare, Medicaid, Social Security, and unemployment insurance. . . . Once investors see entitlements get the ax, they will acknowledge that serious deficit reduction is under way by helping trigger a long-term decline in interest rates." (*Money*, April 1995, p. 186)

**GET THE BALL ROLLING (TO).** Get things started.

**GET/GIVE THE BOOT.** Be dismissed.

"News from Britain today that the London Stock Exchange has given its Chief Executive the boot." (*Marketplace*, National Public Radio, Jan. 4, 1996)

**GET THE BUSINESS (TO).** Be treated roughly.

**GET THE DRIFT/HANG OF IT (TO).** Understand.

**GET THE INK/INK IT (TO).** Get the customer to sign the contract.

**GET THE PINK SLIP (TO).** Be dismissed.

**GET TO WHERE THE ACTION IS (TO).** Find where decisions are made or opportunities can be found.

**GETTING AT (WHAT ONE IS).** The point or essence of what one is saying.

**GETTING ONE'S FEET WET.** Beginning to learn about a new market/product.

**GHOST RIDER.** Person who falsely claims to have been in a vehicle involved in an accident in an effort to collect for alleged injuries.

**GIFFEN GOODS.** Goods that do not obey the law of demand, in that quantity demanded decreases as price decreases (from British economist, Robert Giffen).

**GILT-EDGE.** Of high quality and reliability.
   "Gilt-edged bonds are marketable bonds denominated in sterling that are issued by the Bank of England on behalf of the treasury." (*Euromoney*, Aug. 1995, p. 68)

**GIMMICK.** A special item practice or feature of a product designed to gain customer interest.
   "Repeating a word is an easy mechanical gimmick, but the word should be strong and should be used 3 times." (*Direct Marketing*, Dec. 1993, p. 36)

**GINNIE MAE.** Nickname for GOVERNMENT NATIONAL MORTGAGE ASSOCIATION.

**GIVE A LITTLE (TO).** Compromise.

**GIVE-BACKS.** The surrender by unions of previously agreed upon benefits.
   "Carey's 1991 campaign took a hard line against wage concessions, relaxation of work rules, and other give-backs." (*Traffic Management*, Feb. 1994, p. 34)

**GIVE IT THE ONCE-OVER (TO).** Check something but not spend a lot of time carefully reviewing it.

**GIVE SOMEONE PAPER (TO).** Place an order.

**GIVE THE NOD (TO).** Give approval to a plan; perceive as having an advantage. "You'd have to give the nod to Delcor at this point." (*Wall Street Journal*, May 17, 1995, p. A3)

**GIVE THEM THE NICKEL TOUR.** Make it fast.

**GLAD-HANDING.** Shaking hands with everyone present. See also SCHMOOZING.

**GLAMOR STOCK.** A stock that is widely followed. In the 1990s many technology companies have become glamor stocks.

**GLASS CEILING.** Invisible barrier (discrimination) to career advancement for women and minorities.
   "The consensus at the 4th annual Women's Foodservice Forum (WFF) was that women are breaking through the food service glass ceiling that has blocked them from the executive suite, but progress must be accelerated in this direction." (*Restaurants & Institutions*, June 15, 1995, p. 32)

**GLASS-STEAGALL (ACT OF 1933).** Depression-era banking reforms that prohibited commercial banks from offering stock brokerage and insurance services. Banking reforms in the 1980s and 1990s have gradually removed many of the barriers among these service industries.

**GLIMMER OF HOPE.** A slight chance of success.
   "There remains a glimmer of hope in South Korea's overall business conditions as the prolonged sluggishness appears to be ending." (*Business Korea*, May 1992, p. 12)

**GLITCH.** A small problem or temporary setback.
   "Just weeks before the scheduled launch of Windows 95, Microsoft Corp. has issued a list of software products it says have Windows 95 compatibility glitches." (*Computer Reseller News*, Aug. 7, 1995, p. 1)

**GLITZ/GLITZY.** Flashiness/bright, showy.
   "Boxing is now valued for the incremental revenue it can produce for the people who host the fight. No one realizes that more than casino operators, who attract gamblers to their desert castles with a surreal

mix of glitz, entertainment and fantasy." (*Financial World*, Feb. 14, 1995, p. 54)

**GLOBAL ARENA.** World marketplace.

**GLOBALITY.** Functioning on a global basis.

**GLOBAL PACE OF CHANGE.** Speed of business worldwide.

**GLOBASM.** A company or executive who becomes obsessed with expanding globally is said to be experiencing globasm.

**GO BELLY UP (TO).** Fail; go bankrupt.

**GO BOND.** See GENERAL OBLIGATION BOND.

**GOFER.** Low-ranking employee; errand boy (from "go-for").
"I was a gofer in the studio, says Mr. Iovine. If you bring somebody tea 100 times and get it right each time, they get to like you." (*Wall Street Journal*, Feb. 22, 1996, p. B1)

**GO-GO FUND.** Risky, aggressive mutual fund. These funds tend to do well in BULL markets but poorly in declining markets.

**GOING CONCERN.** Existing business.

**GOING LONG.** Purchasing a stock or other investment.

**GOING SHORT.** Selling a stock without owning the shares. When going short an investor sells shares borrowed from the brokerage firm, expecting the price of the stock to decline. See also SHORT SQUEEZE.

**GOING THE EXTRA MILE.** Paying attention to detail; providing quality service.
"Going the extra mile is the theme of new seminars to help hotel front-desk agents deal with 'challenging check-ins and check-outs' and curb the growth of costly no-shows." (*Wall Street Journal*, March 14, 1996, B1)

**GOLDBRICKER.** Employee who tries to do the least amount of work without getting fired, lazy worker. The author's father told the story of a framing carpenter who, when he heard the 4:00 whistle ending the workday, had a nail halfway into the piece of wood. When asked why he pulled the nail out of the wood rather than nailing it in, the goldbricker replied, "I don't get paid for overtime." (Ex Rel. Morris Folsom, 1970)

**GOLDBUG.** Investor in gold or gold stocks. Goldbugs perceive the commodity to be a safe investment during period of depression or hyperinflation.

**GOLDEN FLEECE AWARD.** Symbol of exorbitant prices (from ancient Greek mythology). For years former U.S. Senator William Proxmire made symbolic Golden Fleece Awards bringing public attention to inflated prices charged by businesses for products sold to the government.

**GOLDEN GOOSE.** The prize; valuable asset. The golden goose is used in many fairy tales as a magical source of wealth.
   "Draconian changes in the province [Hong Kong] may kill the golden goose." (Mary Kay Magstad, "Marketplace," National Public Radio, Jan. 9, 1996)

**GOLDEN HANDCUFFS.** Attractive financial incentive designed to keep executives from leaving a company.
   "Another emerging trend is the use of golden handcuffs, an agreement designed to keep the executive committed to the institution, usually taking the form of deferred compensation arrangements." (*Hospitals*, Feb. 20, 1995, p. 66)

**GOLDEN PARACHUTE.** Special retirement benefits for executives.
   "Investors and analysts argue that top Kemper executives have the wrong incentive to sell—golden parachutes—paying as much as $19 million and new jobs waiting in the wings." (*Journal of Taxation*, Jan. 1995, p. 56)

**GOLD MINE.** A very profitable opportunity.
   "While older folks may fret over long-term care, life insurance companies are coming to see it as a potential gold mine." (*Euromoney*, July 1995, p. 51)

**GO NAKED (TO).** Stock market action of selling a call option without owning the stock.

**GOOD-OLD-BOY CLUB SYSTEM/NETWORK.** See OLD-BOY CLUB/ NETWORK.

**GOOD-TILL-CANCELED ORDER (GTC).** Stock market buy or sell order with no time restriction. Most stock orders are either day-orders or GTC.

**GOODWILL.** The amount by which the purchase price for a business exceeds the value of its real assets.

"Goodwill forms a substantial part of the total asset structure of a typical company, and is therefore of considerable concern to accounting regulators." (*Accounting and Business Review*, Winter 1993, p. 79)

**GO PUBLIC (TO).** Sell shares of stock in a company that was previously privately owned.

"Along with estate taxes that are close to confiscatory of private businesses, such feuds will force many private companies to go public or sell out." (*Forbes*, Dec. 6, 1993, p. 140)

**GO THROUGH THE RANKS (TO).** Start at the bottom of an organization and be promoted upward.

**GO TO BAT FOR (TO).** Support (baseball).

"Utah Insurance Commissioner Robert Wilcox told members that he would go to bat for them if necessary on the issue of residential mortgage limits in the National Association of Insurance Commissioners' proposed model investment law. The model investment law's 50% limit on residential loans may hurt small companies." (*National Underwriter*, Oct. 3, 1994, p. 64)

**GOVERNMENT NATIONAL MORTGAGE ASSOCIATION "GINNIE MAE." (GNMA).** Government corporation which guarantees payment on mortgage-backed securities.

**GRAB YOUR WALLET.** Be careful with your money.

**GRACE PERIOD.** Period of time until a bill becomes due.

"While it is true that distributions from individual retirement accounts (IRA) are not taxed if they are ROLLED OVER to new IRAs within 60 days of receipt, this tax-free grace period, which allows an individual to put the funds to short-term use, can be used only once in a one-year period." (*Small Business Reports*, Sept. 1993, p. 65)

**GRAIN OF SALT (WITH A).** Less than certitude.

"Part of the problem: too-rosy projections. Market studies must be taken 'with a grain of salt,' says Mr. Caden." (*Wall Street Journal*, April 18, 1996, p. A1)

**GRANDFATHER CLAUSE.** A provision in a law exempting existing individuals or businesses from the requirements of a new law.

"Although banks are barred from selling insurance, Chase and a few others have grandfather clauses that exempt them." (*Advertising Age*, May 24, 1993, p. 46)

**GRAPEVINE.** Informal office communication network; gossip.

"People in the human resource department need to manage communications effectively so that the grapevine is not the main source of information." (*Training & Development*, April, 1995, p. 28)

**GRASS STAIN.** Slight damage or signs of strenuous effort. In baseball, the players who have played usually have dirty uniforms, including grass stains, while those who sat on the bench have clean uniforms.

"Because we PLAYED BALL, we came through with a few grass stains but no serious injuries." (*Wall Street Journal*, June 17, 1996, p. A14)

**GRAVE INSULT.** Serious affront.

**GRAVEYARD SHIFT.** Work shift that starts around midnight.

**GREASE (TO).** Make happen by the payment of a bribe.

**GREASY SPOON.** A small, cheap restaurant.

"Today's diners must overcome an image, often incorrect, of a greasy spoon." (*Nation's Restaurant News*, Jan. 16, 1995, p. 7)

**GREAT DEAL OF.** Lots of.

**GREATER FOOL THEORY.** The idea that there is always someone willing to pay a higher price.

"When stocks are selling a 100 times or infinite times earnings they are depending on the greater fool theory." (Scott Black, on *Wall Street Week*, Nov. 3, 1995)

**GREAT SOCIETY PROGRAMS.** Social programs initiated during the Lyndon Johnson administration, 1964–1968.

"With the 'Great Society' programs of the 1960s, and with robust economic growth, the percentage of Americans in poverty fell from 22.4% to 11.1% by 1973." (*Barron's* Jan. 30, 1995, p. 53)

**GREEN CARD.** Immigration permit allowing a person to work in the United States.

**GREEN LIGHT.** Signal to proceed.

"After being left in the dust several times by rivals Ford and Chrysler, General Motors (GM) gave a green light to its first payout boost since February, 1989." (*Barron's*, May 8, 1995, p. 39)

**GREENMAIL.** Payment made to a CORPORATE RAIDER to stop buying up shares of the company.

**GREEN REVOLUTION.** The hoped-for increase in output from the use of Western technology in agricultural production in the developing world.

"The agribusiness revolution will dwarf the impact of the green revolution that swelled crop yields and ended famine in India, says Felipe Mantiega of the U.S. Agency for International Development in New Delhi." (*Wall Street Journal*, March 13, 1996, p. A9)

**GREENPEACE.** International organization which fights for environmental issues using visible symbolic efforts, including protests at nuclear test sites and intervention in the whaling industry.

**GREEN SHOE.** When an underwriter of an INITIAL PUBLIC OFFERING has the option to sell extra shares.

"The deal will consist of 5 million Stripes (Structured Yield Product Exchangeable for Stock), plus a potential 15% green shoe, to be priced at MGIC's closing quote on the night of the offering." (*Investment Dealers Digest*, Aug. 8, 1994, p. 9)

**GREY MARKET.** Legal but unauthorized (by the producer) distribution channel. Many U.S. manufacturers license their technology and brands abroad. Licensees agree not to sell their output in the U.S. but their distributors are not bound by this arrangement.

**GRIND TO A HALT/SCREECHING HALT (TO).** Stop suddenly.

**GROSS.** Total sales or revenue; twelve dozen.

**GROSS IMPRESSIONS.** The total number of exposures to a marketer's message. One person seeing an advertisement four times counts as four exposures.

**GROSS RATING POINTS.** Total gross impressions, expressed as a percentage of the population.

**GROSS REACH.** Total potential viewers of an advertisement.

**GROUNDWORK.** Foundation; preliminary research, or contacts made in establishing business relationships.

"The initial groundwork rests mainly with the project sponsor. The sponsor needs to identify the belief or assumption that the outcome study will investigate." (*HR Focus*, Dec. 1993, p. 14)

**GROUP OF SEVEN (G-7).** The seven largest industrial countries, including Canada, France, Germany, Great Britain, Italy, Japan, and the United States. In the 1990s, representatives of Russia were first invited to attend G-7 meetings.

**GUARANTEED INVESTMENT CONTRACT (GIC).** Retirement investment product offered by insurance companies.

"Most 401(k) plans offer some type of stable-value investment option. Plan sponsors have chosen GICs, which are bond-like obligations issued by insurance companies and pay fixed-interest rates, usually for periods ranging from 3 to 5 years." (*Pension Management*, May 1995, p. 50)

# H

**HACKER.** Computer nerd who illegally enters computer systems; a poor golfer.

**HACK IT (TO).** Succeed; put up with.

**HALF TONES.** Photographs used in advertising pieces.

**HALO EFFECT.** Situation where past positive perceptions influence current judgment.

"The idea is that marketers will also benefit from a halo effect as consumers, seeing the HelpAd logo on a product, choose it over a competing brand in order to help a good cause." (*Journal of Healthcare Finance*, Spring 1995, p. 48)

**HAMMER OUT (TO).** Come to an agreement through difficult negotiation.

"Corporate chieftains, seeking to acquire businesses they know well, sit down and hammer out deals face-to-face." (*Wall Street Journal*, March 6, 1996, p. A1)

**HAMMER THE MARKET (TO).** Sell large quantities of a stock at one time.

**HAND OVER FIST (TO MAKE MONEY).** So profitable that one is overwhelmed just taking in the money.

**HANDS-ON (MANAGEMENT STYLE).** Direct involvement with employees' activities.

"Questioned before Congress about influence peddling at the Department of Housing and Urban Development several years ago, Mr. Pierce swore he had no 'hands on' involvement in his own agency's funding decisions." *Wall Street Journal*, March 21, 1996, p. A1)

**HANG IT UP (TO).** Quit; retire.

**HANG OUT ONE'S SHINGLE (TO).** Start a business, announce the opening of a business.

"Merchants that hang out an electronic shingle in cyberspace don't have to worry about shelf space and can target their marketing to interested customers at a fraction of the cost." (*Wall Street Journal*, June 17, 1996, p. R6)

**HANG TOUGH (TO).** Continue to struggle.

**HAPPY HOUR.** After-work promotional specials at a bar or restaurant. In the United States, happy hour is usually from 4:00 P.M. to 7:00 P.M.

"The group was about to adjourn for happy hour, and 'we told them they were going to have to earn those drinks,' says Kim Chairez, the division's escrow coordinator." (*Wall Street Journal*, Nov. 11, 1995, p. B1)

**HARDBALL.** Aggressive competition (baseball).

"Microsoft Plays Hardball: the Use of Exclusionary Pricing in Markets for Operating System Software." (*Antitrust Bulletin*, Summer 1995, p. 265)

**HARD CURRENCY.** Money easily accepted worldwide.

**HARD HAT.** Manual laborer. See also BLUE-COLLAR WORKER.

**HARD-HITTING.** Forceful; strong-willed (football).

"The catalog is the very antithesis of the soft sell, and its maximum-impact graphics and stand-out prices drive home the message of long-lasting clothing for the budget-conscious buyer. Product stills are hard-hitting close-ups of Wearguard's built-to-last work clothes." (*Material-Handling Engineering*, Sept. 1994, p. 24)

**HARD-NOSED.** critical, inflexible.

"Over the years, and without consistent gains, Washington has tried everything from the GLAD HAND to the hard nose to wrest open the Japanese economy." (*Wall Street Journal*, Aug. 26, 1994, p. A6)

**HARD NUMBERS.** Facts rather than estimates.

"Direct marketing is the only medium that allows you to use hard numbers to plan, engineer and measure programs." (*Target Marketing*, Aug. 1995, p. 24)

**HATCHET MAN.** Junior executive who is given the task of firing employees.

"The employee GRAPEVINE quickly pegged Mr. Mercer as a 'hatchet man,' according to numerous workers." (*Wall Street Journal*, Feb. 10, 1995, p. A1)

**HAUL.** Large sum of money, sometimes obtained illegally.

**HAVE THE INSIDE TRACK.** Have an advantage.

"U.S. firms seem to have something of an inside track: Twenty-three of the 41 pending electricity projects bid on by non-Indian companies have gone American." (*Communications Week*, May 29, 1995, p. 38)

**HAWTHORNE EFFECT.** Study which found that any changes in working conditions improved productivity.

"Hawthorne effect refers to the findings of a 1924 study that measured the correlation between specific working conditions and output. It showed that productivity increased (regardless of particular changes) whenever the workers sensed that they were regarded as valued members of the organization." (*Supervisory Management*, May 1990, p. 6)

**HEAD HONCHO.** Top boss. The term honcho comes from Japanese, *han-cho*, the leader of a small group.

"Once held only by the head honcho, the title of 'chief' is now running rampant through the executive suite—and overuse threatens to dim its luster." (*Wall Street Journal*, July 8, 1996, p. B1)

**HEADHUNTER.** Recruiter who find executives for companies; implies stealing people from other organizations.

**HEADLIGHTING.** To bring issues up for discussion and consideration before they become crises.

"Texas Instruments is doing some headlighting by listing, as much as a year in advance, which jobs are in jeopardy and asking those employees, 'What do we need to do to broaden you out to look for a job inside or outside TI*?' " (*Wall Street Journal*, Oct. 3, 1995, p. B1)

**HEALTH MAINTENANCE ORGANIZATION (HMO).** Healthcare group which charges a fixed fee per member and provides a wide range of services to the members. From World War II until the 1990s, most health insurance programs in the United States allowed the insured person to choose any health provider. The premiums for this insurance were usually paid by the employer. HMOs have expanded rapidly in the 1990s as a means to constrain healthcare costs for employers.

**HEARTLAND.** The noncoastal areas of the United States. The heartland in the United States is perceived to have more "traditional," conservative values.

**HEAVY HITTER/HEAVYWEIGHT.** Very important person, business.
"With dreams of success like that of such heavy hitters as Boston Market and Au Bon Pain, several local Boston-area operators are doggedly fine-tuning their privately held concepts and hunting for suitable real estate in the quest for growth." (*Nation's Restaurant News*, July 31, 1995, p. 3)

**HEDGE (TO).** Insure or protect against losses.

**HELICOPTER (TO).** Maintain a presence in a corporation; to observe the overall economic trends.
"The Ten Deadly Euphemisms, Part 2: 1. Helicoptering. To advance, you must hover over the corporate scene to observe the broad economic tides that push companies into new businesses that create opportunities, or out of old businesses that eliminate them." (*Wall Street Journal*, Oct. 3, 1995, p. B1)

**HEMLINE THEORY.** U.S. stock market phenomenon correlating fashions for short skirts with BULLISH markets and longer skirts with BEARISH markets.

**HERD INSTINCT/MENTALITY.** Everyone follows the leaders.
"In times of crisis, stock markets are propelled largely by psychology. As bandwagons form, investors' herd instincts frequently push prices higher than they ought to go." (*Business Week*, Feb. 13, 1995, p. 84)

**HEYDAY.** Good times.
"The revamp marks a return to the visual strengths which helped the paper to a circulation of 422,000 in its late 1980s heyday." (*HR Focus*, May 1995, p. 14)

**HIDDEN AGENDA.** Important issues that are not officially part of a meeting; personal antagonism between managers.

**HIDDEN COST.** Unexpected or difficult-to-measure costs.

**HIERARCHICAL COMMAND.** Traditional, from-the-top-down management.

**HIGH COTTON (IN).** Conceited (Southern).

**HIGH END.** More expensive; powerful; up-to-date.

**HIGHER GEAR.** A faster pace.

**HIGHER-UPS.** Senior administrators. See TOP BRASS, MUCKY-MUCKS.
    "Whether or not the higher-ups are buying or selling their stock can be a clue about the future of a company, an industry, even the overall market." (*Business Week*, Aug. 7, 1995, p. 74)

**HIGH-FLYER.** A stock or investment whose price has risen rapidly; implies that it may be a risky investment at the time.

**HIGH-WIRE ACT.** Risky decision.
    "Brainchildren have a tendency to become risk junkies. . . . Encourage them to perform their high-wire acts, but install a safety net and keep it there." (*Wall Street Journal*, Oct. 30, 1995, p. B1)

**HIKE PRICES (TO).** Increase prices.

**HILL (THE).** Capitol Hill in Washington, D.C., site of the legislative branch of the U.S. government.

**HIRED GUNS.** Lawyers, accountants, and other business strategy consultants.
    "In the opening rounds, Charleston formed task forces charged with defending specific facilities targeted by the Pentagon, enlisted some hired guns from Washington, and mounted a sophisticated and unrelenting public-relations campaign that ran throughout the Defense Base Realignment and Closure Commission's 4-month decision-making process." (*Government Executive*, Sept. 1994, p. 30)

**HIT.** A success; a huge loss. Rapid sales of a new product suggest the product is a hit, while a sudden, significant decline in a firm's sales or profits is also called a hit.

**HIT LIST.** Projects or programs that may be cut from a budget.

"The Defense Base Closure and Realignment Commission was set in late June 1995 to deliver its latest choices for the base closure hit list, but politics and money could intervene before the selection process ends later in 1995." (*ENR*, July 3, 1995, p. 10)

**HIT THE FAN (TO).** Refers to the onset of chaos or panic. Often the phrase is included in the saying, "when the shit hits the fan."

**HIT THE NAIL ON THE HEAD (TO).** Be exactly right.

**HIT THE PANIC BUTTON (TO).** Become very alarmed.

**HOG-CORN RATIO.** The ratio of the price received for a hog to the price of its primary input, corn. Developed by Dr. Earl O. Heady, the hog-corn ratio is used to determine whether it is more profitable to sell the corn or feed it to the hog.

**HOI POLLOI.** The many, the masses; people who have a high opinion of themselves (Greek).

"Always an iconoclast, Mr. [Oliver] Stone has begun to rent his western getaway to the hoi polloi." (*Wall Street Journal*, Jan. 19, 1996, p. A1)

**HOLD THE LINE (TO).** Not change, as in maintaining on offering price or controlling costs.

**HOLD THE PHONE (TO).** Delay, wait a minute (command).

**HOLY GRAIL.** Sacred creed or value.

"Cost-cutting has become the holy grail of corporate management. . . . But what helps the financial statement up front can end up hurting it DOWN THE ROAD." (*Wall Street Journal*, May 14, 1994, p. A1)

**HOMEGROWN.** Local.

**HOME INDUSTRY ARGUMENT.** Protection of local companies.

**HOME IN ON (TO).** Concentrate, focus.

"Other U.S. investigators expressed surprise that Lockheed Martin's August SEC* filing referred to a subpoena it had received barely weeks earlier, the wording of which made it clear that the investigation was still preliminary and is likely to take many months to home in on individual targets." (*Wall Street Journal*, Sept. 5, 1995, p. B6)

**HOME RUN.** A success (baseball).

"Touted by Wall Street as a demographic home run, Providential Corp.'s INITIAL PUBLIC OFFERING (IPO) in early 1992 was massively oversubscribed." (*Barron's*, July 4, 1994, p. 26)

**HOME TURF.** Domestic or local market.

"Despite decades of slugging it out in the worldwide film market, neither Kodak nor Fuji has made much headway on other's home turf." (*Business Week*, July 10, 1995, p. 34)

**HONEYMOON.** Extra cooperation at the beginning of a relationship.

"The peso's 40% plunge from mid-December 1994 to early January 1995 has shattered Mexico's honeymoon with international investors, disrupted a budding economic recovery, and badly undermined the credibility of President Ernesto Zedillo's 2–month old government." (*Banker*, Feb. 1995, p. 27)

**HONORARIUM.** Stipend, small fee paid to a speaker.

**HONORARY LIFE MEMBER (HLM).** Private groups and organizations often bestow honorary life membership to people who have made significant contributions to their cause.

**HOOK (TO).** Gain control of; promotional device designed to bring in new customers.

**HOOPLA.** Excitement (French).

"For all the hoopla surrounding the Internet, actually finding one's way onto the information superhighway remains surprisingly difficult." (*Business Week*, July 10, 1995, p. 34)

**HOOPS.** Barriers (that must be "jumped through").

"The painters, in particular, have had to jump through regulatory hoops to contain lead in a densely populated area and still keep automobile traffic flowing under the tracks." (*ENR*, April 10, 1995, p. 24)

**HOSTILE TAKEOVER.** Unfriendly buyout, purchase of control of a business by a CORPORATE RAIDER.

**HOTBED.** Popular theme; under pressure to produce.

"Branding began decades ago with Chiquita, Dole and Sunkist fruits, but pre-cut vegetables are the latest hotbed." (*Brand Week*, June 26, 1995, p. 32)

**HOT BUTTONS.** Management philosophy that employees should make decisions themselves without going to upper management; employees should push the hot buttons.

**HOT-DESKING.** Practice of not assigning permanent desks to employees; instead, workers share a pool of desks.

**HOT ISSUE.** A new stock that is popular among investors.

**HOT POTATO.** Something that is controversial.
   "Politically, the minimum wage is a hot potato, traditionally dividing business and labor, Republicans and Democrats." (*Wall Street Journal*, April 24, 1996, A1)

**HOT TIP.** Information received in advance of others.

**HOT UNDER THE COLLAR.** Angry.

**HOUSE-CLEANING.** Reorganization of a business, usually including dismissal of many employees.
   "The securities firm is trying to recover from a $3 million embezzlement scheme that resulted in the 1994 dismissal of two managers accused of stealing the money. It also prompted a house-cleaning at Gruntal which culminated late last year with the resignation of chairman, Howard Silverman." (*Wall Street Journal*, Feb. 7, 1996, p. B4)

**HUD.** See DEPARTMENT OF HOUSING AND URBAN DEVELOPMENT.

**HUDDLE (TO).** Come together to discuss strategy (football).
   "All of this explains why there have been so many drug mergers, as the companies huddle together for greater strength. (*Forbes*, April 24, 1995, p. 88)

**HUMAN RESOURCES (HR) DEPARTMENT.** Department responsible for hiring, training, and the management of worker benefits.

**HUMDRUM.** Mediocre, ordinary.

**HUMP DAY.** Wednesday, the middle of the work week.

**HUSH MONEY.** Bribe; payment to keep someone quiet.
   "The probe revolved around allegations that the company's former chairman, Roy Speer, and other top executives received KICKBACKS

and paid hush money to would-be WHISTLEBLOWERS." (*Wall Street Journal*, April, 14, 1994, p. B4)

**HYPE.** Superfluous promotion.

"If media attention and marketing hype are to be believed, the release will be followed by an avalanche of hardware and software upgrades throughout corporate America." (*Information Week*, Aug. 21, 1995, p. 28)

# I

**ICEBERG PRINCIPLE.** The idea that in any situation only a small part of the problem will be initially visible.

"Adds Andrew Brimmer, an economist and financial consultant who sits on the boards of several major corporations: 'It's like the iceberg principle. The 8% of the iceberg above the water is what we see—large corporations that have institutionalized affirmative action. The vast bulk of firms are below the surface—the smaller corporations have done virtually nothing.' " (*Wall Street Journal*, March 20, 1995, p. B1)

**ILLEGAL ALIENS.** People from another country without proper documentation.

**ILLEGAL PARKING.** Stock market practice of having another firm purchase securities in its name but guaranteed by the real investor.

"Michael Milken and Ivan Boesky made the practice of illegal parking famous in the 1980s. Illegal parking allowed Boesky to circumvent SEC* net capital requirements." (Jim Reilly, Robinson-Humphrey Co., 1996)

**ILLIQUID.** Lacking cash.

**IN ABSENTIA.** In the absence of (Latin).

**IN CAMERA.** In private (Latin).

**INCENT (TO).** Provide incentives for employees.
"A premium can be added to incent the employee to take the assignment." (*Benefits & Compensation International*, April 1994, p.15)

**IN DEEP WATER.** In trouble.

**INDIVIDUAL RETIREMENT ACCOUNT (IRA).** Tax-deferred retirement savings program created in the 1980s to try to get Americans to save. With restrictions, workers can put up to $2,000 per year in an IRA account and not pay income taxes on the money or interest until they withdraw the funds.

**INFANT INDUSTRY.** New manufacturing companies. Infant industries have the potential for economies of scale if they survive long enough to grow. Governments frequently protect these firms from international competition through tariff barriers.

**INFOMERCIAL.** An extended (ten to thirty minutes) television advertisement; a television commercial presented as if it was entertainment or an informative report.
"News organizations should reject advertorials and infomercials altogether. Not just as a matter of ethics, but because they are bad business." (*Editor & Publisher*, Sept. 9, 1995, p. 48)

**INFRASTRUCTURE.** Vital services and capital assets of a country.

**IN-HOUSE.** Done within the company, as opposed to OUTSOURCING.

**INITIAL PUBLIC OFFERING (IPO).** The first time a company's stock is offered to investors. In the 1990s, IPOs have offered significant profits to investors who have FLIPPED the stock.

**IN KIND.** Barter, countertrade.

**IN LOCO PARENTIS.** In the place of a parent (Latin).

**INSIDE CANDIDATES.** Company employees being considered for a new position.
"Diane Bryan is the only valid inside candidate for the new opening but is 5 months pregnant." (*Harvard Business Review*, Jan./Feb. 1994, p. 16)

**INSIDE TRACK.** An advantage. In a footrace the inside runner travels a shorter distance around a curve than other competitors, thereby having an advantage.

"According to pilot evaluations, the Rockwell Ranger 2000 has the inside track in the competition for the US' new primary trainer aircraft." (*Aviation Week & Space Technology*, June 5, 1995, p. 24)

**INTERNAL RATE OF RETURN (IRR).** Discount rate at which the present value of future cash flows from an investment equals the cost of the investment.

**INTERNAL REVENUE SERVICE (IRS).** U.S. government agency charged with collecting most federal taxes, including personal and corporate income, social security, estate, gift, and excise taxes. An audit announcement from the IRS is not a joyous occasion.

**INTERNATIONAL BANK FOR RECONSTRUCTION AND DEVEL-OPMENT (IRBD, WORLD BANK).** Created at BRETTON WOODS in 1944, the World Bank financed the reconstruction of Europe and Asia after World War II. World Bank loans, a major source of financing for global economic development, have recently been criticized for over emphasis on large-scale projects and lack of sensitivity to cultural and environmental impacts.

**INTERNATIONAL ORGANIZATION FOR STANDARDIZATION (ISO).** Swiss-based organization coordinating and setting quality control standards. ISO 9000 certification has become a requirement for many companies wanting to do business in Europe.

**INTERNATIONAL MONETARY FUND (IMF), "THE FUND."** The IMF functions as the regulator of foreign exchange rates and as a source of international liquidity. IMF assistance comes with conditions, including monetary and fiscal spending restrictions which are often painful and controversial.

**IN THE BAG.** Certain.

"A few weeks ago, Carson Pirie Scott & Co. thought it had Yonkers Inc. in the bag. . . . Its hotly contested and unusually nasty 8-month takeover battle had succeeded in forcing 3 directors . . . off the 9-person Yonkers board and replacing them with Carson's representatives." (*Business Week*, July 3, 1995, p. 72)

**IN THE BALL PARK.** Close to what was expected (baseball).

"The result obtained with a specific heuristic can be considered 'good' (i.e., close to optimal) if that result is in the ball park of the result obtained through a maximally different method." (*Decision Support Systems*, Aug. 1995, p. 313)

**IN THE BLACK.** Operating profitably.

"After 4 years of RED INK, Gaylord Container will be in the black in 1995." (*Business Week*, Sept. 4, 1995, p. 41)

**IN THE CARDS.** Likely to happen.

"This time, however, a cyclical BULL market is not in the cards. Traders should instead prepare for a major SHAKEOUT before year end." (*Futures–Cedar Falls*, Sept. 1995, p. 32)

**IN THE CLEAR.** Out of danger.

**IN THE DRIVER'S SEAT.** In charge, control.

"Thomas Loane of Alamo Rent A Car Inc. says IBM's lack of published list prices puts him in the driver's seat at the negotiating table." (*Computerworld*, Oct. 9, 1995, p. 150)

**IN THE KNOW.** Well informed.

"At a time when French advertising is considered lackluster by those in the know, Christophe Lambert's will has produced results at fledgling advertising agency Opera RLC." (*Adweek*, Oct. 31, 1994, p. 30)

**IN THE LONG RUN.** Over a considerable period of time. Economist John Maynard Keynes, whose economic models focused on the importance of short-run economic policy adjustments, is famous for the statement, "In the long run we are all dead."

**IN THE LOOP.** In the circle of power.

**IN THE MONEY.** An option contract where the current market price is greater than the STRIKE PRICE for a call option and below the strike price for a put option.

**IN THE PIPELINE.** Being prepared; not ready for distribution at this time.

**IN THE RED/RED INK.** Operating at a loss.

"However, with the company now awash in red ink that Paine Webber figures may hit $126 million on revenues of $267 million this year, Discovery Zone stock, at about 5, languishes 75% below its 52-week high." (*Business Week*, Oct. 9, 1995, p. 41)

**IN THE RUNNING/RACE.** Under consideration.

"The companies' combined revenue now should exceed $300 million, putting Simple Technology in the running to become a player in what may be a consolidating market." (*Computer Reselling News*, Sept. 4, 1995, p. 101)

**IN THE TANK.** Declining.

**IN THE TRENCHES.** In the workplace (World War I).
The senior systems programmer analyst who once played a key role in the data processing organization is rapidly being replaced by a new breed of technical wizard who learned how to implement and manage networks in the trenches." (*Network World*, June 19, 1995, p. 68)

**IN TRANSITION.** Unemployed, usually executives; changing.
"According to Peter Drucker, American business is in transition, and prominent in the transition is the transfer of power from manufacturing to service sectors." (*Metal Center News*, June 1995, p. 37)

**INVENTORY RUNS.** Computer analysis of inventory levels.

**INVENTORY TURNS.** How many times inventory is sold and replaced per year.
"Overburdened inventories, resulting in poor inventory turns and on-time performance that is far less than desirable, are serious problems for many companies." (*Production & Inventory Management Journal*, Second Quarter 1995, p. 39)

**INVERTED MARKET.** Financial market where short-term interest rates are higher than long-term rates.

**INVESTMENT GRADE.** Bonds that do not have a high default risk. Corporate and municipal bonds that receive at least a Baa rating from MOODY'S or a BBB rating from STANDARD AND POOR'S agencies.

**INVISIBLE HAND.** Power of the marketplace.
"Every individual endeavors to employ his capital so that its produce may be of greatest value. He generally neither intends to promote the public interest, nor knows how much he is promoting it. He intends only his own security, only his own gain. And he is led by an invisible hand to promote an end which was no part of his intention. By pursuing his own interest he frequently promotes that of society more effectively than when he really intends to promote it." (Adam Smith, *Wealth of Nations*, 1776)

**INVOLUNTARY REDUCTION IN FORCE (IRIF).** Corporate lay-offs made after attempting to encourage workers to terminate voluntarily. Large U.S. companies will offer workers a PACKAGE of incentives to avoid involuntary reductions in force.

**IRONCLAD.** Solid, guaranteed, as in an ironclad promise.

"Mr. Ciresi also criticized the pact for its 'lack of an ironclad' requirement that Liggett cease marketing cigarettes to children." (*Wall Street Journal*, March 15, 1996, p. B2)

# J

**JACK-OF-ALL TRADES.** A person with many different skills but who is not an expert in one particular area.

**JAWBONE (TO).** Talk someone into doing what you want; persuade with pressure.

"Business rose up against Mr. Clinton when early in his presidency he sought to enact universal health care by requiring all employers to pay most of their employees' health insurance bills. Now, he has stripped government from the mix and is seeking to do little more than jawbone companies into becoming better corporate citizens." (*Wall Street Journal*, March 25, 1996, p. B7)

**J CURVE.** Graphic representation of the impact of currency devaluation on a country's balance of trade. Currency devaluation results in immediate relative price changes, but the quantity of exports and imports respond more slowly. Initially after devaluation the quantity of exports and imports do not change, but imports become more expensive and exports cheaper, thus, a country's balance of payments will worsen. Over time the change in relative prices will cause exports to increase and imports to decline, improving the country's balance of payments.

**JET LAG.** Tired feeling after an airplane trip that includes changes in time zones.

**JILLION.** A very large number. See also ZILLION.

**JINGLE.** Telephone call; lyrics or melody in a commercial.

"Clients and agencies know that today's world audience will not be persuaded by a jingle or over-dubbed film. International campaigns now have to have as much edge as domestic campaigns." (*Adweek*, July 17, 1995, p. 43)

**JOB HOP (TO).** Change employment frequently.

**JOB LOCK.** Situation of employees who want to leave their current positions but feel they cannot because they would lose their health benefits. In the United States, health benefits are provided primarily by employers, but most benefit programs do not cover pre-existing conditions. This "locks" many employees with health problems to their current job. A new law passed in 1996 is intended to create portability of health benefits, thereby reducing employees' sense of job lock.

**JOB TRAINING PARTNERSHIP ACT (JTPA).** Federal government worker training regulations providing incentives for employer education programs.

**JOCKEY FOR POSITION (TO).** Promote and sell oneself or one's products in order to compete (horse racing).

"Gordon's innovations in customer service and management are 2 key factors that keep Bell Atlantic in a strong leadership stance, as the competition jockeys for position." (*Black Enterprise*, May 1995, p. 54)

**JOG (TO).** Recall after concentration or suggestion, as in to jog one's memory.

**JOHN HANCOCK.** Signature. John Hancock, as president of the Continental Congress, was the first to sign the Declaration of Independence; he did so with such flourish that in the United States his name has become synonymous with signature.

**JOHNNY COME LATELY.** A company late in entering a market.

**JOURNAL (THE).** Nickname for the *Wall Street Journal*.

**JUICE.** Connections, power.

**JUMP BALL.** Undecided situation (basketball).

"As a result, the economic issue stands as one of Mr. Dole's principal opportunities for making inroads in a one-sided race that has hardened in Mr. Clinton's favor in recent weeks. 'It's still a jump ball,' says Democratic pollster Peter Hart." (*Wall Street Journal*, May 16, 1996, p. A16)

**JUMP ON THE BANDWAGON (TO).** Join what is popular.

"Besides its own ad blitz, Microsoft has offered inducements that make it difficult for PC makers not to jump on the bandwagon." (*Brandweek*, June 26, 1995, p. 8)

**JUMP THE GUN (TO).** Start too soon (track and field).

" 'To be honest, we are more concerned about having them [PC makers] jump the gun than be late,' Mr. Silverberg said." (*Wall Street Journal*, June 6, 1995, p. B16)

**JUMP AT IT (TO).** Eagerly take advantage of an opportunity.

**JUMP START (TO).** Initiate, to get something going.

"After Pinochet, the new leaders in Chile jump started the economy by shifting to free market economics." (Prof. Ralph Folsom, University of San Diego, 1996)

**JUMP THROUGH THE HOOPS (TO).** Do all that is required.

"In entering the race at the end of September, he [Steve Forbes] said he wouldn't jump through the hoops needed to qualify for federal campaign matching funds but instead was ready to spend millions of his own." (*Wall Street Journal*, Dec. 6, 1995, p. A1)

**JUNIOR LEAGUERS/JUNIOR LEAGUE.** Affluent nonworking women under forty years old.

"She accepted her appointment to the authority, she says, because it was 'better than the Junior League.' " (*Wall Street Journal*, Nov. 29, 1995, p. F1)

**JUNK BOND.** A high-risk, less-than-INVESTMENT-GRADE corporate bond. Junk bonds became very popular among investors in the late 1980s.

"If an investor wants a risky fixed-income investment with potential for extra return, they should invest in a junk bond fund." (*Forbes*, June 19, 1995, p. 234)

**JUNKET.** A trip, offered to politicians usually with all expenses paid, designed to enlighten or influence them.

**JURY-RIGGED.** Temporarily fixed; not a permanent solution. See also RUBE GOLDBERG.

"The downside is Japan [after the Kobe earthquake] will have to depend on these jury-rigged transport links for some time to come." (*Wall Street Journal*, March 17, 1995, p. A1)

**JUST-IN-TIME (JIT).** Management practice minimizing inventories. Materials arrive just in time to meet production schedules.

# K

**KAIZEN.** Japanese term for continuous improvement through incremental change. In the 1980s, so many American managers studied Japanese production methods that the term has become part of American business jargon.

"Co-workers call him Mr. Kaizen, a reference to the Japanese word for continuous improvement." (*Wall Street Journal*, Aug. 13, 1996, p. B1)

**KEEP A CLOSE EYE/TAB ON (TO).** Watch carefully.

"Snacks are a big market: they contribute 70% of Nabisco's nearly $8 billion in annual revenues. This means that Nabisco must keep a close eye on its competitors." (*Forbes*, Aug. 28, 1995, p. 102)

**KEEP IT SIMPLE, STUPID (KISS).** A business slogan suggesting that plans should be kept clear and logical.

"Most insurance agents in the work site marketing arena were weaned on the KISS (keep it simple, stupid) method of payroll deduction installations." (*Broker World*, Aug. 1995, p. 10)

**KEEP UP WITH THE JONESES (TO).** Strive, especially beyond one's income, to socialize and spend like others in the same neighborhood.

"This allows for the idea that households care about their relative standard of living, or the saying goes, they want 'to keep up with the Jones.' " (*Journal of Money, Credit and Banking*, Feb. 1994, p. 1)

**KEEP ONE POSTED (TO).** Keep one informed.

**KEYSTONE (TO).** Mark up the price of a good 100% of its cost.
"The art dealer will double the price I give him, and the retailer will keystone it too." (Chet Allenchey, CAMMEO Art and Photography, 1996)

**KICKBACK.** A bribe.
"An investigation into bribery and kickbacks at General Motors Corp.'s Adam Opel AG unit and German construction firms will encompass more than 200 people and 40 Opel employees." (*Ward's Auto World*, Aug. 1995, p. 17)

**KICK BUTT (TO).** Outwit or overwhelm the competition.

**KICKER.** Something added to a contract proposal to make it more attractive. *See* SWEETENER.
"Traditionally, private debt placements for companies rated B or lower contained equity kickers—commonly warrants for 5% to 10% of the company." (*Corporate Cashflow*, Nov. 1994, p. 15)

**KICK OFF (TO).** Beginning; to initiate (football).
"IBM PC Co. is targeting the midrange, general business segment of the notebook computer market. To kick off its plan, IBM will announce in the next few weeks a new line of ThinkPads equipped with many features formerly found in the HIGH END—but now with a LOW-END price." (*Computerworld*, Oct. 9, 1995, p. 4)

**KICK/PUSH UPSTAIRS (TO).** Promote out of the way.
"Some observers saw the Keshner move as a 'kick upstairs' that removed him from power." (*Investment Dealers Digest*, June 27, 1994, p. 5)

**KILLING.** A large, quick profit.
"Yet almost no one expects to make a killing by selling or licensing browser software. The real money is in the overall Internet products and services business, of which the browser business is but a small part." (*Informationweek*, Oct. 23, 1995, p. 81)

**KILLJOY.** Unenthusiastic person.

"Enter the killjoys. The Web's JURY-RIGGED INFRASTRUCTURE, they say, will continue to frustrate all but the most persistent computer-literate consumers." (*Wall Street Journal*, June 17, 1996, p. R1)

**KIND OF NEAT.** Somewhat interesting.

**KINGPIN/FISH.** Boss, important person.

"Prince Alwaleed bin Talal bin Abdulaziz Alsaud of Saudi Arabia is probably the most important financial kingpin." (*Business Week*, Sept. 25, 1995, p. 88)

**KISS OF DEATH.** Final blow; signal that something will fail.

**KISS A LOT OF FROGS (TO).** Keep looking until one finds what one wants. The saying comes from the story *The Frog Prince*, wherein a prince is doomed to be a frog until he is kissed by a princess.

**KISS UP TO.** Flatter; BROWN-NOSE.

**KIT AND CABOODLE.** Including everything.

**KITCHEN CABINET.** Close advisors to a president of the United States. The term originated with President Andrew Jackson, when he suspended Cabinet meetings and met with close friends.

**KITE A CHECK (TO).** Write a check without sufficient funds to cover it.

**KNEE-JERK REACTION.** To act without thinking, thoughtless response.

"Insurance industry leaders must set aside their knee-jerk hostility to federal involvement and push Washington for help in covering the catastrophe risks that have driven carriers from hurricane—and earthquake-prone states." (*National Underwriter*, Sept. 25, 1995, p. 1)

**KNOCKOFF.** An unlicensed copy of a product.

"Every time P&G or Kimberly-Clark comes to market with product innovations, Paragon has a knockoff in short order." (*Forbes*, Oct. 10, 1994, p. 78)

**KNOCK OUT COLD, KO (TO).** Overwhelm the competition (boxing).

**KNOCK THEIR SOCKS OFF (TO).** Defeat the competition.

"In what AT&T declared was the largest interactive quality conference ever conducted, over 9,000 participants from 13 countries learned about giving customers knock-their-socks-off service." (*Quality Progress*, July 1995, p. 14)

**KNOW-HOW.** Knowledge.

**KNOW-IT-ALL.** Someone who shows off their knowledge; conceited person.

"People to think twice about giving training assignments include: 1. know-it-alls." (*Supervisory Management*, March 1995, p. 1)

**KNUCKLE DOWN (TO).** Focus; work hard.

"MGN is fiercely commercial, and media buyers are predicting that, if the deal goes ahead, the Independent will have to knuckle down under a new commercial regime. (*Marketing News*, Jan. 27, 1994, p. 1)

**KNUCKLE UNDER (TO).** Give in, concede.

**KOHLBERG, KRAVIS, ROBERTS (KKR).** KKR is a merger and acquisition firm most famous for arranging the $29 billion buyout of R. J. Reynolds Company in 1989.

"Kohlberg, Kravis, Roberts is preparing an offer for Aetna's property-casualty insurance operations that could top $4 billion." (*Wall Street Journal*, Nov. 13, 1995, p. A1)

**KONDRATIEFF CURVE.** Economic theory, named after a Soviet statistician, suggesting that the world economies move in fifty-year cycles. Stalin was not pleased with this analysis, and Kondratieff spent time in Siberia.

**KOOSHING.** Rejecting someone for a job.

**KOWTOW (TO).** Cater to; defer to (Chinese).

"But will Washington kowtow and stay out of the strait as ordered or will it make the 'show of force' that Li Peng warned it not to make?" (*Wall Street Journal*, March 19, 1996, p. A22)

**K&R INSURANCE.** Kidnap and ransom insurance.

"K&R may also provide the services of a protection consultant who can assist acompany to avoid difficult situations and respond appropriately." (*Across the Board*, Nov./Dec. 1994, p. 52)

**KUDOS.** Congratulations, approval (Greek).

"Singapore has a lot of selling points, but geography may be the country's real drawing card. . . . Singapore's communications infrastructure also gets kudos from bankers." (*Global Finance*, Aug. 1995, p. 86)

# L

**LABOR FORCE.** Workers. U.S. Department of Commerce labor force statistics include employed and unemployed persons sixteen years old or older who either have jobs or are actively looking for and available for employment.

**LABOR-INTENSIVE.** Production method requiring many workers relative to other inputs.

**LAFFER CURVE.** 1980s economic idea, espoused by Arthur Laffer, suggesting that lowering marginal tax rates stimulates increases in output thereby increasing government tax revenue. See also SUPPLY-SIDE ECONOMICS, DYNAMIC SCORING.

**LAISSEZ-FAIRE.** Hands off, to let be free (French). Laissez-faire economic doctrine was advocated by Adam Smith in *The Wealth of Nations* (1776). Conservatives in the United States have latched on to the term as a symbol for reducing government influence in the economy.

**LAME DUCK.** Politician who is still in office but who has announced retirement or has been defeated in a recent election. The term originated

in Britain in the eighteenth century, when it meant a bankrupt businessman.

**LARGE SCALE.** Big picture; broader view.

**LAST IN, FIRST OUT (LIFO).** A method of assigning cost to the ending inventory which assumes that the cost of the remaining units
consists of the costs of the earliest units purchased.

**LAST STRAW.** Mistake or problem that causes a manager to take action.
    "The company asked respondents for the precipitating event—or 'last
straw' as the questionnaire put it—that led to their decisions to file [for
bankruptcy]." (*Wall Street Journal*, May 23, 1996, p. A4)

**LAUNDER (TO).** Put illegal funds through a legitimate business, thereby
cleaning the money of its "dirty" origin.
    "Harvey Weinig, a New York lawyer, was sentenced to 11 years and
three months in prison for participating in a $100 million scheme to
launder money from drug proceeds for the Cali cocaine cartel." (*Wall
Street Journal*, March 25, 1996, p. A1)

**LAYING-OFF.** Terminating workers because there is no work.

**LEAD BALLOON.** A dismal failure.
    "Hong Kong Governor Chris Patten said that the colony's 3.2m
holders of British Dependent Territories Citizen passports should be
given the right to live in Britain. The comment went over like a lead
balloon in London." (*Far Eastern Economic Review*, Oct. 5, 1995, p. 22)

**LEAD TIME.** Time between the initiation of a new project and its
delivery date.
    "Given such uncertainties as the Middle East and the long lead time
needed to develop major oil fields, rising prices seem inevitable." (*Fortune*, Oct. 30, 1995, p. 88)

**LEAPFROG (TO).** Bound forward. Employees climbing the CORPO-
RATE LADDER sometimes leapfrog past others on the way to the top.
    "To catch up—and perhaps even leapfrog American competitors—
Genset plans to bring economies of scale to gene discovery." (*Wall Street
Journal*, March 1, 1996, p. B5)

**LEAP TO NEW HEIGHTS (TO).** Attain levels never before reached.
    "Management may have chosen the logo to inspire the inefficient
government-owned bank to leap to new heights of financial activity."
(*Euromoney*, April 1995, p. 20)

**LEAPS AND BOUNDS.** Large jumps, amounts, or quantities.

"In a recent test of mobile computing from a 13,000 foot high mountain trail in Colorado, it was determined that . . . the mobile world has advanced by leaps and bounds." (*Forbes*, Oct. 9, 1995, p. 116)

**LEAVE IN THE DUST (TO).** Leave behind; defeat one's competitor.

**LEFT-BRAIN PERSON.** A person with strong organizational and mathematical skills; someone obsessed with order.

**LEFT FIELD (FROM).** Out of nowhere, a total surprise (baseball).

**LEFT-HANDED COMPLIMENT.** Praise that is in fact subtle dispraise.

**LEGAL EAGLE.** Clever lawyer.

**LEGAL MACHINE.** The legal system; a machine meeting legal standards.

**LEMON.** A defective product, especially a car. Lemon laws in the United States typically allow a manufacturer four attempts to fix a recurring problem.

"Now chairman Steve Roth has been presented with another lemon: the recent announcement that Bradlees had filed for bankruptcy protection." (*Barron's* July 10, 1995, p. 13)

**LESS THAN TRUCKLOAD (LTL).** Transportation prices are usually quoted for full loads and LTL shipments.

**LET SLIDE (TO).** Ignore; not criticize.

"And while preparing for debate today on the party's landmark Medicare bill, the leadership has let slide its schedule for deficit-reduction legislation next week." (*Wall Street Journal*, Oct. 19, 1995, p. 24)

**LEVEL (PLAYING) FIELD.** Everyone being treated the same (sports).

"Now that the country is playing on a level field, business people are taking a hard look at how it [Vietnam] measures up as an investment destination against regional competitors such as Malaysia, Indonesia, Thailand, the Philippines, Burma and China." (*Far Eastern Economic Review*, Sept. 22, 1994, p. 72)

**LEVERAGE (TO).** Use borrowed funds to make an investment; the ratio of borrowed funds to invested capital in a business; influence.

"The Buick would be one of many individual car-line programs GM is expected to implement to leverage its estimated $5 million Olympic 2nd-tier sponsorship." (*Brandweek*, Oct. 2, 1995, p. 8)

**LEVERAGED BUYOUT (LBO).** The purchase of a company with borrowed funds.

"It seems to have escaped people's memory that RJR* was the subject of the biggest restructuring in history, all of six years ago. What's more, this KKR*-led LBO was a FLOP. As a private entity, RJR spent its energy trying to pay off $29 billion in debt." (*Wall Street Journal*, Nov. 2, 1995, p. C1)

**LEVITTOWN.** Suburbia; specifically, a town on Long Island, New York, built by Arthur Levitt as the first mass-produced suburban housing constructed to meet consumer needs after World War II.

"The Toronto area made planning history in the early 1950s with the development of Don Mills—the region's quintessential automobile-dependent community and distant cousin to the U.S. Levittowns." (*Planning*, March 1995, p. 18)

**LIE DOWN ON THE JOB (TO).** Not be productive.

**LIFELONG STUDENT.** Someone who is always learning.

**LIGHTNING ROD.** Person who initiates change, particularly dramatic and potentially dangerous changes in an organization.

"Hillary Rodham Clinton is a key figure in the Whitewater affair, her poll numbers are sinking, and she has become a lightning rod for Republican attacks on the President." (*Business Week*, March 21, 1994, p. 40)

**LIKE A MILLION BUCKS.** Very good.

**LIKE AN EDSEL.** A failure. Ford Motor Company introduced the Edsel with great fanfare in the 1950s. The car, which was based on out-of-date research and contained gimmicks rather than added value for consumers, was a dismal failure.

**LIMIT ORDER.** An order to buy or sell a stock at a specific price.

**LINE.** Profession; products one sells.

**LINGO.** Slang.

"The cost of getting 'Between Brothers' in the can—film-making lingo for getting a film shot, which doesn't take into account editing and other post-production costs—was $80,000." (*Wall Street Journal*, March 27, 1996, p. A1)

**LION'S SHARE.** Largest part.

"Airbus came in a distant second in the race to provide the world with commercial aircraft last year, capturing just 15 percent of the global market. The United States-based Boeing won the lion's share, some 70 percent, and its compatriot McDonnell Douglas took 10 percent." (*Worldbusiness*, March/April 1996, p. 11)

**LIP SERVICE.** Officially agreeing with, while having private reservations about the issue.

"Though both sides continue to pay lip service to the notion of balancing the budget, odds for a bipartisan agreement are extremely low." (*Wall Street Journal*, March 21, 1996, p. A22)

**LIQUID.** Easily converted to cash.

"By focusing on its vegetable bioengineering activities, Monsanto could become the only highly liquid, cash-positive biotech investment play around." (*Financial World*, Sept. 26, 1995, p. 16)

**LITMUS TEST.** Basis for determining (chemistry).

"What this is going to be, in a way, is a litmus test on whether or not a cartel with all the money and profits of the tobacco industry can defeat a state and prevent it from collecting taxpayer funds." (*Wall Street Journal*, March 27, 1996, p. F1)

**LITTLE GUY.** Small investor.

"In the bitter arbitration wars between the securities industry and investors who contend that they have been fleeced, WALL STREET, in the past year or so, has suffered some significant routs. Conversely the 'little guys' have enjoyed some very profitable and possibly portentous victories." (*Barron's*, Sept. 1995, p. 16)

**LIVELIHOOD.** Job, how one earns one's living.

**LIVING ON BORROWED TIME.** Being in a situation about to fail.

"Without backup, a company's data is living on borrowed time, and its business could suffer." (*Forbes*, Aug. 29, 1994, p. 54)

**LIVING PROOF.** Actual evidence.

"But the Japanese are not mere bystanders in the evolution of a European style. NTT Europe's managing director Kageo Nakano is living proof that Japanese management is part of Europe." (*Management Today*, June 1994, p. 21)

**LOAD.** Sales charge associated with the purchase of a mutual fund.

**LOADED.** Very rich; fully equipped.

**LOAN-TO-VALUE RATIO (LTV).** The ratio of the amount of money borrowed to the fair market value of the asset against which the loan is secured.

**LOCAL AREA NETWORK (LAN).** Group of computers that are linked together.

**LOCKED INTO.** Forced to stay with, having no other option.

**LOCK HORNS (TO).** Disagree.
"The Detroit Department of Transportation and the Suburban Mobility Authority for Regional Transportation have locked horns over a merger debate that has polarized the population and the politicians." (*ENR*, Sept. 25, 1995, p. 12)

**LOCK, STOCK, AND BARREL.** Everything.
"Under terms of the agreement, Oracle will use Acorn's expertise, but Oracle will own the resulting reference design 'lock, stock, and barrel' said Andrew Lauren, Oracle's vice president of networking computing." (*Wall Street Journal*, Nov. 11, 1996, p. B2)

**LOCK UP (TO).** Complete, finalize, gain control of.
"Toy companies pay TV stations to clear their shows, committing advertising dollars to lock up a time period." (*Brandweek*, June 19, 1995, p. 36)

**LOG (TO).** Official records; to record.

**LOMBARD.** An acronym for "Lots of Money but a Real Dodo." A wealthy, simple person.

**LONDON INTERBANK OFFERED RATE (LIBOR).** The interest rate charged to highest-quality customers for loans in the Eurodollar market. Less creditworthy customers pay the LIBOR rate plus varying percentage points. Like the PRIME RATE in the United States, the LIBOR is the standard by which interest rates are established.

**LONELY AT THE TOP.** The price of leadership may be a lack of friends.

**LONG BOND.** Thirty-year U.S. Treasury bond.

**LONG ON (TO BE).** Supportive of; to own a financial interest in; to consist mostly of.

"Thus far, the latest round of congressional proposals to rein in Medicare spending have, once again, been long on generalities and short on specifics." (*HR Focus*, Aug. 1995, p. 1)

**LONG RUN.** Time frame in which all inputs are variable.

**LOOPHOLE.** Legal way to get around the law.

"Trimming corporate welfare is back in vogue . . . House Budget Committee Chairman John R. Kasich wants to save that much just by closing corporate tax loopholes." (*Business Week*, July 3, 1995, p. 36)

**LOOSE CANNON.** An uncontrollable person (nautical).

"The White House has reason to be wary of Reich. He has a tendency to become a loose cannon, publicly floating controversial ideas that have not been cleared by the President." (*Financial World*, Feb. 28, 1995, p. 18)

**LOOT.** Money.

"In just three years, a slew of new products has catapulted Chrysler Corp. from near death to one of the world's most profitable car companies. Many investors would like some of the loot to be divvied up." (*Business Week*, Nov. 28, 1994, p. 29)

**LOSE ONE'S SHIRT (TO).** Lose a significant amount of money.

"U.S. investors did venture abroad from time to time. But they often lost their shirts—especially in the Latin American and Weimar Republic bond defaults of the 1930s." (*Wall Street Journal*, May 28, 1996, p. R24)

**LOSS LEADERS.** Products offered at very low prices to attract customers.

"One of the main reasons that price erosion may not affect Microsoft Office or Office upgrades is that Windows 95 is being positioned as a loss leader. Once the platform is installed, resellers can make profits on installing solutions." (*Computer Reseller News*, Aug. 14, 1995, p. 25)

**LOW-BALL.** Reduce, as in a bid; a very low estimate.

"To compete profitably in the new low-fare environment, the major airlines know they must continue to slash costs, introduce BARE-BONES products and use fare sales that low-ball the market." (*Advertising Age*, Sept. 28, 1994, p. 22)

**LOW-END.** Lowest priced. See also TOP-OF-THE LINE.

"International Business Machines Corp. plans to announce tomorrow that it is re-entering the low-end printer business, a market it agreed to stay out of for five years following the spinoff of its low-end printer division in 1991." (*Wall Street Journal*, June 17, 1996, p. B4)

**LOW MAN/WOMAN ON THE TOTEM POLE.** Lowest position in an organization (offensive to Native Americans).

**LUDDITES.** Workers who feel their jobs are threatened by changing technology. The original Luddites, early 1800s British craftsmen, were followers of the mythic figure, Ned Ludd. They rioted, destroying textile machines that had replaced them.

"The original Luddites made bad choices in resorting to violence, but they were trying to protect their way of life." (*Wall Street Journal*, April 22, 1996, p. B1)

**LUMP SUM.** One-time payment.

"The program offered by Bancorp Hawaii provided employees with a decision to take a lump sum and gain the opportunity of substantial investment growth." (*Trusts & Estates*, Oct. 1995, p. 52)

# M

**MA BELL.** American Telephone & Telegraph.

"The latest breakup, announced September 20, 1995, gets AT&T out of the computer business and creates 3 separate companies out of what was once known as Ma Bell." (*Information Week*, Oct. 2, 1995, p. 14)

**MACHIAVELLIAN.** Ruthless person (reference to Niccolò Machiavelli, author of *The Prince*, 1532).

"Irony thus becomes an escape route for journalists who would rather describe Newt Gingrich with an adjective like 'slimy' or 'Machiavellian.' " (*Wall Street Journal*, Feb. 16, 1995, p. A14)

**MAD MONEY.** Money saved and spent on impulsive purchases.

**MADE UP OF.** Consists of.

**MADISON AVENUE.** Advertising agencies; New York City street with many ad agencies.

"Despite Polaroid's surprise in learning that it would have to replace BBDO, the company's affection for Madison Avenue is not likely to change as it looks for an advertising agency to handle its $25-million consumer account." (*Adweek*, Aug. 7, 1995, p. 3)

**MAGIC (THE).** Art, charm.

**MAKE A BUCK (TO).** Make money.

**MAKE A FEDERAL CASE OUT OF IT (TO).** Overreact, overemphasize.

**MAKE A MARKET (TO).** Be willing to buy or sell. In the stock market, a dealer who buys and sells over the counter shares of a stock is called a MARKET MAKER.

**MAKE ENDS MEET (TO).** Get by, be barely able to pay the bills.
"Small service businesses and service-oriented retail outlets tend to be labor-intensive and not particularly profitable, so even though entrepreneurs imagine themselves hiring someone to do all the dirty work, they usually end up having to do it themselves to make ends meet." (*Working Woman*, Oct. 1995, p. 49)

**MAKE GOOD (TO).** Make an adjustment or special allowance when a problem arises; a free repeat of an advertisement when there has been a mistake.
"They [global managers] seriously doubt the U.S. Treasury would fail to make good its interest payments on its debt." (*Pensions & Investments*, Sept. 15, 1995, p. 3)

**MAKE IT WORK (TO).** Be successful.

**MAKE OUT LIKE A BANDIT (TO).** Emerge from a business transaction very successfully.

**MAKING IT.** Becoming successful.

"Making it is relative, though, and even the most optimistic estimates are now a far cry from the original BULLISH projections." (*Wall Street Journal*, July 19, 1996, p. R6)

**MALARKEY.** Nonsense.

**MALTHUSIAN.** Person who advocates population control; follower of the ideas of Thomas Malthus, nineteenth-century philosopher who predicted that population would grow faster than our ability to produce food. Malthusians ignored the contribution of technology improvements to increasing productivity.

**MANAGED CARE.** Healthcare system where a third party, usually the government or an insurance company, reviews and controls payments to healthcare providers.

**MANAGEMENT-BY-EXCEPTION.** Theory that managers should focus their attention on areas that differ from normal.

"The model developed provides a management-by-exception approach to highlight problem items and identify the degree to which total inventory is operational versus nonfunctional." (*Production & Inventory Management Journal*, 4th Quarter 1995, p. 1)

**MANAGEMENT BY OBJECTIVES (MBO).** Management technique of setting goals and then reviewing performance against them.

"On the one hand, MBO is seen as a traditional management tool which forms part of the foundation of effective public management, while at the same time it is viewed by others as being out of date, ineffectual, and inconsistent with contemporary management and thought practices." (*Public Administration Review*, Jan.–Feb. 1995, p. 48)

**MANAGEMENT BY WALKING AROUND (MBWA).** Informal management style where decisions and changes are made based on the observations of supervisors.

"Managers literally walk around making informal visits to work areas. This enables them to collect data, form impressions, and generally keep their finger on the company's pulse." (*Across the Board*, Nov./Dec. 1993, p. 42)

**MANAGEMENT GURU.** Well known management author or consultant.

"Management gurus tend to give too much importance to establishing objectives and . . . give far too little thought to the question of who we are attempting to reach these objectives with." (*Management Today*, Aug. 1995, p. 76)

**MANUFACTURER'S SUGGESTED RETAIL PRICE (MSRP).** Manufacturers are not allowed to dictate prices to retailers in the United States but many have "suggested" prices. Fair Trade laws enacted in the 1930s allowed manufacturers to stipulate prices retailers could charge. The Consumer Pricing Act (1975) ended resale price maintenance agreements.

**MAQUILADORA.** Foreign-owned or controlled factories in Mexico that assemble parts and materials primarily for export to the United States.

**MARATHON SESSION.** Lengthy business meeting.

**MARGIN.** Profit margin, the difference between the selling price and the initial cost of a good.

**MARGIN CALL.** Brokerage house requirement that a stock trader either put up more funds against stock purchased with borrowed money or the stock will be sold.

**MARK.** Person who is the object of a deceptive business practice.

"The company had acquired a reputation as an easy mark in the claims business." (*Business Marketing*, Feb. 1994, p. 34)

**MARKDOWN.** Downward revision of the value of a security due to changes in market prices.

**MARKET MAKER.** Market specialist who commits to buying and selling particular stocks.

**MARKET PENETRATION.** Marketing strategy designed to increase sales of existing products in present markets.

"Fearing that it may be losing a new generation of diners and worried by the rapid market penetration of several upstart competitors, . . . S&A Restaurant Corp. is experimenting with an ambitious reimaging project to make the Steak and Ale chain more competitive and appealing." (*Nations Restaurant News*, Aug. 28, 1995, p. 1)

**MARKETING CONCEPT.** The idea that businesses should focus their efforts on anticipating and fulfilling the needs of customers.

"The idea that all markets can be profitably segmented has now received almost as widespread acceptance as the marketing concept itself." (*Marketing Management*, Summer 1995, p. 59)

**MARK TO MARKET (TO).** Banking term for valuing assets at their market price.

**MARRY UP.** Auctioneering technique of putting low-valued goods with more-valued merchandise.

**MARSHALL PLAN.** United States investment and loans to redevelop Europe after WW II. Also known as the European Recovery Program, this foreign-aid program was named after then U.S. Secretary of State George C. Marshall.

**MASSAGE (TO).** Manipulate; carefully or gently adjust; manipulate data.

**MASS CUSTOMIZATION.** Mass production with special features to meet individual customer needs. Allows consumers to customize options. Also called flexible manufacturing or targeted mass production.

**MAVEN.** An expert, often self-taught.
"In its zeal to develop a range of markets, Kodak was simply piling too much responsibility onto salespeople, expecting them to be marketing mavens for some customers, and product experts for others." (*Sales & Marketing Management*, Sept. 1995, p. 56)

**MAX OUT (TO).** Reach the limit.
"Riskier applicants include not only those who had payback problems in the past but also those who tended to 'max out' on their available credit." (*Wall Street Journal*, March 15, 1996, p. A1)

**McCARTHYISM.** Character assassination. Joseph McCarthy was a senator from Wisconsin in the 1950s who gained national attention by his claims that the State Department and other agencies of the U.S. government were full of communist sympathizers.
"He [Bob Dole] has served in elective office continuously since 1950, the year the Korean War and McCarthyism began." (*Wall Street Journal*, Jan. 22, 1996, p. A12)

**McJOB.** Low-paying positions in service companies. The term is a derogatory reference to McDonalds Company. One survey predicted that by the year 2000, 10 percent of the American labor force would have at one time worked for McDonalds.

**MEA CULPA.** My fault (Latin).
"Mr. Gates, meanwhile, just hopes his mea culpa will permanently shelve the issue. He writes, 'I personally apologize for any offense caused.'" (*Wall Street Journal*, Feb. 14, 1996, p. B1)

**MEAT AND POTATOES.** Basics; main ideas.
"The meat and potatoes of the market is credit card receivables. These deals account for about 45% of the overall market and will continue to dominate the business." (*Investment Dealers Digest*, May 22, 1995, p. 62)

**MEALYMOUTHED.** Garrulous; will not concisely state their concern.

**MEANS TEST.** Criteria used by government agencies to determine eligibility for social welfare programs.

**MEDIA BLITZ/HYPE.** Short-term, intense advertising campaign.

"The U.S.' largest import auto-seller [Toyota] will use the Web site as a springboard for an integrated new media blitz which will feature CD-ROMS, computer diskettes, on-line services, and INFOMERCIALS for its array of vehicles." (*Adweek*, March 27, 1995, p. 3)

**MELT-DOWN.** Product failure (nuclear reactors). See also ECONOMIC MELTDOWN.

**MERC.** Nickname for Chicago Mercantile Exchange.

**MERGE AND PURGE.** Marketer's term for combining mailing lists and eliminating duplications.
"A mailer is charged only for the names that remain after a merge/purge against the mailer's house file." (*Target Marketing*, July 1995, p. 19)

**MESSAGE CENTER.** Answering service.

**METROPOLITAN STATISTICAL AREA (MSA).** Census Bureau classification of a city with at least fifty thousand residents.

**MICKEY MOUSE.** Unsophisticated.
"Jim Bartlett warns of the dangers of not knowing your audience. He tells of a software salesman who reassured Walt Disney executives that his was no 'Mickey Mouse' system." (*Wall Street Journal*, Jan. 9, 1996, p. B1)

**MICROMARKETING.** Marketing strategy targeting very small groups or individual customers.
"A 4-market test of a new micro-marketing program will customize Heinz ketchup TV ads for specific grocery stores." (*Brandweek*, June 26, 1995, p. 3)

**MILE-HIGH CITY.** Denver, Colorado.

**MILITARY-INDUSTRIAL COMPLEX.** The combined influence of military manufacturers and government bureaucracies.
President Dwight D. Eisenhower warned, "In the councils of government, we must guard against the acquisition of unwarranted influence, whether sought or unsought, by the military-industrial complex." (Farewell Address, Jan. 17, 1961)

**MILK (TO).** Exploit, to get the maximum out of. See also COW.
"With a lot of those thrifts, we hadn't gotten around to milking the cow, Mr. Allison notes." (*Wall Street Journal*, June 13, 1996, p. B4)

**MIND THE STORE (TO).** Take care of routine business.

**MIND YOUR OWN BUSINESS (MYOB).** Don't get involved (impolite).

**MINT (TO).** New; place where money is produced; to make.

**MISERY INDEX.** The combined inflation and unemployment rates in a country. Republicans created the term during the 1980 U.S. presidential elections as a "sound bite" criticism of the Carter administration.

**MISSIONARY SALESPEOPLE.** Sales support people who concentrate on promotional activities and new product introductions.

**MISSION-ORIENTED.** Focused on a particular goal.

**MISS THE MARK (TO).** Fail.
    "Environmental laws and rules, now 17 volumes of fine print, often seem to miss the mark or prove counterproductive." (*Across the Board*, May 1995, p. 40)

**MODIFIED AMERICAN PLAN.** Hotel price that includes the room, breakfast, and dinner.

**MODUS OPERANDI.** Method of operating (Latin).

**MOGUL.** Powerful, rich person.
    "Cable mogul Ted Turner's Turner Broadcasting System Inc. owns the Atlanta Braves baseball team and controls the Atlanta Hawks basketball team and Tribune Co., which has various media holdings, also owns the baseball Chicago Cubs." (*Wall Street Journal*, March 18, 1996, p. B7)

**MOM-AND-POP.** Small store.
    "Additionally, the technological leverage chains now wield is hastening the end of the 'mom-and-pop' pharmacist." (*Chain Store Age*, Aug. 25, 1995, p. 15)

**MOMENTUM.** Stock market technical analysis charting price and volume of trade changes.

**MOMMY TRACK.** Damaging, dead-end career status often afforded people with family responsibilities.
    "But in practice, many women (and men too, though in smaller number) who need to use them [flexible schedules] resist for fear of being relegated to the Mommy Track." (*Wall Street Journal*, Dec. 13, 1995, p. B1)

**MONEY ILLUSION.** The false perception of increased income when inflation is greater than the increase in income.

"Smokers experience money illusion in that they respond more to nominal price changes than to real changes." (*Journal of Business Research*, Sept. 1995, p. 33)

**MONDAY MORNING QUARTERBACK.** A critic after something has gone wrong; a KNOW-IT-ALL (football).

**MONKEY BUSINESS.** Pranks, being silly; less-than ethical behavior.

"The Truth in Lending Act and the Real Estate Settlement and Procedures Act are supposed to PUT A DAMPER ON monkey business at settlement." (*Wall Street Journal*, Dec. 1, 1995, p. B14)

**MOONLIGHT (TO).** Work a second job.

"David Hardie, president of Hardie's Fruit & Vegetable Co. of Dallas, never thought he would moonlight as a fashion model." (*Wall Street Journal*, March 27, 1996, p. T2)

**MORAL SUASION.** Pressure, influence, as opposed to citing laws and regulations. The FED has been known to use moral suasion to influence bank practices.

**MOST FAVORED NATION (MFN).** GATT* trade understanding that no other nation will receive special privileges. If a trade barrier is reduced between any two members of GATT, the benefit is extended to all other GATT members under MFN principle.

**MOTHER-OF-ALL/MOTHER LODE.** Largest, huge (Persion Gulf War/mining).

"Broadcast television is poised to leap into the digital age. The transformation will mean 2 things for public network carriers: a revitalized competitor for video customers and a mother lode of spectrum greater than the PCS bonanza." (*America's Network*, July 15, 1995, p. 18)

**MOTOWN/MOTOR CITY.** Detroit, Michigan, home of Motown music and the BIG THREE automobile manufacturers.

**MOUTHPIECE.** Spokesperson; sometimes refers to a lawyer.

**MOVE UP IN LIFE (TO).** Make more money.

**MOVERS AND SHAKERS.** Important people.

"The Wall Street movers and shakers who dominated the late 1980s acquisition boom have been reshuffled to new places of employment." (*Global Finance*, Sept. 1994, p. 124)

**MUCKY-MUCKS/MUCK-A-MUCK.** People in charge, decision-makers.

"The expression is still often heard as 'high muck-a-muck' because of its probable derivation from Chinook [Native American] jargon, hiu (plenty) muckamuck (food); hence, one who has plenty to eat, or a man of power, a BIG WHEEL." (*Safire's New Political Dictionary*, 1993, p. 469)

**MULTI-LEVEL MARKETING.** Direct marketing system where sellers recruit other people into the organization as sales representatives, earning a commission on their sales. Critics refer to such practices as PYRAMIDING; multi-level marketing sounds more professional.

**MULTIPLE LISTING SERVICE (MLS).** Cooperative real estate system advertising each company's properties.

**MURPHY'S LAW.** If something can go wrong, it will.

"Delivery promises are susceptible to Murphy's Law, the more desperately the system needs to be delivered on time, the less likely it is that will happen." (*Computerworld*, Jan. 31, 1994, p. 120)

**MUSHROOM (TO).** Expand.

"Few mainland Chinese have actually logged on to the Internet. . . . But those numbers are bound to mushroom as China rushes headlong to connect." (*Far Eastern Economic Review*, July 27, 1995, p. 71)

**MUSHROOM JOB.** Derogatory reference to any distasteful work; deceive. From the joke, "Treat them like mushrooms: keep them in the dark, and feed them shit."

**MYSTERY SHOPPER.** Company representative who poses as a customer in another business. See SECRET SHOPPER.

"Wilson sent out mystery shoppers to visit a total of 2,000 randomly selected pro shops to see if the shops had at least 3 different models of the Ultra balls on display and in stock." (*Incentive*, Feb. 1995, p. 14)

# N

**NADER'S RAIDERS.** People working with noted consumer advocate and environmental lawyer Ralph Nader.

**NAKED CALL.** An option to buy a stock that is not actually owned by the seller of the option.

"Some employ an array of strategies such as buying on credit, writing naked call options and using other forms of LEVERAGE." (*Wall Street Journal*, March 14, 1996, p. C1)

**NANNY STATE.** A NEWT description of excessive government involvement in social issues and problems.

"The book effectively lays out the neoconservative arguments against the nanny state—which, he points out, is anything but 'compassionate' in its effects." (*Wall Street Journal*, Feb. 28, 1996, p. A12)

**NARROWCASTING.** Broadcasting to a small, specific audience. Technological advances increasingly allow marketers to appeal to small target markets.

**NARROWING THE SPREAD.** Reducing of the difference between the bid and asked prices for a stock.

**NATIONAL ASSOCIATION OF PURCHASING MANAGEMENT (NAPM).** Trade organization of purchasing managers.

"Bond prices jumped on the heels of the National Association of Purchasing Management report [which] showed surprising weakness in the nation's manufacturing sector. The NAPM October index fell to 46.8%." (*Wall Street Journal*, Nov. 2, 1995, p. C1)

**NATIONAL ASSOCIATION OF SECURITIES DEALERS AUTO-MATED QUOTATIONS (NASDAQ).** Computerized market for securities of smaller companies in the United States.

**NATIONAL CREDIT UNION ADMINISTRATION (NCUA).** Federal agency supervising credit unions in the United States.

**NATIONAL INSTITUTE OF HEALTH (NIH).** Federally funded center for health-related research.

**NATIONAL LABOR RELATIONS BOARD (NLRB).** The NLRB administers the National Labor Relations Act (1935), which prohibited employers and employees from engaging in unfair labor practices.

**NECK AND NECK (TO BE).** In close competition.

"Dreyer's is now neck and neck with Unilever Plc.'s Breyers in the premium-priced—$4.50 per half gallon—ice cream market, each with around 12%." (*Forbes*, Aug. 14, 1995, p. 42)

**NEGATIVE CASH FLOW.** A business situation requiring more cash than it produces from existing sales.

**NEGAWATT.** The conservation of electrical power. The term was coined by Amory Lovins, leader of the Snowmass Institute and critic of government energy policies that encourage production rather than conservation.

**NERVE.** Self-importance; willingness to take risks.

"Investment opportunities abound in today's bank merger wave and so do the risks. If an investor has the nerve for it, the obvious way to play bank mergers is to identify those with low P/Es in good markets and wait until they get swallowed up at a premium." (*Fortune*, Aug. 14, 1995, p. 48)

**NEST EGG.** Funds set aside for a specific purpose, often for retirement.

"In the past, he said, investors looked at their BLUE-CHIP investments as a combination nest egg and income-generating vehicle." (*Wall
Street Journal*, March 25, 1995, p. A5)

**NET.** Amount left after expenses and taxes.

**NET ASSET VALUE (NAV).** The value per share of a mutual fund; the
total assets of a company less liabilities and intangible assets, divided
by the number of shares outstanding.

**NETIQUETTE.** Internet etiquette.
"Direct marketers seeking to maximize the World Wide Web and
Internet for commercial purposes should heed to the generally accepted
rules of 'Netiquette' if they don't want to end up on the Blacklist of
Internet Advertisers." (*DM News*, May 20, 1996, p. 1)

**NET THIRTY.** The balance is due in thirty days.
"The advertisers pay 50% when they order and 50% net 30 days."
(*Folio*, May 1, 1994, p. 9)

**NETWORKING.** Building friends and contacts.

**NEWBIE.** Someone new to an online computer network.

**NEW KID ON THE BLOCK.** New competitor.

**NEW DEAL.** The economic programs of the Franklin Roosevelt administration (1932–1945). Elected during the height of the Great Depression,
Roosevelt enacted numerous social and economic programs, including
Social Security, the Works Project Administration (WPA), and the Civil-
ian Conservation Corps (CCC).

**NEWLY INDUSTRIALIZED COUNTRIES (NICs).** Developing countries that pursue an outward-oriented market strategy. The original
NICs included Hong Kong, South Korea, Taiwan, and Singapore. Based
on their success, many other countries are pursuing similar strategies.

**NEWT.** Referring to or related to Newt Gingrich.
"Newt Portfolio, stocks that would do well with the policies Congress-
man Gingrich advocates." (*Wall Street Journal*, Feb. 14, 1995, p. C1)

**NICE GUYS FINISH LAST.** Look out for yourself (Leo Durocher, famous baseball manager).

**NICKEL-AND-DIME (TO).** Small amounts; quibble over minor issues.

"Compared to what has been done in the past, the theft . . . is nickel-and-dime stuff." (*Far Eastern Economic Review*, Jan. 27, 1994, p. 34)

**NICHE MARKETING.** Marketing strategy of serving a unique (often small) market segment. Niche marketing is considered a step toward RELATIONSHIP MARKETING, because it reinforces the concept that companies must anticipate and satisfy customer needs.

**NIELSEN.** A C. Nielsen rating of the number of households watching a television program.
    "It is argued that the sooner a Nielsen or ARBITRON of the Internet emerges, the faster the billion-dollar commercial potential of the interactive era will be unleashed." (*Brandweek*, Sept. 25, 1995, p. IQ38)

**NIFTY.** Creative, well done.

**911.** (Pronounced nine-one-one); Emergency telephone number in the United States.

**NINE-TO-FIVE.** A regular day job, usually salaried.

**NINTH INNING.** At the last moment (baseball).
    Even though Schwab, based in San Francisco, is getting into the 401(k) game in the ninth inning, its arrival is sure to ruffle some competitors, especially given Schwab's reputation for low-cost service." (*Wall Street Journal*, April 3, 1996, p. C1)

**NITTY GRITTY.** Most basic parts.
    "The prestigious Zagat Surveys measure the nitty-gritty of U.S. restaurants." (*Nation's Restaurant News*, Aug. 21, 1995, p. 18)

**NO-BRAINER.** An easy decision.
    "You want people to see an ad once with significant impact, and of course as close to the point-of-purchase as possible. But that's a no-brainer." (Leah Martin, Eller Media, 1996)

**NO CEILING.** No limit.
    "In a Vietnamese joint venture, the foreign party is required to contribute at least 30% of the legal capital, but there is no ceiling on the foreign party's equity contribution." (*Law & Policy in International Business*, 1994, p. 481)

**NO-FRILLS.** Without any extra features. See also VANILLA MODEL.

"Air travelers on the new no-frills EuroBelgian Airlines Express will get no meals, no newspapers, and no connecting flights." (*Business Week*, Nov. 28, 1994, p. 72)

**NO LOAD.** Without any added fees.

**NOLO CONTENDERE.** Choosing not to contest (Latin), as in a legal dispute. Many Americans first learned the term when Vice President Spiro Agnew resigned from office in 1973, pleading nolo contendere to charges of tax evasion.

**NON-ACCELERATING INFLATION RATE OF UNEMPLOYMENT (NAIRU).** An inflation rate that creates jobs but not pressure to raise wages.
    "NAIRU fanatics, Treasury Secretary Rubin and his followers have narrowed the growth potential of the Home of the Brave to a band between 2.3% and 2.5%." (*Wall Street Journal*, June 20, 1996, p. A18)

**NO SCRAPS HIT THE FLOOR.** Competitors will immediately replace firms which make mistakes.
    "There is so much competition out there that no scraps will hit the floor." (Jami Martin, USC Corp., 1995)

**NOTE.** A promise to pay.

**NOT IN MY BACKYARD (NIMBY).** Local oppostion to environmental threats. Critics have suggested that environmentalists are not really concerned with pollution but instead are interested in making sure it is not in their backyards.
    "Perhaps surprisingly, prisons do not generally provoke a not-in-my-backyard reaction. The prospect of jobs and spinoff economic development is typically enough to head off opponents." (*Planning*, June 1995, p. 14)

**NO WONDER.** Not surprising; "I'm not surprised."
    "It is no wonder that Exec-U-Net reports that 60% of its members earning more than $100,000 a year believe that they will be forced out of their jobs in 1995." (*Barron's*, July 10, 1995, p. 12).

**NOISE.** Anything that distracts from a marketer's message.

**NONCOMPETITIVE BID.** A bid accepting the average price at an auction.

**NUKE (TO).** Eliminate, terminate.

"But only a family with a very committed ownership with a long-term perspective could make a decision to nuke earnings for three years." (*Wall Street Journal*, Nov. 28, 1995, p. A3)

**NUMBER CRUNCHER.** Accountant; technical financial analyst.

"Because risk managers are by nature number crunchers and because they do not have hard data on workplace violence, it is difficult for them to appreciate the value of violence-prevention investments." (*National Underwriter*, Aug. 14, 1995, p. 33)

**NUMERO UNO.** One's own self; Spanish/Italian for "number one."

"And a survey this month by the American Society of Travel Agents found Mexico was numero uno among those who wanted a 'value-oriented' respite." (*Wall Street Journal*, Feb. 16, 1995, p. B1)

**NURSE AN ACCOUNT (TO).** Give special attention or consideration to a problem account.

# O

**OCCUPATIONAL SAFETY AND HEALTH ADMINISTRATION (OSHA).** OSHA was created in 1970 to protect workers. The many confusing and contradicting OSHA regulations have turned the acronym into an epithet in management circles.

**ODD-BALL.** Loner, person or thing left out of the group; strange, unusual.

"In the past 3 weeks alone, racy convertibles have been sold by Reynolds Metals, First Chicago, Bowater, and Kaiser Aluminum. . . . The attraction of these odd-ball securities is simple—high yield." (*Barron's*, Feb. 14, 1995, p. 14)

**ODD LOT.** Stock trades of less than one hundred shares. One hundred shares is considered a ROUND LOT.

**ODD MAN OUT.** All alone.

"That would leave Sprint the odd man out among AT&T and MCI Communications Corp. in the race to establish global partnerships." (*Network World*, Feb. 13, 1995, p. 1)

**OFF BASE (TO BE).** Not informed, not understand.

"John Banzhaf, . . . believes the advertising industry is off base in its arguments. 'We restrict advertising of drugs,' says Mr. Banzhaf. 'If we are going to treat nicotine as a drug, then such restrictions are justified and needed.' " (*Wall Street Journal*, Aug. 11, 1995, p. B3)

**OFFICE OF THE INSPECTOR GENERAL (OIG).** The OIG is the internal investigation division within the federal government.

**OFFICE OF MANAGEMENT BUDGET (OMB).** The NUMBER CRUNCHING arm of the executive (White House) branch of government.

**OFFPEAK PRICING.** Energy pricing with lower rates during periods when demand is low.

**OFFSHOOT.** Derived from or variation of.

"But the creation of Pentium offshoots, and a series of chips from competitors, will make it more confusing for PC buyers who are after the latest and greatest technology, he said." (*Wall Street Journal*, Sept. 20, 1995, p. B8)

**OFFSHORE FUNDS.** Investments registered outside one's home country for tax advantages.

"In the 1960s the late Bernie Cornfield's Investors Overseas Services sold offshore funds to U.S. citizens living in Europe." (*Financial World*, April 15, 1995, p. 71)

**OFFSHORE PRODUCERS.** Overseas companies.

**OFF-THE-BOOKS.** Cash or barter; Business done without records to avoid taxation.

"So many Spaniards do off-the-book jobs that they've adopted a word for it, chapuza, which literally means slipshod." (*Wall Street Journal*, Nov. 30, 1995, p. A14)

**OFF-THE-CUFF.** Informal, initial opinion.

"In off-the-cuff remarks at Stanford, Microsoft's CEO* recalled the letters he'd written a decade ago, urging Apple's management to license out the Macintosh operating system for CLONING." (*Wall Street Journal*, Feb. 6, 1996, p. A15)

**OFF THE RECORD.** Unofficially, not for quotation. Many times politicians and government bureaucrats will only speak off the record.

**OFF-THE-SHELF/RACK.** Readily available, not custom made.

"Italy's Brioni, maker of the most expensive, hand-sewn, off-the-rack suits in the world, had sales in 1994 of $46 million up 20%." (*Forbes*, July 31, 1995, p. 96)

**OFF THE TOP.** Before any deductions are made; from the most profitable part.

"However, in an effort to prevent SKIMMING off the top, telecom operators will not be permitted to only take part in the more lucrative international sector." (*Business Korea*, July 1994, p. 33)

**OFF-THE-WALL.** Crazy.

"Tango's latest burst of off-the-wall advertising, which breaks tonight, goes one step further than previous ads with a new interactive element for the mainstream orange brand." (*Marketing*, March 23, 1995, p. 5)

**OIL PATCH.** The U.S. oil industry; specific regions of the United States noted for oil production and refining, including Texas, Oklahoma, Louisiana, California, and Alaska.

"Messman was the rare executive that clicked immediately on things like redesigning processes and squeezing unit costs—notions common in many industries but still uncommon in much of the oil patch." (*Wall Street Journal*, Jan. 23, 1996, p. A1)

**OK.** All right. The term may have come from President (1837–1841) Martin Van Buren's nickname, "Old Kinderhook."

**OLD AGE, SURVIVORS, AND DISABILITY INSURANCE (OASDI).** The official name for Social Security.

**OLD-BOYS CLUB/NETWORK.** Closed network of established business relationships.

"Private placements, a market that was once a secretive, old-boys club for a few huge life insurance companies and a handful of WHITE-SHOE investment bankers, is now being overrun with commercial banks, money managers and other institutions." (*Investment Dealers Digest*, Aug. 28, 1995, p. 14)

**OMBUDSMAN.** Third party who acts as an arbitrator within an organization. The term comes from the Swedish word *ombud*, meaning authority to act for another.

**ON A BACK BURNER.** In reserve; waiting to be developed.

"Congress and the EPA have put legislation that would protect the confidentiality of a company's self-audits on a back burner." (*Chemical Week*, Nov, 1, 1995, p. 34)

**ON ACCOUNT.** In partial payment of a debt.

**ON ALL FOURS.** Ready to go.

**ON A MISSION (HE/SHE IS).** Highly motivated.

**ON A ROLL (TO BE).** A series of successes.
    "And New York Fires has been on an acquisition roll, growing to more than 100 units by buying up half a dozen small competitors." (*Success*, Sept. 1995, p. 2)

**ON A SIGNATURE BASIS.** Based on one's reputation or signature, without review.
    "While credit cards operate almost exclusively on a signature basis, debit transactions in the majority of countries are undertaken by using the cardholder's PIN*, or by a combination of signature and PIN." (*Credit Card Management*, April 1994, p. 100)

**ON BOARD (TO BE).** Hired. The phrase is most often associated with jobs in government.
    "Among the most common pitfalls of buying practices are paying too much for a practice and paying the doctor too much once on board as an employee." (*Modern Healthcare*, Sept. 25, 1995, p. 64)

**ONCE-UNHEARD-OF.** Never happened in the past.

**ONE FELL SWOOP.** All at once (Shakespeare).
    "Acquisition also eliminates competition and delivers geographic penetration in one fell swoop." (*Success*, Sept. 1995, p. 83)

**ONE-MAN-SHOW.** To work alone, sole proprietor.
    "The business was designed almost by accident over the years to fit the founder like a glove, but the one-man show must be redesigned to accommodate a new cast." (*Agency Sales Management*, June 1995, p. 20)

**ONE-TWO PUNCH.** Two actions taken quickly one after the other (boxing).
    "At the same time, the one-two punch from the shutdown of the U.S. government and a devastating blizzard in the Northeast region of the U.S. is likely to weigh on the economy." (*Barron's*, Jan. 15, 1996, p. MW10)

**ONE-UPMANSHIP.** Keeping a subtle psychological advantage over an opponent.

**ON PAPER.** In theory.

"As wealthy as the Shupes are on paper, they find themselves constantly short of cash." (*Money*, Oct. 1995, p. 112)

**ON THE BALL.** Alert, effective.

"Pressler has become Capitol Hill's own Forrest Gump—a nice guy with not much on the ball who succeeds astoundingly just by being in the right place at the right time." (*Adweek*, May 8, 1995, p. 18)

**ON THE CARPET (CALLED).** In trouble.

"A physician that is called on the carpet should ask the accusers if there is a written policy on the alleged misdeed." (*Medical Economics*, Jan. 9, 1995, p. 48)

**ON THE CHEAP.** Inexpensively.

"Health Management buys existing hospitals in small cities, mainly in the southeastern U.S., usually financially ailing hospitals that can be had on the cheap." (*Forbes*, Aug. 28, 1995, p. 90)

**ON THE CLOCK.** Working.

*Customer:* "He's on the clock. He can't sit down."
*Manager:* "Yes I can, I'm SCHMOOZING with customers!"
(A conversation overhead by the author
while working on this book, June 6, 1996)

**ON THE FENCE.** Undecided.

"That's why Greg Quick, first vice president at Commerce Mortgage Corp., says, 'many people basically are sitting on the fence to see what happens.' " (*Wall Street Journal*, March 26, 1996, p. A2)

**ON THE FIRING LINE.** In the path of the action, under pressure.

"Distribution and supply problems with ethanol could put marketers on the firing line with the public once the reformulated gasoline program begins on January 1, 1995." (*National Petroleum News*, July 1994, p. 22)

**ON THEIR OWN TURF.** In their market or offices.

"Outsiders cannot challenge Japanese airlines on their own turf." (*Director*, July 1995, p. 32)

**ON THE LINE.** At risk.

"Now, a growing number of companies is asking RANK-AND-FILE employees to put a portion of their pay on the line. The schemes may link compensation to company TRACK RECORDS, unit performance, team success, or individual achievement, but all have one thing in common: By offering big incentives when things go well but withholding raises when things go sour." (*Business Week*, Nov. 14, 1995, p. 62)

**ON THE MONEY.** Accurate.

"Besides the small fact that the BULLS have been absolutely on the money and the BEARS dead wrong all year, what has fed investor complacency has been the supposed lack of feverish speculation, that universally perceived telltale sign that trouble is brewing." (*Barron's*, Aug. 28, 1995, p. 3)

**ON THE SIDELINES.** Not involved, not participating in decision or action. The term comes from football, where if you are on the sidelines you are not in the game.

**ON THE SPOT.** Immediately; under pressure.

"The problem with getting discussion groups going is that people feel that they are being put on the spot." (*Personnel Journal*, Oct. 1995, p. 141)

**ON THE TABLE.** UP FRONT, up for discussion.

"Peter Sprague again has his chips on the table, this time as chairman and CEO* of Wave Systems." (*Chief Executive*, Oct. 1995, p. 22)

**ON THE TAKE.** Accepting bribes or illegal payments.

"Carriers say shippers and receivers are on the take, while shippers say carriers are more unabashed than ever about trying to buy their business with entertainment and bribes." (*Distribution*, March 1994, p. 34)

**ON THE WINGS OF.** With the support or assistance of.

"The NASDAQ* is up some 35% since 1995 started, mostly on the wings of the technology stocks." (*Barron's*, Aug. 28, 1995, p. 3)

**OP. CIT. (OPERE CITATO).** In the work cited (Latin).

**OP/ED.** Opinion/editorial section of a newspaper.

**OPEN DOOR POLICY.** Management policy advocating access for employees from all levels within the organization.

"Other examples abound, such as 'right-sizing' for job cuts and 'open door policy' for come talk to me any time, but don't bring any bad news.'" (*Wall Street Journal*, Feb. 26, 1996, p. A12)

**OPEN INTEREST.** The number of outstanding futures contracts.

"Trading volume and open interest in options and futures contracts on stock indices, equities, and interest rate instruments traded on world exchanges have experienced remarkable growth." (*New England Economic Review*, July 8, 1995, p. 25)

**OPEN ORDER.** An order that is good until canceled.

**OPEN SKIES.** Available to everyone.

"An open-skies policy allows carriers from signatory nations to fly from any city in the country to any point in the other." (*Traffic Management*, May 1995, p. 19)

**OPERATING EXPENSES (OE).** All the expenses of running a business except the cost of goods sold.

**OPPORTUNITY COST.** The value of the next best use of a resource.

"Other costs, such as the opportunity cost of wasted time spent by employees playing computer games or surfing the net are not typically calculated." (*Internal Auditing*, Fall 1995, p. 49)

**OPTIMIZE (TO).** Develop to full potential.

**ORDERING AND SHIPPING IMPROVEMENT SYSTEM (OASIS).** Computerized shipping and production control system.

**ORDER OF THE DAY.** Common; objectives being pursued (military).

"New products, new brands combined with new advertising is the order of the day." (*Marketing*, Sept. 7, 1995, p. 9)

**ORGANIZATION OF AMERICAN STATES (OAS).** U.S. dominated regional political alliance including South and Central American countries.

**ORGANIZATION OF PETROLEUM EXPORTING COUNTRIES (OPEC).** Thirteen-member international commodity organization which seeks to limit petroleum production in order to the increase price of oil.

**ORPHAN STOCK.** A stock that is not followed by research analysts, usually because the company is quite small.

**OTHER PEOPLE'S MONEY (OPM).** Borrowed funds.

**OUT OF THE BALLPARK (TO KNOCK).** Beyond the predicted range, excessively high (baseball).

"This [increasing the minimum wage] is going to knock the budget numbers out of the ballpark." (*Wall Street Journal*, April 24, 1996, p. A1)

**OUT OF THE LOOP.** Not part of the decision-making group, not in the network. During the Iran-Contra investigations, then Vice President George Bush claimed that he was out of the loop.

"On the eve of a major brand image overhaul, Mazda Motor of America's National Dealer Council is disbanding and regrouping, irked at being left out of the loop." (*Brandweek*, Aug. 7, 1995, p. 1)

**OUT OF THE MONEY.** A stock option that has no value.

**OUT OF THE WOODS.** No longer in danger.

"Still, convinced that it is not out of the woods yet, Aqualon recently turned to the The Manager's Network to help it tackle new challenges." (*CIO*, May 1995, p. 31)

**OUT OF THE WOODWORK.** Appear unexpectedly.

**OUT OF TOUCH.** Not informed, not understanding.

"Plus, the skills of local workers, coddled by years of job security may be out of touch with the times." (*Business Week*, Sept. 11, 1995, p. 112)

**OUT OF WHACK.** Not right, out of balance.

**OUTPLACEMENT.** Services provided to recently terminated employees.

"By withholding part of the retainer as a bonus for a job well done, the outplacement firm will be motivated to achieve the best results possible." (*HR Magazine*, July 1995, p. 66)

**OUTSOURCE (TO).** Replace company production with subcontractors.

"Should the word outsource be heard around the office, the end is in sight." (*Supervision*, Jan. 1994, p. 4)

**OVERHANG.** A large quantity of stock that is available in the market.

"Risks to Lucent's share price include CUTTHROAT COMPETITION, a huge overhang of 524 million shares that AT&T plans to offer at year end, and doubts about whether Lucent will actually be able to cut 23,000 jobs as planned in an increasingly anti-layoff climate." (*Wall Street Journal*, April 3, 1996, p. C3)

**OVERHEAD.** Management cost associated with a specific activity.

**OVERRUN.** Production in excess of requirements.

**OVER THE COUNTER (OTC).** Stock market transactions which take place through telephone and computer networks rather than through market specialists on the exchanges.

**OZONE-FRIENDLY.** Products without chlorofluorocarbons.

"At issue is a 1990 California statute that established rules for marketers to follow when using environmental terms—such as recyclable, ozone-friendly and recycled—and prescribed specific definitions." (*Advertising Age*, Sept. 12, 1994, p. 13)

**OZZIE AND HARRIET (LIKE).** Traditional two-parent two-children household.

"Ozzie and Harriet Don't Live Here Anymore. . . . An editorial notes that by the year 2000, consumers are more likely to be minorities, immigrants, female heads of households and low-wage earners than they have been in any decade since World War II." (*National Underwriter*, Aug. 15, 1994, p. 18)

# P

**PACESETTER.** Person or product that sets the standards for others who follow (horse racing).

**PACKAGE (TO).** Parts of an agreement; to bring together parts of a business strategy.

**PACK IT IN (TO).** Quit, close a business.

**PACKAGE DEAL.** An agreement including several parts.
   "Americans who want an affordable way to travel to Europe should consider package deals." (*Forbes*, May 8, 1995, p. 164)

**PAC-MAN STRATEGY.** Corporate strategy of buying up the shares of the company attempting to take over one's company (computer games).

**PAD (TO).** Add to, as in a budget or an expense account.

**PAINTING THE TAPE.** Illegal stock market tactic where a large order is divided into many small orders to give the appearance of interest on the part of many investors.

"The action on the floor was dominated by pools, which would rig the market and paint the tape with phony trades. The public would see a stock moving and figure that something must be going on. The suckers would all rush in, . . . and then the pool operators would sell at a profit." (*Wall Street Journal*, May 28, 1996, p. R18)

**PANDORA'S BOX.** An array of potential problems. In Greek mythology, Pandora, the first mortal woman, opened a box, releasing the ills of the world.

**PAPER.** A contract, agreement; abbreviation for COMMERCIAL PAPER.

**PAR.** Face value of a security.

**PARADIGM SHIFT.** A change in focus, or of fundamental assumptions.
"In a paradigm shift: a) your company's structure and work will change profoundly, forever altering your career; b) someone in management has been to a seminar—don't worry, it will pass; or c) many people will be fired to convince investors that real change is taking place." (*Wall Street Journal*, Oct. 3, 1995, p. B1)

**PARALLEL ECONOMY.** Informal, unregulated economy. See also BLACK MARKET.
"Hernando de Soto is the leading scholar documenting the parallel or unlicensed economy. His book, *The Other Path: The Invisible Revolution in the Third World* portrays the extent of this sector in the Peruvian economy." (*Understanding NAFTA and Its International Business Implications*, 1996, p. 247)

**PARKING.** Financial strategy of placing assets in a safe investment while looking for other opportunities. See also ILLEGAL PARKING.

**PARKINSON'S LAW.** The observation that work expands to fill the time available to do it.

**PARLIAMENTARY PROCEDURE.** Rules of order for running meetings based on those used in the British Parliament.

**PARTNERING.** Searching for business opportunities.
"Never do business with anyone who talks freely about 'partnering' because it will cost you." (*Supervision*, Jan. 1994, p. 6)

**PARTY LINE.** The official response or position.

**PAT ON THE BACK.** Support; to encourage.

"Unfortunately, not everyone knows what constitutes recognition, or what, if any, awards should accompany that pat on the back." (*Incentive*, March 1995, p. 62)

**PAVE THE WAY (TO).** Make easier for, provide access to.

"Jencks and other social scientists controlled for all sorts of variables that might pave the way to wealth and power, including parental income, the neighborhood a person grows up in, education, occupation, and test scores." (*Fortune*, Oct. 16, 1995, p. 148)

**PAVLOV'S DOGS.** Reference to conditioned responses; people who respond to management's stimuli. Refers to the research of the Russian psychologist Ivan Pavlov, who conducted stimulus-response experiments with dogs.

**PAYOLA.** Bribe, secret payments.

**PAY ON THE LINE (TO).** Pay promptly.

**PAY THE PIPER/FIDDLER (TO).** Pay what one owes; take the consequences. The phrase comes from the proverb "He who dances must pay the piper."

"Eastern Europe's banks pay the piper after the heady days of the early '90s." (*Wall Street Journal*, April 18, 1996, p. A12)

**PAY THROUGH THE NOSE (TO).** Pay an excessive amount.

**PEARL-DIVING CONTEST.** A sales-force incentive program.

**PECKING ORDER.** Rank, seniority (social behavior of fowl).

"While the impact of their legislative counsel is just being felt, the rising prominence of Gingrich's corporate KITCHEN CABINET has already shaken up the pecking order within the BELTWAY." (*Business Week*, June 26, 1995, p. 80)

**PEEK.** A very brief look or reading.

"On the basis of his knowledge of history and observations about today, Peter Bishop of the University of Houston at Clear Lake provides a peek at tomorrow that is both exciting and frightening for business communicators." (*Communication World*, Oct. 1995, p. 34)

**PENETRATION PRICING.** Marketing strategy of initially setting a low price to gain market-share with the goal of raising prices once one's product is the established leader in the market.

"It is shown that when there is repeat purchases the forward-looking firm should tend towards penetration pricing." (*Marketing Science*, Summer 1994, p. 310)

**PENDULUM SWING.** A change of direction, attitude.

"It has been left to a man—and an economist—to sight a pendulum swing that seemed unthinkable just a short time ago: the exodus of women from the workforce." (*Barron's*, March 21, 1994, p. 33)

**PENNY-ANTE.** Of little consequence or importance.

"So far, the exchanges have been anteing up only lower-volume, penny-ante goods, thereby avoiding the head-to-head competition in key stocks that the SEC* had intended." (*Barron's*, May 2, 1994, p. 9)

**PENNY STOCK.** Stocks that sell for less than $1 per share. Penny stocks are traded over-the-counter at regional stock exchanges. The penny stock market has frequently been the subject of investigations for price manipulation.

**PEOPLE PILL.** Anti-takeover tactic where managers all threaten to leave if the company is purchased by outsiders.

**PEP TALK.** Motivational speech.

"Although inspirational pep talks may help, most employees need more tangible motivation to produce outstanding performance." (*Supervision*, April 1994, p. 2)

**PER DIEM.** Expense allowance per day (Latin).

**PERK/PERC.** Special benefits, privileges.

"Examples of the extensive perks enjoyed by United Nations employees are discussed." (*Money*, Nov. 1995, p. 27)

**PER SE.** By or in itself, as such (Latin).

**PERSONAL IDENTIFICATION NUMBER (PIN).** Secret number used to secure telephone communications or financial transactions.

**PERSONA NON GRATA.** A person who is not welcome (Latin).

**PER STIRPES.** Legal formula for allocating the assets of an estate when the deceased did not leave a will.

**PETER PRINCIPLE.** Tendency of management to promote people one level above their competence. Dr. Lawrence Peter of the University of Southern California coined the term.

"The Peter Principle may be responsible for some employees' performance problems." (*Supervisory Management*, June 1994, p. 14)

**PETRODOLLARS.** Surplus revenues accumulated by oil exporting countries. When OPEC* was established in the 1970s, members insisted on being paid in U.S. dollars.

**PHANTOM INCOME.** A tax and accounting issue in limited partnerships where tax credits taken earlier in the life of the investment result in a reportable income when otherwise there would be a loss. Tax shelters prior to 1986 often resulted in phantom income.

**PHILLIPS CURVE.** Graph of the relationship between inflation and unemployment in an economy.

**PHONE BOOTH GLUT.** 1990's overabundance of telephone booths due to the introduction of cellular phones.

**PHONY AS A THREE-DOLLAR BILL.** Deceitful; con-artist.

**PICKET (TO).** Demonstrate. Union workers form PICKET LINES, and protesters against government policies picket the White House.

**PICKET LINE.** Union protest technique, creating a line of union members which nonunion workers and customers would have to pass in order to enter or leave a business.

"The picket line, once largely honored by unionized and nonunion workers alike, appears to be losing its legs. 'There used to be families that grew up believing that crossing a picket line is the equivalent of pushing an old lady off a curb.' " (*Wall Street Journal*, Jan. 17, 1996, p. A1)

**PICK UP (TO).** Start where one left off; a stimulant; a casual encounter.

**PICK ONE'S BRAIN.** Solicit ideas from someone.

"A survey of more than 100 retailers, marketers, and consumer advocates resulted in these strategies to get freebies: . . . 4. Seek out local experts to pick their brains and get free services." (*Money*, July 1994, p. 96)

**PICKS UP.** Increases.

**PIECE OF CAKE.** Easy.

**PIECE OF THE ACTION.** Part ownership; involvement in a project; some of the sales or profits.

"The prospect of one-stop financial services shops has a lot of insurance agents worried and a lot of banks, securities firms and large insurers anxious to get a piece of the action." (*Best's Review*, June 1995, p. 28)

**PIECE RATE.** Amount a worker is paid per unit when doing PIECE-WORK.

**PIECEWORK.** To be paid based on the quantity of goods produced.

**PIGEON.** A person who is easily deceived. See also MARK.

**PIGEONHOLE (TO).** Place in a category.

"The Animated Series on the Fox Children's Network—continue to pigeonhole Arabs in negative roles." (*Broadcasting & Cable*, July 11, 1994, p. 19)

**PIGGYBACK.** Intermodal transportation combining rail and truck transport.

**PIGGYBACKING.** Practice of one firm marketing another firm's products; making use of existing efforts. In stock markets, when a broker buys or sells based on the actions of a client it is considered illegal piggybacking.

"The new service piggybacks onto existing channel capacity enabling cable-TV viewers to address data, such as weather forecasts and traffic reports." (*Electronic Business Today*, Sept. 1995, p. 44)

**PIGS.** Thirty-pound blocks of aluminum or other metal; greedy people.

**PILOT FISH.** Junior executives who follow close behind senior management. See also BROWN-NOSER, ASS-KISSER.

"Our nations' bulging inventory of business cliches is spun out by pundits, picked up by senior executives, and regurgitated by pilot fish imitating their bosses." (*Fortune*, Feb. 20, 1995, p. 22)

**PILOT LAUNCH.** Test marketing by limiting the initial distribution of a product.

"The test follows pilot launches from Safeways' 2 largest rivals, Sainbury and Tesco." (*Marketing*, Jan. 13, 1994, p. 3)

**PINCH HIT (TO).** Substitute for (baseball).

"Many internal support organizations are now moving toward establishing one number for users to call when reporting difficulties. Some organizations have users pinch hit for the help desk." (*Infoworld*, Aug. 8, 1994, p. 53)

**PINK SHEETS.** Daily publication of stock quotations on the NASDAQ*.

"In 1992, Frontier went public on the NASDAQ bulletin board or pink sheets." (*Oil & Gas Investor*, June 1995, p. 18)

**PINK SLIP.** Dismissal notice.

"In many cases, employees at First Boston will be getting pink slips along with bonus notifications." (*Investment Dealers Digest*, Feb. 20, 1995, p. 7)

**PIN MONEY.** A small amount of money allocated for a trip.

**PISSED.** Angry.

"Two Cheers for the Pissed Off." (*Forbes*, April 10, 1995, p. 17)

**PIT.** The center of activity in futures and options markets.

**PITCH.** High-pressured sales presentation.

"At a meeting sponsored by the Advertising Club of Greater Boston, U.S. Senator John Kerry lashed out at what he called Republicans' snake-oil sales pitch." (*Adweek*, Oct. 16, 1995, p. 4)

**PITCH MAN.** Sales person.

**PLAIN-VANILLA.** Ordinary, without any extras.

"Ultimately he was assigned to new-product development—helping KPMG escape its stigma as a plain-vanilla financial-statements auditor." (*Wall Street Journal*, Jan. 19, 1996, p. B1)

**PLASTIC.** Credit card.

"With retail card executives questioning the relevance of their plastic, retailers are approaching a crossroads. They can either surrender to 3rd-party cards or retrench and find new ways to profit from growing their cards' share of sales." (*Credit Card Management*, July 1995, p. 6)

**PLAY BALL (TO).** Cooperate; get started (baseball).

"Because we played ball, we came through with a few GRASS STAINS but no serious injuries." (*Wall Street Journal*, June 17, 1996, p. A14)

**PLAYBOOK.** Corporate plans (football).

"Borrowing a page from software developers, playbooks, Intel will launch an early-testing program in the 3rd quarter of 1995 that will let hundreds of sophisticated users do the TROUBLESHOOTING on P6-based systems." (*Informationweek*, May 29, 1995, p. 16)

**PLAY CLOSE TO THE CHEST/VEST.** Keep one's thoughts or plans secret.

"Current Yield: As the FED Plays It Close to the Vest, the Market Moves as If It's Got a Handful of Aces." (*Barron's*, Aug. 28, 1995, p. MW10)

**PLAY HARDBALL (TO).** Be demanding, difficult to negotiate with (baseball).

"The problem is that the Republican-controlled Senate is vowing to play hard-ball over the FED vacancies. GOP lawmakers are all but demanding that Clinton reappoint Greenspan, a conservative Republican, to a 3rd 4-year term." (*Business Week*, Sept. 25, 1995, p. 60)

**PLAY THE FLOAT (TO).** Write a check today and deposit the funds to cover it tomorrow.

**PLAYER.** A noteworthy competitor in the market.

"Hughes developed the first successful communications satellite and was an early player in this lucrative business." (*Business Forum*, Winter/Spring 1995, p. 5)

**PLEAD THE FIFTH (TO).** Refuse to divulge information. The Fifth Amendment to the U.S. Constitution allows citizens not to answer questions in court when their response would incriminate themselves.

**PLOW BACK (TO).** Put back into.

"Many invest in companies that plow back most or all of their earnings into their businesses to become more profitable—which, in turn, raises their stock prices." (*Medical Economics*, May 9, 1994, p. 40)

**PLUG A PRODUCT (TO).** Promote.

**PLUM.** A good investment.

**POINT-OF-PURCHASE (POP) DISPLAY.** Retailing strategy of placing impulse items near where customers make their purchases.

**POINT PERSON.** Person designated to take charge of a crisis situation.

**POISON PILL.** A financial maneuver to avoid being taken over by another company.

"First Brands Corp. said its board adopted a shareholder-rights plans, commonly known as a poison pill." (*Wall Street Journal*, March 27, 1996, p. C1)

**POLITICAL ACTION COMMITTEE (PAC).** Group created to lobby government.

"The $17 billion in cuts in this year's budget affect the weakest groups in society, without PAC money or lobbying clout." (*Business Week*, April 3, 1995, p. 138)

**POLITICALLY CORRECT (PC).** Accepted terminology; espousing non-Western culture and values.

"Multiculturalists and politically correct people, while bad-mouthing white men and Western culture and values, celebrate cultural relativism and pluralism." (*Vital Speeches*, June 1, 1995, p. 492)

**POLLUTION CREDIT.** Market-based pollution control credit program, allowing firms which reduce their levels of pollution below what is required by law, to sell the difference between the maximum amount allowed and their current amount produced to other firms. The economic logic is that firms which can easily reduce pollution will do so, while those firms for whom it would be expensive to reduce pollution will purchase credits instead.

**PONZI SCHEME.** A fraudulent financial proposition where initial investors are promised very high rates of return; Eventually the scheme collapses. The phrase is named after Charles Ponzi, who in 1919 created the Security and Exchange Company, promising investors a 40% return. Ponzi paid off the initial investors with funds of later investors. Auditors eventually revealed the scheme, and Ponzi went to jail. He later sold real estate in Florida. See also PYRAMID.

**POOL OF APPLICANTS.** Potential employees.

**POOL TOGETHER (TO).** Combine.

"In private banking the aim is to pool together the various international operations HSBC [Hongkong and Shanghai Bank] runs and group them under the umbrella, HSBC Private Banking." (*Director*, Oct. 1994, p. 60)

**POOR-MOUTH (TO).** Deny one's wealth.

**PORK BARREL.** Government spending designed to favor a politician's constituents.

"The reason freight railroads make good profits and render excellent service whereas Amtrak loses heavily and delivers shoddy service, is pork barrel politics and labor unions that still live in the 1950s." (*Business Week*, May 15, 1995, p. 86)

**PORTFOLIO.** A collection of securities.

**PORTFOLIO INVESTMENT.** Purchasing stock in a number of companies.

**POSITION.** A company's financial condition; an investor's interest in a venture.

**POSITIVE CASH FLOW.** More cash produced than used.

**POSTAL PRICING.** Pricing telephone calls the same regardless of distance, like postal (mail) rates.

**POTHOLES.** Problems; obstacles.

"It is tough enough to deal with the potholes of any career path. However, for those at the top, the going can get especially rocky." (*Personnel Journal*, Oct. 1995, p. 100)

**POUND OF FLESH.** An exorbitant demand or payment. In Shakespeare's *Merchant of Venice*, SHYLOCK demands a pound of flesh as payment for his loan to Antonio.

**POWER HITTERS.** Strong, forceful individuals (baseball).

**POWER NAP.** A short, five-to-ten-minute rest. Some people have the ability to sleep for short periods of time and awaken refreshed and ready to go again.

**POWER LUNCH.** Lunchtime business meeting between MOVERS AND SHAKERS.

"Advertising executive Phil Guarascio recently flew to New York to meet with top executives of Conde Nast and its parent, Advance Publications, at a pre-Christmas power lunch." (*Advertising Age*, Dec. 19, 1994, p. 34)

**POWER OF THE PRESS.** Media's ability to change or affect public opinion.

"Just as television should not be PIGEON-HOLED, the power of the press to brand strongly should not be underestimated." (*Marketing*, May 18, 1995, p. 3)

**POWERHOUSE.** Forceful person or group.

"Marvel Entertainment Group's consumer marketing unit . . . has proven to be a youth marketing powerhouse, able to score value-added points for McDonald's Happy Meals, General Mills' fruit snacks and Nabisco Cookies." (*Adweek*, Oct. 9, 1995, p. 112)

**POW-POW.** Meeting, discussion. The term comes from a Native American word for conjurer or medicine man.

"The Travel Industry Association of America's Discover America International Pow Wow for 1997 and 1998 will be held in Nashville and Chicago, respectively." (*Hotel & Motel Management*, Sept. 18, 1995, p. 13)

**PREFAB.** Abbreviation for prefabricated: already manufactured and ready for assembly.

**PREMIUM.** The excess of market price over the value of the good; in insurance the payment due.

**PREMIUMS.** Items given away or for a reduced price when customers purchase another product. Premiums are used to motivate consumers to try a new product or brand.

**PRESS THE FLESH (TO).** Shake hands. See also GLAD HAND.

**PRESSURE-COOKER.** Stressful environment.

"Because working-age Americans often spend 1/2 of their waking hours on the job, life in this pressure cooker frequently builds up excessive levels of stress." (*HR Magazine*, Dec. 1994, p. 92)

**PRICES TUMBLING.** Prices going down rapidly.

"News of a profits shortfall sent the share price tumbling from its 447p high to 174p last year." (*Director*, May 1995, p. 56)

**PRIMA DONNA.** Show-off (Italian).

**PRIMA FACIE.** On first appearance (Latin).

**PRIME.** Prime rate. The rate charged by banks to their highest-quality borrowers for short-term, uncollateralized loans.

**PRIVATIZATION.** The selling-off by government of nationalized industries; contracting privately for services previously done by government employees.

"The candelilla wax market remains stable, having smoothly made the transition from government control to privatization." (*Chemical Marketing Reporter*, Oct. 2, 1995, p. 10)

**PROACTIVE.** Taking a position in advance rather than reacting.

"An increasing number of progressive companies have been proactive in offering paid and unpaid family leaves as part of their employees' benefit package." (*Public Personnel Management*, Fall 1995, p. 271)

**PROBLEM CHILD.** A low-market-share product in a fast-growing market.

**PRO BONO.** For the (public) good (Latin), i.e., without charge.

Most state law associations require lawyers to do some work pro bono annually.

**PRODUCER PRICE INDEX (PPI).** The PPI measures inflation at the wholesale level. Changes in the PPI usually precede changes in inflation at the consumer level.

**PRODUCT LIFE CYCLE (PLC).** Stages a product goes through in the marketplace, including introduction, growth, maturity, and decline. PLC was once used exclusively among marketers, but in the 1990s it is used by accountants and finance managers concerned with whether a product will remain marketable long enough to be profitable.

**PRO FORMA.** As a matter of form (Latin). New companies often issue pro forma, hypothetical income and expenditure statements.

**PROGRAM TRADING.** Computerized purchase or sale of a group of securities, usually in amounts of $1 million or more.

**PROGRESSIVE TAX.** A tax which increases as income increases.

**PROMO.** Promotion.

"The only damper may be the Hands-off-Halloween campaign, coordinated by the Coalition on Alcohol Advertising to lobby against Halloween promos, charging they contribute to alcohol consumption by minors." (*Brandweek*, Oct. 23, 1995, p. 1)

**PRO RATA.** According to shares (Latin), a percentage based on past performance.

**PROS AND CONS.** Advantages and disadvantages.

"Shana Robison, vice president of the Newton Systems Group, has a tough job ahead as the industry weighs the pros and cons of the emerging handheld computer market." (*Computer Reseller News*, June 5, 1995, p. 77)

**PROSPECT.** A potential customer.

"The more that is learned about customers and prospects, the less they fit into the normally distributed theory." (*Journal of Direct Marketing*, Winter 1995, p. 5)

**PROTECTION MONEY.** Bribe; money paid to avoid problems with authorities or criminals.

"On May 3, Farooq Sumar, a leading Karachi industrial magnate, came out of 3 weeks in hiding to explain publicly how he, his family, and his employees had been threatened by the local mafia after he refused to continue to pay protection money." (*Far Eastern Economic Review*, May 25, 1995, p. 52)

**PROXY.** Agreement allowing another person to represent one's interests.

**PRUDENT-MAN RULE.** U.S. legal standard for the actions of someone charged with investing funds in trust for others. The administrator of the funds is expected to ask, "Would a prudent man or woman make this investment?"

**PSYCHIC INCOME.** Non-monetary value or satisfaction from a work activity.

**PUBLIC DOMAIN.** Available to all citizens. In the United States, government documents are public domain.

**PUBLIC EYE (IN THE).** Visible, widely publicized.

"The firm was looking to reach a large audience with a large easy-to-read message that was in the public eye every day." (*Journal of Accountancy*, July 1995, p. 93)

**PUBLICITY STUNT.** An outrageous act designed to get media coverage.

"Although the media attention for General Motors" Saturn automobile homecoming was impressive, the event should be less remembered as a publicity stunt than as a milestone of RELATIONSHIP MARKETING. (*Brandweek*, Aug. 8, 1994, p. 18)

**PUBLIC SERVICE ANNOUNCEMENT (PSA).** Free advertising time for socially important messages. As part of their licensing requirements, radio and television stations in the United States are expected to provide time for public service announcements.

"TV clutter is defined as all non-programming time, including commercials, PSAs, promos, station IDs, and programming credits." (*Advertising Age*, May 8, 1995, p. 42)

**PUFF PIECE.** HYPE; extravagant praise.

"Ways to make an executive HEADHUNTER come calling before one has to send out resumes are discussed: . . . 5. Have a public relations consultant plant puff pieces about oneself." (*Across the Board*, Jan. 1995, p. 49)

**PULL IN (TO).** Bring in, as in people or money. See also DRAW.

"Hogan hopes the new programs and formats will pull in some younger viewers, but the emphasis is on getting more business from existing customers." (*Business Week*, July 31, 1995, p. 83)

**PULL IT OFF (TO).** Succeed.

"However, WALL STREET is not so sure the company can pull it off. The rush into new markets comes at a time when trouble is brewing for MCI's core long-distance business." (*Fortune*, Oct. 2, 1995, p. 107)

**PULL PUNCHES (TO).** Hold back, (boxing).

"Mary Shapiro, . . . says she plans to quickly 'send out some clear signals' that her office won't pull any punches in policing brokers and dealers." (*Wall Street Journal*, Dec. 6, 1995, p. C1)

**PULL STRINGS (TO).** Use one's influence.

**PULL THE PLUG (TO).** Terminate something.

"Cathay Pacific Airways Ltd.'s January decision to pull the plug on plans for a flight-training center in Australia—despite the promise of a multi million-dollar tax break—dealt a serious blow to the Australian government's strategy for expanding foreign investment down under." (*Worldbusiness*, March/April 1996, p. 8)

**PULL THE RUG FROM UNDER (TO).** Undermine; suddenly cease support for.

"Worse, foreign commercial banks might be tempted to pull the rug from under Japanese banks in the interbank markets." (*Banker*, Aug. 1995, p. 6)

**PULL THE STRING(S) (TO).** Track a problem to resolution; manage, control.

"Future graduates of Ecole Nationale d'Administration . . . manage big companies, and pull the strings of the centralized economy" (*Business Week*, Nov. 18, 1994, p. 31)

**PULL THE WOOL OVER SOMEONE'S EYES (TO).** Deceive.

**PUNCH IN/PUNCH THE CLOCK (TO).** Report for work; punch a time card at a factory.
"If a student is late, she must punch in on the keypad and report to the feared attendance office." (*Automatic ID News*, Sept. 1994, p. 37)

**PUNT (TO).** Give up (football).

**PURE PLAY.** Investment in a company that is in only one market or industry.

**PURGE AND MERGE (TO).** See MERGE AND PURGE.

**PUSH COMES TO SHOVE (WHEN).** A hostile situation.
"However, the federal government is more nearly synonymous with politics, programs and agencies that most Americans value highly and, when push comes to shove, want to preserve more than they want either to cut the deficit or balance the budget." (*Brookings Review*, Fall 1995, p. 40)

**PUSH THE ENVELOPE (TO).** Always trying to do better (aeronautical engineering).
"Crystal is always pushing the envelope. When he gave her the go-ahead, the child . . . would race down the base path and score." (*Wall Street Journal*, April 24, 1996, p. B1)

**PUSH UPSTAIRS (TO).** Promote someone out of the way.

**PUT A DAMPER ON (TO).** Discourage.
"The demise of President Clinton's healthcare reform plan has not put a damper on employer's efforts to reduce healthcare costs by joining forces." (*Compensation & Benefits Review*, March/April 1995, p. 15)

**PUT EVERYTHING ON THE LINE (TO).** Risk everything on the business.

**PUT IT IN THE ROUND FILE (TO).** Throw it away.

**PUT ON THE SPOT (TO).** Challenge or pressure someone openly.

**PUT OUT TO PASTURE (TO).** Pressure someone to retire.

**PUT THE MEAT ON THE TABLE (TO).** Discuss the important parts of a business negotiation.

"My boss always used to say, 'let's put the meat on the table.' As a Hindu this seemed very strange to me." (Dr. Niren Vyas, USCA, 1995)

**PUT THE SQUEEZE ON (TO).** Put under pressure.

"Windows 95 will not necessarily put the squeeze on Apple Computer Inc.'s Macintosh operating systems." (*Computer Reseller News*, Aug. 24, 1995, p. 14)

**PUT UP OR SHUT UP (TO).** Become part of the team or keep quiet; prove what you say is true.

"In addition, 1995 will be the year that vendors have to 'put up or shut up.' Instead of issuing yet another round of future oriented press releases, vendors must demonstrate successful implementations of large-scale management solutions in customer environments." (*Computer World*, Jan. 16, 1995, p. 56)

**PUT YOURSELF IN YOUR PARTNER'S SHOES (TO).** Try to understand the other person.

**PYRAMID.** An unethical or illegal financial scheme. See also PONZI SCHEME.

"In the wrong hands, the pyramid-commission concept can easily be manipulated into a pyramid scheme, in which the driving philosophy is to corral as many new distributors as possible and then ride their backs until the pyramid collapses." (*Working Woman*, April 1995, p. 44)

# Q

**Q.E.D. (QUOD ERAT DEMONSTRANDUM).** That which was to be proven (Latin).

**Q RATING.** A measure of a celebrity's name recognition. Advertisers frequently use celebrity testimonials and want to know in advance which "stars" are currently most popular.

**Q 1, 2, 3, 4.** Abbreviation for first, second, third, and fourth quarter of a business year.

**QT (ON THE).** Quiet, without others knowing.

**QUALITY AWARDS.** Citations given by governments recognizing organizations that are leaders in TQM*. The three major awards are: the Malcolm BALDRIDGE Award (U.S. private sector), The President's Award for Quality (U.S. public sector), and the Deming Prize (Japan). The Baldridge Award has become quite competitive, with winning corporations using the award in their marketing promotions.

**QUALITY CIRCLES.** Management and worker groups that focus on improving the substance and value of their products.

"Muscadine, Iowa based Grain Processing Corporation began implementing quality circles in 1982 as a means of getting employees to work together to identify, analyze, and solve problems that negatively affect quality, productivity and safety." (*Supervisory Management*, July 1995, p. 7)

**QUALITY MANAGEMENT.** Analysis of production processes and statistical error to improve efficiency and performance.

"Quality gurus W. Edward Deming, J. M. Juran, Philip B. Crosby, Armand V. Fiegenbaum, Kaoru Ishikawa, and other pioneers of quality management who wrote influential works between the 1950s and 1970s, . . . developed and refined many of the statistical process measurement techniques used in TQM*." (*The Public Manager*, Winter 1992–93, p. 45)

**QUALITY OF LIFE.** Living conditions.

**QUALITY TIME.** Short but satisfying periods of time spent with family members. Harried executives often talk about spending quality time with members of their family.

**QUEEN BEE.** Office matron; woman in charge of an office. The phrase is considered offensive, sexist.

"The jury is the Queen Bee of the American legal system, reputedly all-powerful but in practice immobilized, groomed and force-fed by a swarm of functionaries." (*Wall Street Journal*, July 21, 1995, p. A12)

**QUICK AND DIRTY.** Cheap, easy, but often second-rate solution to a problem.

"The poverty researchers couldn't have known at the time that their quick and dirty index would guide social and economic policy in the U.S. for decades to come." (*Wall Street Journal*, April 22, 1996, p. A22)

**QUICK BUCK.** Money made fast.

"Quick Buck story: If some hell of a nice guy offers you a high-return, can't lose investment, keep your check book in your pocket." (*Forbes*, June 21, 1993, p. 236)

**QUID PRO QUO.** Something for something (Latin). Many business agreements have implicit quid pro quo understandings.

"That suited the IRA [Irish Republican Army] fine, until Prime Minister John Major attached his quid pro quo: Elections must precede all-party talks." (*Wall Street Journal*, Feb. 13, 1996, p. A14)

# R

**RACE THE CLOCK (TO).** Work feverishly to complete something before a deadline.

"The two sides raced the clock to resolve a conflict over China's piracy of music, movies and computer services." (*Wall Street Journal*, June 17, 1996, p. A 11)

**RACKET.** Noise; special business deal that is very profitable and may or may not be legal.

"But the king of this racket is New York's inimitable Alfonse D'Amato, parlaying his dual role as Banking Committee chairman and head of the Senate Republican Campaign Committee." (*Wall Street Journal*, July 7, 1995, p. A15)

**RACKETEER INFLUENCED AND CORRUPT ORGANIZATION ACT (RICO).** A federal law designed to address problems of organized crime in the United States. RICO has also been used to convict people of insider trading and other financial industry violations.

**RACK-JOBBER.** Distributor who monitors and stocks store shelves.

**RACK UP (TO).** Gain large amounts.

"The firm said that its review of the accounts used by Nick Leeson to rack up massive losses in Japanese stock-index futures were 'conducted with all required professional skill.' " (*Wall Street Journal*, Jan. 26, 1996, p. B12D)

**RAGS TO RICHES.** Poor to rich.

**RAG TRADE.** Clothing industry.

**RAIDER.** Outside investor trying to take over a company.

"Marty Whitman: Corporate Raider?: 'Enter Whitman, who scoops up 6.3% of Piper's shares. . . . Whitman, a savvy investor in distressed and reorganizing companies, runs a number of investment vehicles." (*Financial World*, Oct. 29, 1994, p. 28)

**RAIN CHECK.** A postponement. When an unscheduled conflict arises many Americans will apologize saying, "I'll have to take a rain check." Businesses also offer rain checks to customers when they have run out of something. The rain check promises to allow the customer to purchase the product at the price advertised.

**RAINMAKER.** Person who uses his or her influence to benefit a client. The term originally referred to Native American shamans who would attempt to make it rain.

**RAISE MONEY (TO).** Find investors.

**RAKE IN/OFF (TO).** Bring in large amounts, usually money.

"If just 15% of Windows customers upgrade to the new version, Microsoft will rake in close to $1 billion in the first year." (*Business Week*, July 10, 1995, p. 94)

**RANDOM WALK THEORY.** Stock market theory that past share movements are of no use in predicting future changes.

**R-AND-R.** Rest and recreation (military).

**RASPBERRY (THE).** Disapproval, usually associated with a flatulent sound.

"Japan has given Snapple the raspberry." (*Wall Street Journal*, April 15, 1996, p. B1)

**RATCHET.** Incentive system where management increases its equity in a company if the firm does well.

**RATEBUSTER.** Worker who produces more than other workers doing the same task.

**RATE CARD.** Standard advertising prices for media. In the 1990s, increased competition has forced most media in the United States to discount from published rates.

**RATING.** The television or radio audience, expressed as a percentage of the total population; evaluation of credit risk. The major rating services in the United States are Duff & Phelps, Fitch, Moody's, and Standard & Poors. Their rating scales vary slightly but range from AAA* to D.

**RAT RACE.** Today's high-pressure business environment.
"Money can't buy the kind of approval many executives crave, they say. And as far as leaving the rat race to set up the ideal life-style: for many 'that day never comes.' " (*Wall Street Journal*, Feb. 26, 1996, p. R5)

**REACH.** The number of different people who see or hear a commercial.

**READ MY LIPS.** A promise. President George Bush pledged, "Read my lips, no new taxes," but he then agreed to a compromise budget plan that raised taxes.

**REAGANOMICS.** The economic programs of the Reagan administration (1980–88). Reaganomics emphasized lower marginal tax rates, increased defense spending, and placed constraints on social programs. Originally the Reagan program also included promises to balance the budget, but Reaganomics resulted in the highest U.S. budget deficits ever.

**REAL ESTATE INVESTMENT TRUST (REIT).** A company that manages a portfolio of real estate properties. REITs are usually publicly held trusts which, under special investment laws, must distribute 95% of its NET income annually to investors.
"REITs invest in real estate or mortgages. As publicly traded stocks, REITs produce portfolio income." (*Fortune*, Dec. 8, 1986, p. 36)

**REALITY CHECK.** Comparison of perceptions with available evidence. Suggesting that someone needs a reality check is an unflattering comment that they have a distorted perspective of what is happening.

**REALLY!** That is amazing!

**REAL WAGES.** Wages adjusted for inflation.

**RECORD PACE.** Fastest rate.

**RED CARPET/RED CARPET TREATMENT.** Plush, fancy; fit for royalty.

"Cities weren't rolling out the red carpet for $6-an-hour jobs during the fourth quarter." (*Wall Street Journal*, Jan. 3, 1996, p. F1)

**RED CHIPS.** Shares of top-quality Asian companies.

"As if to confirm the vote of confidence in Hong Kong's future a growing number of red chip companies, Hong Kong–listed companies with substantial interests in mainland business, are seeking a listing on the Hong Kong Stock Exchange." (*Institutional Investor*, July 1994, p. 176)

**RED-EYE (THE).** Overnight flight.

**RED FLAG.** Warning sign.

"What are the red flags that he, and to some extent analysts at Alex. Brown & Sons and Hambrecht & Quist, among others missed?" (*Wall Street Journal*, March 7, 1996)

**RED HERRING.** An act of deception; an advance copy of a prospectus for the issue of new securities.

"Some consumers, environmentalists and public-power advocates believe the Energy Policy Act of 1992, which was supposed to bring consumer choice to the electric power market, is just another red herring that will let the utilities continue to operate as unregulated monopolies behind a facade of competition." (*Electrical World*, July 1995, p. 68)

**RED-LINING.** Illegal practice wherein lenders do not make loans in certain geographic areas red-lined on a map.

**REDNECK.** Low-class person (derogatory).

"The local convention and visitors bureau has stepped up marketing efforts, pitching the beach once dubbed the Redneck Riviera to 20 campuses and initiating plans to slip brochures into thousands of college dorm rooms in the Southeast, Northeast and Midwest." (*Wall Street Journal*, Jan. 3, 1996, p. F1)

**RED TAPE.** Bureaucratic delays.

"Foreign investors, he points out, can now buy up an Indian company with a minimum of red tape." (*Worldbusiness*, March/April, 1996, p. 37)

**REDUCTION IN FORCE (RIF).** LAYOFFS.

**RE-ENGINEERING.** Reorganizing a company. See also DOWNSIZING.

"Therefore, a commitment was made to provide workshops to help employees through the adjustments caused by re-engineering, training to upgrade the skills and competency of the work force, and education and development programs to improve employee's problem-solving capabilities." (*Wall Street Journal*, Nov. 13, 1995, p. B1)

**REHAB.** Rehabilitation. Someone who has gone to rehab has been treated for substance abuse.

**RELATIONSHIP MARKETING.** Firm's attempt to develop long-term links with customers.

**RENAISSANCE CONSULTING.** Supposedly new ideas.

"Renaissance consulting is the new spin on what was called 'process consulting'—a continuing cycle of testing and monitoring." (*Wall Street Journal*, May 30, 1996, p. A1)

**RENEGADE.** Maverick, one who refuses to conform to norms.

**REP.** Representative.

**REPURCHASE AGREEMENT (REPO).** Financial market agreement where the seller agrees to repurchase a security at a set price and stated time in the future. Repos are used in money markets for short-term investments and cash management.

**REQUEST FOR PROPOSALS (RFP).** Government agencies and grant foundations announce RFPs to solicit projects related to the issues and objectives of the group.

**RESOLUTION TRUST CORPORATION (RTC).** U.S. government agency created in 1989 to address the Savings & Loan crisis. The RTC took over bankrupt S&Ls, merging some with financially sound banks and liquidating the assets of others.

**REST ON ONE'S LAURELS (TO).** Sit back, relax based on past performance.

**RETIREMENT.** Repayment of a debt.

**REVENUE-MANAGEMENT.** 1990s use of computers to analyze past sales, predict patterns of consumer purchases, and adjust prices accordingly.

"The guru of revenue-management consultants, Robert Cross, . . . will publish a book on the practice this year. 'It's knowledge-based pricing,' he says. 'Sometimes it's analyzing gigabytes of marketing data, and sometimes it's basic observation." (*Wall Street Journal*, Jan. 5, 1996, p. B1)

**REVENUE STREAM.** Flow of money coming in over time.

"The company has 'a high recurring revenue stream, expanding profit margins and experienced management,' says Mr. Mullins." (*Wall Street Journal*, March 4, 1996, p. C1)

**REVOLVING-DOOR SYNDROME.** When government officials and regulators quit or retire and then take employment with the companies they regulated.

"Ann Eppard for months has been Exhibit A for what critics call the revolving door between government service and lobbying. She became the transportation industry's most successful new lobbyist when her old boss, Rep. Bud Shuster, assumed the chairmanship of the committee that oversees such issues last year." (*Wall Street Journal*, Feb. 9, 1996, p. A4)

**RICHES TO RAGS.** Rich to poor.

**RIDE THE MARKET (TO).** Make money with the general growth in the economy.

**RIDE SHOTGUN (TO).** Oversee; to be ready to take on problems or conflicts (nineteenth-century American West).

"Ingrassia says the Kerkorian effort, which includes Lee Iacocca to ride shotgun, stems strictly from the personalities of the two protagonists." (*Wall Street Journal*, April 19, 1995, p. A14)

**RIDING HIGH.** Confident; successful.

**RIG (TO).** Fix a machine; illegally predetermine an election; illegally manipulate a market; a truck or other piece of large machinery.

**RIGHT-BRAIN PERSON.** A person with creative skills.

**RIGHT-HAND MAN/WOMAN.** Trusted assistant; a person who works closely with the manager.

**RIGHT OF FIRST REFUSAL.** Part of a business contract giving a company the first chance to produce or distribute a new product. In the publishing industry, a publisher frequently asks for the right of first refusal of an author's next work.

**RIGHT OFF THE BAT.** From the beginning (baseball).

**RIGHT TO WORK.** Rule allowing employees to work without being required to join a union. Most Southern states in the United States have "right to work" laws.

**RING A BELL (TO).** Stimulate memory.
   "Initial public stock offerings were red hot, as well, with several new issues making jaw-dropping leaps. (Does Netscape ring a bell?)" (*Wall Street Journal*, Jan. 2, 1996, p. R1)

**RINGER.** An expert or professional who pretends to be an amateur. A ringer might be brought in to gain an advantage over the competition.

**RING UP (TO).** Record a sale; to telephone.
   "Such a process would diversify ownership of the plants among dozens of companies, both Mexican and foreign, and ring up high prices in the process." (*Wall Street Journal*, March 13, 1996, p. A7)

**RIPOFF.** A swindle, scam.

**RISK-FREE RETURN.** The interest rate on the lowest-risk investment, usually a U.S. government security, for that period of time. Investors compare the yield premium over the risk-free return versus the risk of the investment.

**RISING STAR.** Someone who is being promoted quickly within the organization.
   "Mr. Shoemaker, who grew up in a union family in a working-class neighborhood in Davenport, Iowa, long has been a rising star in the powerful UAW." (*Wall Street Journal*, March 21, 1996, p. B4)

**R. J. REYNOLDS (RJR).** Originally a U.S. tobacco company, in 1989 RJR was the object of the largest takeover in U.S. corporate history.

**ROAD MAPS.** Guides.
   "Such attention to detail includes defining the target market, evaluating the company's position in the marketplace, sizing up the competition and studying trends. Collectively, this information is a road map showing how to position the product, how to design and package it, how

to advertise it or even whether to advertise." (*Nation's Business*, Aug. 1995, p. 32)

**ROAD SHOW.** Seminars held by investment underwriters to attract investors to a new issue.

**ROBBER BARONS.** Powerful companies who manipulate a market; American Industrial Revolution industrialists who monopolized markets.

**ROBERT'S RULES OF ORDER.** Book providing guidelines for managing official meetings.

**ROB PETER TO PAY PAUL (TO).** Take funds from one account or project for use in another.

**ROCK THE BOAT (TO).** Cause trouble.
    "Mr. Krol, says S. G. Warburg analyst Paul Reman, is a detail-oriented, low-key manager 'who won't rock the boat' but is the 'right person' for DuPont at this time." (*Wall Street Journal*, Sept. 28, 1995, p. B12)

**ROLL BACK (TO).** Return prices to a previous lower level after regulatory action by government.

**ROLL-OUT.** A full advertising campaign; the sale of corporate assets to investors; ceremony introducing a new aircraft.

**ROLLOVER.** The movement of money from one investment to another. Employees switching jobs will often rollover their retirement funds from one plan to another, avoiding the problem of creating taxable income.

**ROLODEX.** Brand name for a popular business card index file.

**ROOF OVERHEAD.** A building or shelter; basic necessities.

**ROOT CAUSE.** Primary reason.

**RO-RO.** Roll-on/roll-off maritime shipping.

**ROSY SCENARIO/"ROSIE SCENARIO."** Very optimistic prediction.
    "The full name, Rosie Scenario, serves as a personification of hope. One political take on George Bush's election in 1988 was that it means Rosie Scenario assumptions on economic growth and interest rates." (*Safire's New Political Dictionary*, 1993, p. 672)

**ROUND FILE.** Waste basket.

**ROUND LOT.** A hundred shares of stock.

**RUB ELBOWS WITH (TO).** Interact with; work together.
"Erlene Mikels . . . attended the group's BOOT CAMP a year ago to rub elbows with experts in the field and to polish up rusty marketing techniques." (*Wall Street Journal*, Jan. 16, 1996, p. B1)

**RUBBER CHECK.** A check for which there are not sufficient funds, a bounced check.

**RUBBER-STAMP (TO).** Approve without review.
"The 107-year-old Bar falls under the purview of the state Supreme Court, whose members belong to the Bar and nearly always rubber-stamp the Bar's budget." (*Wall Street Journal*, Feb. 21, 1996, p. F1)

**RUBE GOLDBERG.** Less-than-professional, especially a repair job. Rube Goldberg was an early twentieth-century cartoonist whose works depicted complex machinery with improbable parts. The machines involved enormous effort that resulted in very little.
"These Rube Goldberg routes may sound costly and inefficient and they are!" (*Wall Street Journal*, March 17, 1995, p. A1)

**RUG RANKING.** Situation where a secretary or assistant's career path is tied to the fate of the boss.

**RULE OF 72.** Financial formula for determining how long it will take for an investment to double in value. Dividing 72 by the interest rate will yield the number of years needed.

**RULE OF THUMB.** Basis for measuring, deciding.
"If you followed all of WALL STREET's rules of thumb, your hands would be full—and your pockets empty. Many of these financial-planning edicts are undoubtedly helpful. But oftentimes, you will find that the rules are just too costly to implement." (*Wall Street Journal*, Dec. 5, 1995, p. C1)

**RUN.** In banking, a sudden surge in withdrawals. During the Depression, many banks suffered runs and went bankrupt.

**RUN BY (TO).** Visit; repeat; discuss briefly with an associate or supervisor, usually as a courtesy rather than as a request for their input.

**RUN INTERFERENCE FOR (TO).** Assist, protect (football).

**RUN IT UP THE FLAG POLE AND SEE WHO SALUTES (TO).** Introduce a new product or idea and see what happens.

**RUN-OF-THE-MILL.** Ordinary.

**RUN THE SHOW (TO).** Be in charge.

**RUN UP (TO).** Incur.

**RUN WITH IT (TO).** Implement an idea.

**RUST BELT.** Manufacturing areas in the Midwest that have lost jobs to competitors in other regions using newer technology.

# S

---

**SACK (TO).** Fire, dismiss. See also SEND PACKING.

**SACRED COW.** Something which cannot be questioned or eliminated (Hinduism). Managers sometimes have favorite projects that become sacred cows even if they are not profitable and have little chance of becoming so.

"The French government, already under intense pressure from unions striking today to protect its Social Security reform, is preparing to attack another deficit-ridden sacred cow, the French railways." (*Wall Street Journal*, Nov. 24, 1995, p. A1)

**SAFE HARBOR LEASING.** Financial measure to reduce tax liability.

**SAFEKEEPING.** Out of danger; to be responsible for.

**SAFETY NET.** Government social welfare programs designed to assist the poor. The term is derived from the net protecting circus high-wire performers should they fall.

"What's more, farmers are more cautious because they expect the government safety net to drop." (*Wall Street Journal*, March 21, 1996, p. A1)

**SAIL THROUGH (TO).** Successfully complete or be approved with little or no difficulty.

"By understanding how the system works and avoiding some common missteps, investors can increase the odds that their accounts will sail through the transfer process smoothly." (*Wall Street Journal*, Jan. 19, 1996, p. C1)

**SALARY COMPRESSION.** Situation where new employees are paid more than current employees.

**SALLIE MAE.** Nickname for government student loan marketing program, college loans. See also SLMA.

**SALT MINE.** Work, drudgery.

**SAMURAI BONDS.** Bonds denominated in Japanese yen but issued by non-Japanese firms.

**SANDBAG (TO).** Mislead; attack from behind; sales representative's practice of not reporting sales in the current year once quota or bonus standards are reached.

"Every other company has used them, too—preannouncements to try to sandbag their competitors." (*Wall Street Journal*, Feb. 16, 1995, p. B1)

**SATELLITE OFFICES.** Branch offices.

**SATISFICING.** Aiming for a predetermined level of profit or sales, rather than profit maximizing.

**SATURDAY NIGHT SPECIAL.** Sudden attempt to buy a large share of stock in a company; a cheap gun.

**SCAB.** A non-union worker; strikebreaker.

"Keith Butterfield, Caterpillar's chief spokesperson, . . . also notes that the rules apply to managers, too. And that while offensive or inflammatory language—'scab' for example—is banned, calm discussion of the labor dispute isn't." (*Wall Street Journal*, Jan. 12, 1996, p. A1)

**SCALABLE.** Easily enlarged or reduced in size or scope.

**SCALE.** The wages paid for different types of jobs in a company.

**SCALP (TO).** Sell tickets at prices above their face value.

**SCAM (TO).** Cheat someone out of something; swindle.

**SCAPEGOAT.** Person who is blamed for a mistake.

**SCARLET LETTER.** Symbol of shame. The term comes from Nathaniel Hawthorne's *The Scarlet Letter*.
"Executives at Wal-Mart Stores Inc. are wearing something new on their lapel these days: a quarter . . .—representing the retailer's dismal fourth quarter—as a sort of scarlet letter." (*Wall Street Journal*, Feb. 23, 1996, p. B1)

**SCHLEMAZEL.** Bad luck; a person who has bad luck (Yiddish).

**SCHLEMIEL.** An awkward person; a nerd (Yiddish).

**SCHLEP.** Stupid, awkward person (Yiddish).

**SCHLOCK.** Inferior merchandise (Yiddish).

**SCHMOOZE.** Mingle with the crowd at a business function. See also GLAD-HANDING.
"Somebody at a supplier house has been reviewing the day's orders and noticed that Mr. Fukuda has dropped their wheat beer from his line-up. Two kegs a week is worth $10,000 a year in sales, so Mr. Fukuda gets schmoozed by a lot of beer distributors." (*Wall Street Journal*, April 2, 1994, p. A15)

**SCHMUCK.** Obnoxious person (Yiddish).
"Jacob, the SCHLEMIEL, has worked in the kitchen of a restaurant for years. One night the regular waiter is sick and Jacob is given the chance to replace him. Henry, the schmuck, is a rich powerful businessman who comes to the restaurant each night. David, the SCHLE-MAZEL, is also at the restaurant on his first date with the girl of his dreams. Henry orders Jacob to bring him fresh soup, and when it is brought, angrily and loudly sends it back as too little. As Jacob, the Schemiel, turns to return to the kitchen, Henry, the schmuck, sticks out his foot sending Jacob tumbling and the soup flying, landing all over David, the Schlemazel." (Jerry Rosenthal, Zip's Business Services, 1996)

**SCOOP.** A news story one is the first to report.

**SCORCHED-EARTH STRATEGY.** Anti-takeover defense of selling off a company's most attractive assets (military).

**SCORE POINTS/BIG (TO).** Impress.

"The ruling coalition is using the banking mess to score points against its opponents." (*Wall Street Journal*, June 14, 1995, p. A1)

**S CORP.** See SUBCHAPTER S CORPORATION.

**SCRAP (TO).** Terminate a project.

**SCUTTLEBUTT.** Rumors, gossip.

"Perhaps predictably, there's a certain amount of stock-market scuttlebutt that another suitor might surface for Intuit of Menlo Park, California." (*Wall Street Journal*, May 23, 1995, p. C2)

**SECOND-CLASS.** Not as good, inferior.

**SECONDS.** Products with defects.

**SECOND STRING.** Not the top-quality people (sports).

"He says hotels are often staffed with second-string employees, trainees or temporary workers over the major holidays." (*Wall Street Journal*, Dec. 22, 1995, p. A1)

**SECULAR TREND.** Long-term, as opposed to cyclical or seasonal, trend.

**SECURITIES AND EXCHANGE COMMISSION (SEC).** Federal agency set up after the collapse of the stock market during the Depression. The SEC is responsible for oversight of the securities market.

**SEED MONEY.** Initial funds needed to start an enterprise.

**SEIGNORAGE.** The profit made by government from the production and issue of coins.

**SELF-ADDRESSED STAMPED ENVELOPE (SASE).** Preaddressed, postage-included, envelope. When requesting information or submitting work to a publisher an SASE is often expected.

**SELL ONE, MAKE ONE (SOMO).** Production management slogan or policy.

"SOMO companies enjoy increased efficiency: no inventory pileups, no excess paperwork." (*Across the Board*, Nov./Dec. 1993, p. 42)

**SELL SHORT AGAINST THE BOX (TO).** In the stock market to sell borrowed shares while owning the same or similar shares that one delivers later to complete the transaction.

"The most popular is to 'sell short against the box.' To do this, you arrange through a broker to sell borrowed securities (a short sale) while owning essentially identical securities that you deliver later to complete the short sale." (*Wall Street Journal*, Oct. 27, 1995, A1)

**SEND PACKING (TO).** Dismiss, fire from a job.

"Mr. Foley isn't the only Washington state incumbent the voters may send packing." (*Wall Street Journal*, Sept. 23, 1994, p. A14)

**SEND TO SIBERIA (TO).** Transfer an employee to an insignificant or out-of-the-way division of the company.

**SET UP SHOP (TO).** Open for business.

"So Mr. Volchok and others have set up shop as on-call fixers for the many professionals who depend on computers but don't have a clue about how to fix them." (*Wall Street Journal*, March 29, 1996, p. B1)

**7 BY 24 SCHEDULE.** Seven days per week and twenty-four hours per day. An overworked employee's perception of his or her workweek.

**SEVEN S MODEL.** Seven factors can be used to measure a company's performance: strategy, structure, systems, style, shared values, skills, and staff. The model was developed by Richard Pascale, Tom Peters, and Robert Waterman when they were consultants for McKinsey & Co.

**SEVEN TOOLS OF QUALITY.** An inclusive term for seven key statistical tools used in analyzing quality through SPC*: control of Shewart charting, check sheets, flowcharts, histograms, scatter diagrams, Pareto charts, and fishbone or Ishikawa charts." (*The Public Manager*, Winter 1992–1993, p. 45)

**SHAKEDOWN.** Pressuring someone for a bribe to ensure things work out correctly. See PROTECTION MONEY.

**SHAKE OUT.** Period in which unprofitable businesses leave the market.

"For now, industry observers give GM's competitors the nod but acknowledge that it will be some time before the winners and losers fully shake out." (*Wall Street Journal*, March 20, 1996, p. B1)

**SHAPE UP OR SHIP OUT.** Do the job or leave (command).

**SHARE.** The percentage of TV watchers (or radio listeners) who are watching (or hearing) a particular show.

**SHARK.** Swindler.

**SHARK REPELLENT.** Any measure taken by a company to avoid a takeover attempt. See also POISON PILL.

**SHELTER FROM THE ELEMENTS (TO).** Protect from the weather or adversity.

**SHIFT DIFFERENTIAL.** Added pay for working less desirable hours.

**SHINDIG.** Big party. See also BASH.

**SHOESTRING (ON A).** Small budget.

**SHOOT FOR (TO).** Attempt, set as a goal.
"Should small-cap investors shoot for the stars or root around in the dirt looking for bargains in the coming months?" (*Wall Street Journal*, March 4, 1996, p. C1)

**SHOOT THE BREEZE (TO).** Talk casually.

**SHOOT-THE-BULL (TO).** Exaggerate; engage in casual conversation.
"The innovative course is seen by some as a 'neat shoot-the-bull session' which cheats the kids, and by others as a remedy for teens who haven't been exposed to healthy relationships at home." (*Wall Street Journal*, Nov. 9, 1994, p. B1)

**SHOP FLOOR EMPLOYEES.** Lower level employees.

**SHOP TALK.** Discussion of the latest business news or rumors.
"At one Scott facility he clambered over machines, discussed their workings with the factory crew and easily slipped into shop talk." (*Wall Street Journal*, June 27, 1994, p. B3)

**SHORT (TO).** Sell stock not owned by the seller, based on the assumption that the stock's price will decline.
"Traders who sell securities 'short' borrow stock and sell it, betting that the stock's price will decline and they can buy the shares back later at a lower price for return to the lender." (*Wall Street Journal*, Oct. 20, 1995, p. C20)

**SHORT INTEREST.** The number of borrowed shares that have not been purchased for return to the lender.

**SHORT SQUEEZE.** Situation where prices of a stock rise sharply, forcing traders who have SHORTED the stock to buy the stock in order to cover their position, in the process pushing the price of the stock even higher.

**SHORT SHRIFT.** Ignored, lack of respect.

"Tougher labor and environmental standards, which the Clinton Administration says would protect Americans from unfair competition, are favored by labor unions and environmentalists, two Democratic constituencies. But they get short shrift in Latin America." (*Wall Street Journal*, Jan. 9, 1996, p. A12)

**SHORT-TERM DISABILITY (STD).** Temporarily not able to work.

"I once met an employee who proudly announced to me that she had STD. I beat a retreat, unsure of what sexually transmitted disease she had. Later, I discovered she meant short-term disability." (*Wall Street Journal*, Aug. 1, 1994, p. A14)

**SHOTGUN APPROACH.** A marketing campaign without a specific target audience/goal.

"But many analysts remain skeptical about its [Rubbermaid's] vaunted growth plans, including doubling to 30% its foreign sales as a percent of total sales by 1998. . . .'It's an aimless, shotgun approach,' said Bonita Austin of Prudential." (*Wall Street Journal*, June 12, 1995, p. B4)

**SHOT/SHOOT ACROSS THE BOW.** A warning, to warn.

"The lawsuit, she says, is a 'shot across the bow' to municipalities using illegal means to keep out competitors, which 'seems to be a much more common practice than we were aware of.' " (*Wall Street Journal*, June 3, 1996, p. A1)

**SHOUTING MATCH.** Loud, noisy argument.

**SHOW THE DOOR (TO).** Get someone to leave; to dismiss someone.

**SHRINK.** Losses due to shoplifting.

**SHYLOCK.** Moneylender, especially one who charges exorbitant interest rates (Shylock is a character in Shakespeare's *Merchant of Venice*). See also POUND OF FLESH.

**SICKOUT.** When workers by pre-arrangement CALL IN SICK (a form of union protest).

**SIDECAR.** New York Stock Exchange CIRCUIT-BREAKER that restricts trading when the S&P 500* index falls twelve points in one day.

**SIDE EFFECT.** Additional impact or consequence of an action.

**SIGNATURE LOAN.** An unsecured loan.

**SILICON VALLEY.** Santa Clara Valley, California, center of the U.S. computer industry.

**SIMPLIFIED EMPLOYEE PENSION (SEP) PLAN.** Retirement plan where both the employee and employer can contribute.

**SINK ONE'S TEETH IN (TO).** Become involved in.

**SINKING FUND.** Funds set aside to pay off a bond or preferred stock. Many companies create sinking funds, managed by a custodian, as a means to increase investor confidence and reduce the cost of borrowing.

**SINKING INTO THE SUNSET.** Slowly disappearing. Products, like records and cassettes, that have reached the maturity stage of the product-life-cycle slowly sink into the sunset.

**SIN TAX.** Taxes on cigarettes and alcohol. The Clinton administration wanted to pay for expanded healthcare coverage through increases in sin taxes.

**SIPHON OFF (TO).** Remove or steal (usually refers to money).
"Indeed, Osceola County officials are now considering projects intended to siphon off business from Orange County: a new merchandise mart, a world trade center and a convention complex." (*Wall Street Journal*, Feb. 7, 1996, p. F1)

**SIT ON ONE'S WALLET (TO).** Refuse to purchase or spend.

**SITTING DUCK.** Defenseless target.
"Because of its size, diabolical complexity, and lax management practices, the Medicare program is a sitting duck for con artists, thieves and degreed opportunists." (*Wall Street Journal*, Aug. 25, 1995, p. A8)

**SITUATION NORMAL, ALL FOULED UP (SNAFU).** Half-serious, half-humorous employee comment implying inept management.

**SIX OF ONE, HALF A DOZEN OF ANOTHER.** It is all the same.

**SKELETONS IN THE CLOSET.** Problems that others are not aware of.

**SKIMMING.** Pricing policy where a firm initially charges a high price but later gradually lowers the price to increase sales.

**SKULL SESSION.** An intense briefing or discussion among members of a business team.

**SKY-HIGH.** Extremely lofty.

**SKY'S THE LIMIT.** Anything you want, there is no limit.

**SKYROCKETING.** Increasing rapidly.
   "Reeling from 1995's skyrocketing price increases in raw materials, specialty surfactant suppliers in the U.S. are struggling to recoup eroding profit margins and maintain growth in an increasingly competitive industry." (*Chemical Marketing Reporter*, Jan. 22, 1996, p. SR24)

**SLAM-DUNK.** Something that is easily accomplished (basketball).
   "Bancomer officials think those performance goals are a slam-dunk and say the option adds a full 20 centavos a share to the final purchase price." (*Wall Street Journal*, Feb. 28, 1996, p. B2)

**SLAP IN THE FACE.** An insult.

**SLEEPING BEAUTY/SLEEPER/SLEEPING GIANT.** A company with many attractive assets but not well known to investors.

**SLIPSTREAM (TO).** Include something hoping no one will notice.

**SLOWDOWN.** A decrease in activity or growth.

**SLUSH FUND.** Money available to use without review. During the Richard Nixon administration, the Committee to Re-Elect the President was accused of keeping slush funds for campaign efforts, including Watergate.

**SMALL BUSINESS ADMINISTRATION (SBA).** Government agency which provides information and credit to small businesses in the United States. The SBA has been criticized as a welfare program for corporate America.

**SMALL CAP.** In the U.S. financial market, small cap companies or mutual funds include those with less than $500 million in value.

**SMALL FRY.** Unimportant individual.

**SMALL POTATOES.** Small amount of money, number.
   "In fact, most MUD players today are science-fiction and fantasy fans who are also university students—a group that numbers itself in the thousands. That's 'small potatoes' compared with an estimated 35 million to 40 million players of action games made by Nintendo Co. and Sega Enterprises Ltd., says Lee Isgur." (*Wall Street Journal*, Sept. 15, 1995, p. R16)

**SMART MONEY.** Informed prediction.

**SMOKE AND MIRRORS.** Deception, the use of "magic" to make appear real.

**SMOKING GUN.** Evidence of a problem.
   "The INTERNAL REVENUE SERVICE thought it had evidence of a smoking gun. An internal report late last summer showed a tax-credit program for building low-income housing had produced $6 billion in 'potential fraud and abuse.' " (*Wall Street Journal*, Jan. 10, 1996, p. B1)

**SMOOTH SAILING.** Without problems or restrictions.

**SNAKE-CHECK.** Reviewing a plan for hidden consequences.

**SNAKE OIL.** A product that is represented to do more than it actually will; a misrepresentation.

**SNOWBALL (TO).** Increase rapidly, get out of control.

**SNOW JOB.** Persistent persuasion; deception.

**SOFT CURRENCY.** A currency that is not readily accepted for payment in international trade.

**SOFT LANDING.** An economic slowdown without going into a recession.

**SOFT MONEY.** Campaign contributions which can be used for a variety of purposes by the political party.

**SOIL BANK.** Department of Agriculture program which pays farmers not to use part of their land, conserving these resources.

**SOMETHING IS ROTTEN IN THE STATE OF DENMARK.** Corrupt, not like it should be. The phrase is from *Hamlet* by William Shakespeare.

**SONG AND DANCE (ROUTINE).** Lively sales presentation meant to be entertaining as well as informative.

**SORRY.** Ineffective; incompetent (Southern).

**SOS.** International distress signal; abbreviation for "same old shit."

**SO-SO.** Not very good; barely OK*.

**SOUNDING BOARD.** A person or group who provide feedback for ideas.

**SOUP-TO-NUTS.** Everything.
   "Schwab will pitch itself as a soup-to-nuts provider. At a time when employers are clamoring for more investment options, Schwab will dazzle them with a choice of more than 1,300 funds at 185 fund companies." (*Wall Street Journal*, April 3, 1996, p. C1)

**SPAMMING.** Mass marketing using e-mail addresses.
   "The proliferation of unsolicited commercial messages, regarded by many 'Net surfers' to be 'junk e-mail,' has taken on new proportions with the availability of 27 million e-mail addresses. . . . The use of such a list is known in the Internet world as 'spamming.' " (*DM News*, Jan. 13, 1996, p. 4)

**SPECIAL DRAWING RIGHTS (SDRs).** International money first created by the INTERNATIONAL MONETARY FUND in the late 1960s. SDRs are considered part of a country's official reserve assets and can be transferred between the country's accounts.

**SPIN.** Sales technique; implication.

**SPIN-DOCTORING.** See DOCTORING.

**SPIN-OFF.** A separate product or business created from an existing one.

**SPOT MARKET.** The open market for petroleum or other commodities.

**SPREAD.** The difference between two prices: in the stock market, the difference between the bid and ask price; in bond markets, the difference between the yield for two securities of different maturities or quality.

**SPRING FOR (TO).** Pay for.

**SQUARE ONE.** The beginning.

**SQUEAKY-CLEAN.** Immaculate; honest.

**SQUEEZE OUT (TO).** Pressure to eliminate or reduce.

**STACK THE DECK/CARDS (TO).** Dishonestly prearrange something.

**STAKE.** A financial interest, investment.

**STAKE A PLACE (TO).** Win the honor of being included.

**STANDARD & POOR'S (S&P).** One of the two (with Moody's) major investment information and rating services in the United States.

**STANDING ROOM ONLY (SRO).** Sales technique where buyers are given the impression that there are many other customers waiting in line to purchase the product.

**STAR STATUS.** Celebrity.

**START UP (TO).** To begin.

**STAR WARS.** Nickname (from a movie) for the Strategic Defense Initiative, a Defense Department program designed to use satellites with lasers to protect the U.S. from attack. President Ronald Reagan embraced the Star Wars program, spending billions of dollars on it. It is still in the "development" stage.

**STATE-OF-THE-ART.** Modern, the latest technology.

**STATISTICAL MASSAGE.** Make the numbers show what one wants. See also FORCE THE NUMBERS.

**STATISTICAL PROCESS CONTROL (SPC).** A variety of statistical measurement techniques to control work processes.

**STATS.** Statutes (law); statistics (business).

**STEALTH MARKETING.** Strategy designed to target market customer groups without competitors knowing what one is doing.

**STEM THE TIDE (TO).** Stop or slow a negative trend.

**STICKER PRICE.** List price, full retail price. See also MANUFAC-
TURER'S SUGGESTED RETAIL PRICE.

**STIFF (TO).** Swindle; refuse to pay; cheap person.

**STOCK KEEPING UNITS (SKU).** Inventory control codes.

**STOCK-OUT.** When a particular item is not available.

**STONEWALL (TO).** Refuse to cooperate.
  "Because of the legal obligations under Delaware law, it is harder—
though clearly not impossible —for companies and their managements
to stonewall a hostile bidder." (*Wall Street Journal*, Nov. 8, 1995, p. C1)

**STORM BACK (TO).** Recover, return to the contest.

**STRADDLE.** Simultaneously selling puts and buying calls in a stock
at the same STRIKE PRICE.

**STRAIGHT UP.** A drink without ice; honest.

**STRAIGHT YEARS.** Years in a row.

**STRANGLE.** Simultaneously selling call options or buying put options
in a stock at different STRIKE PRICES equally OUT OF THE MONEY.

**STRATEGIC ALLIANCE.** Currently important business partner.
  "Strategic alliance is pure puff and simply a gimmick to make someone feel important enough so that they are lured into a costly proposition. Stay away from anyone who uses strategic in combination with any
other term, as in strategic marketing, strategic decisions, strategic
opportunity and so forth." (*Supervision*, Jan. 1994, p. 6)

**STRAW MAN.** Initial proposal created to elicit responses and changes.
  "Using a straw man, the group has something to critique and change as
opposed to having a meeting and just asking what should we do." (Mary
Grace Allenchey, AT&T, 1996)

**STRAW THAT BROKE THE CAMEL'S BACK.** Issue or problem that
destroys one's patience.
  "I was just starting to get into the story when there it was, at the end
of the third paragraph—the proverbial straw that broke the camel's
back. 'Internet—enabled.' " (*Business Marketing*, Sept. 1995, p. 6)

**STREAMLINE (TO).** Reduce or cut back.

**STREET NAME.** Securities held in the name of the brokerage house rather than the customer.

**STREET SMARTS.** Practical experience; not easily deceived.

"Often, he has ousted genteel, well-respected publishers in favor of street-smart assiduously non-Ivy league types like himself." (*Wall Street Journal*, Jan. 4, 1996, p. A1)

**STRENGTHS, WEAKNESSES, OPPORTUNITIES, AND THREATS (SWOT).** Market analysis technique comparing a firm to its competitors.

**STRETCH OUT PAYABLES (TO).** Pay over a longer period of time.

**STRIKE OUT (TO).** Fail; initiate a new activity or enterprise.

"But when Mr. DiCarlo threatened to strike out on his own, Mr. Boudreau offered a compromise: John Hancock agreed to become a minority owner of a new hedge-fund firm that Mr. DiCarlo would run." (*Wall Street Journal*, March 22, 1996, p. C23)

**STRIKE PRICE.** The price at which the stock or commodity underlying a call or put option may be purchased or sold until the option expires.

**STRING ALONG (TO).** Deceive, to be not fully honest with someone.

"The Bosnian Serbs' prevarication over the peace plan seems to be another attempt to string along negotiations and to sow division between Russia and the West until the Serbs get what they want." (*Wall Street Journal*, July 21, 1994, p. A10)

**STRIP (TO).** Separating a bond's principal from its interest payments.

**STRIP-AND-SELL (TO).** Sell off assets.

**STRIP MALL.** Small shopping mall designed to be convenient to suburban consumers.

**STRIPPED-DOWN.** Basic model. A product without added features. See also BARE-BONES.

"On Tuesday the House postponed action on a stripped-down bill to lend compliance flexibility to small businesses and require periodic reviews and phase-outs of ineffective regulations." (*Wall Street Journal*, March 7, 1996, p. A20)

**STRONGHOLD.** Powerful area.

**STRUCTURAL UNEMPLOYMENT.** Unemployment due to changes in technology which eliminate the need for some people's skills.

**STUDENT LOAN MARKETING ASSOCIATION (SLMA), "SAL-LIE MAE."** Federally created stock-held corporation designed to increase the availability of loans for college students. Sallie Mae purchases loans from financial institutions lending to students.

**STYLIN' DUDS.** Nice clothes.

**SUBCHAPTER S CORPORATION.** Special provisions in the INTERNAL REVENUE SERVICE Code allowing a corporation under certain conditions to be taxed as if it were a partnership, thereby avoiding corporate taxation.

**SUB PAR.** Substandard.

**SUNBELT.** Warmer areas in the United States.

**SUNSET PROVISIONS.** Terms written into laws that cause the law to expire unless reinstated by the issuing legislature.

**SUNSHINE LAWS.** Laws providing for open government. Under sunshine laws most government proceedings cannot be held in secret.

**SUPER.** Supervisor.

**SUPER BOWL INDICATOR.** Stock market phenomenon that if the team from the National Football League wins the Super Bowl, the stock market moves higher.

**SUPER 301.** U.S. trade law which identifies countries violating trade agreements and requires sanctions against them unless corrective action is taken.

**SUPPORT LEVEL.** Price at which investors come back into the market and buy a stock.

**SURE THING.** Yes; a certainty.

**SURFING THE NET.** Exploring the Internet.

**SURVIVAL OF THE FITTEST.** The strongest competitor will survive. See also ECONOMIC DARWINISM.

**SUSTAINABLE DEVELOPMENT.** Economic development based on the principles of conservation and of using renewable rather than non-renewable resources.

**SWEAT BULLETS (TO).** Be very worried; to work very hard.

**SWEAT EQUITY.** The time and effort that goes into early stages of a project without compensation.

**SWEATSHOP.** Low-wage, unhealthy factory, often hiring illegal aliens.

**SWEETEN THE DEAL (TO).** Increase the offer.
   "You had better be prepared to be better next year, and the next year after that; to continually sweeten the deal. Today's consumers expect it." (*Wall Street Journal*, Feb. 12, 1996, p. A14)

**SWEETENER.** Special bonuses to make an investment more attractive. See also KICKER.

**SWEETHEART CONTRACT.** A labor contract that favors the employer.

**SWEETHEART DEAL.** A mutually profitable but illegal arrangement, usually between a business and a government agency.

**SWIPE (TO).** Run a credit card through a scanner; steal.

**SYNERGY.** Mutually beneficial interaction, as between components of companies.
   "The Paramount-QVC-Viacom menage a trois is predicated on the idea that Paramount's activities have so much synergy with those of its suitors that the resultant merger will establish a streamlined, efficient communications conglomerate capable of dominating its industry into the 21st century." (*Institutional Investor*, Jan. 1994, p. 176)

# T

**TAB.** The bill or check, especially for drinks at a bar.

"The Wisconsin Supreme Court has ruled that a government order does not trigger an insurer's obligation to pick up the tab for environmental cleanups." (*National Underwriter*, Nov. 7, 1994, p. 4)

**TAFT-HARTLEY (ACT).** 1947 law that amended the Wagner Act (1935), protecting the rights of workers to join unions and allowing government injunctions to stop strikes in times of national emergencies.

**TAG (TO).** Price tag; label; to assign.

**TAG LINE.** Last few words of a commercial, designed to enhance listener recall.

"Falcon Candy Co. has obtained the licensing rights to manufacture Forrest Gump Chocolates, an assortment of chocolates with the tag line 'Life Is Like a Box of Chocolates.' " (*Discount Store News*, April 3, 1995, p. F12)

**TAIL OFF (TO).** Decline.

**TAILOR-MADE.** Specially designed.

**TAKE.** Revenue from an event.

**TAKE A BATH (TO).** Suffer a financial loss. See also TAKE A BEATING.

**TAKE A BEATING (TO).** Lose; get a bad deal; be crushed.
   "U.S. exports to Mexico will take a beating from the peso devaluation, but the beating may be less severe than it has been in the first few months of devaluation." (*Forbes*, April 24, 1995, p. 49)

**TAKE A FLIER (TO).** Make a speculative investment in.

**TAKE A PASS (TO).** Decide against.

**TAKE A POSITION (TO).** Make an investment in.

**TAKE ADVANTAGE OF (TO).** Avail oneself of an opportunity, sometimes at the expense of others.

**TAKE CARE OF BUSINESS (TO).** Deal with what needs to be done.

**TAKE DOWN A PEG (TO).** Deflate or lower someone.

**TAKE FIVE.** Take a break (may or may not mean a five-minute break).

**TAKE FOR A RIDE (TO).** Swindle or cheat.

**TAKE-HOME (PAY).** Worker's income after all deductions are taken out.

**TAKE IT ON THE CHIN (TO).** Be defeated, lose a large amount of money (boxing).

**TAKE NO PRISONERS.** Management exhortation to be highly competitive.
   "Ken Dooley, president of the Holland Sweetener Co., noted that today's beverage business is evolving from an era of take no prisoners, CUT-THROAT COMPETITION into one in which open-minded firms share the wealth in partnerships." (*Beverage World*, Aug. 1995, p. 64)

**TAKE THE KNOCK (TO).** Sell at a loss.

**TAKE THE PACKAGE (TO).** Agree to severance benefits being offered by a company.

**TAKE ON PARTNERS (TO).** Add more owners to a business.

"Drug makers are beginning to look beyond their own labs and take on partners such as biotech mavericks, smaller drug companies and academic researchers." (*Business Week*, Oct. 17, 1994, p. 204)

**TAKEOVER.** Buying control of another company.

**TAKEOVER TARGET.** A business investors want to buy.

**TALK OUT OF TURN (TO).** Speak too candidly.

**TALK TURKEY (TO).** Speak seriously.

"Little Pluto wants to talk turkey about the dangers of plutonium exposure." (*Wall Street Journal*, Jan. 21, 1994, p. B1)

**TALKING HEADS.** A derisive advertising term for commercials that consist of a pitch man/woman extolling the virtues of a product.

"The latest ground-breaking feature in the convergence technology of desktop videoconferencing is the ability to view several talking heads on one computer screen simultaneously." (*Computer Reselling News*, July 3, 1995, p. 49)

**TANK FARM.** Collection of oil tanks.

**TAP INTO (TO).** Access, make contact with.

**TAPE.** Ticker tape. Before computers, stock market investors and specialists would watch the tape for the latest prices of stocks.

**TAPPED OUT.** Broke, penniless; lacking opportunity.

"Although many professionals contend that Asian hotbeds such as Japan and Hong Kong are tapped out for the moment, they cite Malaysia, Australia, and New Zealand as hot prospects." (*Black Enterprise*, Jan. 1994, p. 35)

**T-BILLS.** Treasury bills, short-term borrowing instruments of the U.S. government.

**TAX HAVEN.** Country where individuals are protected from tax scrutiny. The Cayman Islands are known as a tax haven.

**TAX HOLIDAY.** A period during which a firm is exempt from taxes. Cities and states in the United States will offer a variety of incentives including tax holidays as a way to attract new businesses.

**TAX IDENTIFICATION NUMBER (TIN).** Internal Revenue Service identification number.

**TAX SHELTERED ANNUITY (TSA).** Insurance product that allows an investor avoid or reduce tax liabilities. Taxes are usually deferred until the end of a specified period of time.

**TEACHERS INSURANCE AND ANNUITY ASSOCIATION (TIAA).** Pension fund targeting teachers throughout the United States. In the 1990s TIAA, like CALPERS*, became an important force in U.S. markets, using its financial power to influence corporate and government policy.

**TEAM PLAYER.** Someone who works for the betterment of the group (sports).
   "Team player, an employee who substitutes the thinking of the herd for his own good judgment." (*Fortune*, Feb. 20, 1995, p. 22)

**TEASER.** A low introductory rate on a loan, or a high initial rate on a deposit.

**TECHNO-SHIFT IDIOCY.** Constant upgrades of technology requiring continuous retraining in order to be able to use the equipment.

**TECHNOMICS.** Economical technology; cheap, accessible technology.

**TEETERING ON THE BRINK.** Almost failing.
   "The economy teeters on the brink of a domestic debt trap." (*Euromoney*, Sept. 1994, p. 175)

**TEMPUS FUGIT.** Time flies (Latin).

**TEMPS.** Temporary workers.
   "Fewer than 10 people, some of them temps, are working in Ally & Gargano's Manhattan offices." (*Advertising Age*, Aug. 21, 1995, p. 33)

**TENDER LOVING CARE (TLC).** Careful handling.

**10–K.** Annual financial report required for all large, publicly held companies.

**TEN-SPOT.** A ten-dollar bill.

**TENDER FORM.** Bid form used for buying U.S. Treasury securities.

**TEQUILA EFFECT.** The impact of the decline in the Mexican economy (1994) on securities from other Latin American countries.

**TESEBONOS.** Mexican bonds that are convertible to dollars.
"In the aftermath of the peso crisis financial market readers learned a new word, tesebonos. These short-term notes issued by the Mexican government were denominated in pesos but their value was indexed to the U.S. dollar. In effect the Mexican government was assuming the risk of devaluation." (*Understanding NAFTA and Its International Business Implications*, 1996, p. 307)

**TEST THE WATERS (TO).** Look for opportunities; experiment.
"In Poland, Microsoft will test new waters of HYPE when it takes journalists there on a submarine ride to see what a world without windows looks like." (*Advertising Age*, Sept. 28, 1995, p. 33)

**TEXAS LEAGUER.** A person of minor importance (baseball).

**THANK GOODNESS IT'S FRIDAY (TGIF).** Expression of relief that the workweek is over.

**THAT AIN'T PEANUTS.** That's a large sum of money.

**THAT DOG WON'T HUNT.** That idea will not work. A Southernism popularized by President Lyndon Johnson.
"That Dog Won't Hunt: Why what you've always done won't work anymore." (*Cornell Hotel & Restaurant Administration Quarterly*, Oct. 1994, p. 82)

**THIN ICE.** Unlikely to succeed; dangerous situation.
"As they vie for Vietnamese readers, foreign publishers tread on thin ice. A handful of foreign publishers have gained a toehold in Vietnam, but their presence has clearly alarmed elements of the government." (*Far East Economic Review*, Dec. 29, 1994, p. 98)

**THINK TANK.** Institute that studies social or other issues.
"Sedgwick Noble Lowndes is seeking funds to establish a foundation that will act as a think tank to formulate proposals for a new welfare system for China as it moves from a centrally managed economy to a socialist market economy." (*Business Insurance*, June 19, 1995, p. 32)

**THINKING OUT OF THE BOX.** Creating new processes, not just changing existing methods.

"Hilliard speaks of customer service, relationship marketing, asset utilization, and thinking out of the box with the zeal of a fast-growth company entrepreneur." (*INC.*, July 1995, p. 45)

**360-DEGREE FEEDBACK.** Performance appraisal by all of the people one works with, including bosses, peers, subordinates, and customers.

"So it goes on the controversial subject of so-called 360–degree feedback, which is reaching fad status in corporate America." (*Wall Street Journal*, July 9, 1996, p. B1)

**THIRD DEGREE.** Intense questioning.

"The Third Degree: Financial institutions should hold an interrogation, not an interview, with any employee it reasonably suspects has taken funds." (*Savings & Community Banker*, July 1994, p. 45)

**THREE-MARTINI LUNCH.** A business meal with large quantities of alcohol to loosen up the customer. During the Carter administration, the term came to represent special tax privileges accorded to business, the ability to include lavish entertainment as a business expense.

"There's a sense that the daily slack of earlier eras—the weekday golf foursome, the bridge games and vegetable gardens, the three-martini-lunches, chats across the fence, and pure, uncontrollable laughter—is fast disappearing." (*Wall Street Journal*, March 8, 1996, p. R1)

**THREE MILE ISLAND.** Location (Pennsylvania) of a 1979 nuclear reactor accident that became a symbol of the dangers of nuclear energy.

**THREE STEPS AND A STUMBLE.** Rule of thumb that stock market prices will decline if the Federal Reserve increases interest rates on three consecutive occasions.

**THRIFTS.** Savings banks, savings and loans.

**THROUGH THE MILL.** Subjected to a difficult experience.

"Instead, they're putting the analysts through the mill as third-party witnesses. Their files no doubt contain many documents relevant to Castano's issues, and tobacco executives who have spoken to them might have made comments unrecorded elsewhere but preserved in their notes." (*Wall Street Journal*, Aug. 30, 1995, p. A11)

**THROW IN THE TOWEL (TO).** Admit defeat.

"A look at household finances show why consumers are not ready to throw in the towel. The Federal Reserve reports net financial assets acquired by households continued to rise in the first quarter of 1995, at an annual rate of $556.6 billion." (*Business Week*, June 26, 1995, p. 31)

**THROW IT AGAINST THE WALL AND SEE IF IT STICKS (TO).** Try a new idea and see if it works (cooking).

"It seems like every day, someone is throwing something new up against the wall to see if it sticks." (*Wall Street Journal*, April 8, 1996, p. C1)

**THROW MONEY AT (TO).** Spend large sums of money in hope of solving a problem.

"Companies can throw money at economic problems all day, but low-cost interventions may work as well, at least in the short term." (*Training*, May 1995, p. 47)

**THROW ONE'S WEIGHT AROUND (TO).** Use one's influence.

**THUMBS DOWN.** A negative response.

"Some TOP-GUN economists at the Federal Reserve Bank of Kansas City were thumbs-down on FED Chairman Alan Greenspan when it came to the dollar. They challenged his view." (*Business Week*, Sept. 18, 1995, p. 46)

**TICKER TAPE.** See TAPE.

**TIDAL WAVE.** An overwhelming amount.

"In releasing this tidal wave of HYPE, Microsoft has positioned Windows 95 not as something as dull and vaguely nerdish as an improved operating systems, but as a bona fide cultural event." (*Marketing Computers*, Aug. 31, 1995, p. 37)

**TIED UP.** Very busy.

**TIE-IN.** Joint promotion; two or more promotion campaigns that are linked together.

"General Mills is aiming up with a 4th-quarter promotion for Berry Berry Kix that puts 3 super heroes in every box. The tie-in with Marvel Comics' popular X-Men characters is designed to attract kids older than Kix's 6 to 8 year old core group." (*Brandweek*, Sept. 11, 1995, p. 14)

**TIE UP MONEY (TO).** Cause money to be unavailable for use.

**TIGER BY THE TAIL (TO HAVE).** A big, fast moving issue; situation/problem that could easily be lost, with grave consequences.

"Companies moving into groupware with a passion are finding they have a tiger by the tail. Groupware is hard, both technically and culturally." (*Forbes*, June 5, 1995, p. 76)

**TIGHT-ASS.** Person who is inflexible.

**TIGHT MONEY.** When the money supply is constrained, resulting in higher interest rates.

**TIGHTWAD.** A miser, stingy person.
   "He is such a tightwad. Ninety-three years old and flying coach to save money." (Kathy Folsom, Aiken, SC, 1996)

**TILL.** Cash register.

**TIME FRAME.** A clearly scheduled process with specific beginning and ending points.

**TINKER (TO).** Make small adjustments.

**TINSEL TOWN.** Hollywood, California.

**TIREKICKER.** Person who inspects a product (car) with little intention of making a purchase at that time.

**TOASTMASTERS.** Nonprofit organization that helps business people develop their speaking skills.

**TOE THE LINE (TO).** Follow orders.
   "To its credit, Snapple tried to toe the line with regard to discounting and CMAs." (*Beverage World*, Feb. 1995, p. 94)

**TOE TO TOE (TO GO).** Compete directly and aggressively (boxing).
   "If Coke is going to improve in the U.S., as well as overseas, we can go toe to toe." (*Wall Street Journal*, Feb. 26, 1996, B3)

**TOKENISM.** The hiring or placing of minorities in visible positions to make the company look like it promotes and values its minority employees.

**TOMBSTONE.** A newspaper advertisement listing the underwriters of new stock.

**TOO RICH FOR MY BLOOD.** Too expensive.

**TOP BANANA.** Leader.

**TOP BRASS.** Senior executives.
   "Since 1988, when founder Frank Stronach left to start a political career, auto-parts supplier Magna has had trouble keeping its chief

executives. However, all of the squabbling among the top brass has not stopped Magna from becoming one of the most successful automotive suppliers in North America." (*Financial World*, Jan. 31, 1995, p. 48)

**TOP DOG.** Boss.
"Unfortunately, there are still a lot of DINOSAURS in the executive suites, according to the authors, but if they do not learn new tricks, these top dogs may not be around long enough to experience the other facets of the job." (*Public Relations Journal*, May 1994, p. 20)

**TOP GUN.** Important, powerful people.

**TOP-OF-THE-LINE.** The brand leader in a market.
"The 83 MHz chip is Intel's top-of-the-line upgrade processor." (*Computerworld*, Sept. 18, 1995, p. 45)

**TOP NOTCH.** The best, most important.
"Top-notch leaders think of themselves as master storytellers. They use anecdotes to teach, chart complex social territory, perpetuate important values, and point the way through change." (*Working Women*, Sept. 1995, p. 14)

**TOPPED OUT.** Stuck in a position without hope of promotion or opportunity.
"Some executives have become victims of corporate cost cutting initiatives and have been eliminated because they are too costly for their organizations. They have topped out." (*Executive Excellence*, Dec. 1994, p. 15)

**TOPPING THE LIST.** Number one, the best.

**TOPSY-TURVY.** Disorderly.
"Not only has NSC Corp. survived the topsy-turvy asbestos abatement market intact, but it seems to have landed atop the heap of its competitors." (*ENR*, July 31, 1995, p. 35)

**TOTAL QUALITY MANAGEMENT (TQM).** Continuous improvement.
"While implementing total quality management (TQM) procedures, many companies have focused so much on management, that the quality of their products has suffered." (*Journal of General Management*, Autumn 1995, p. 47)

**TOUCH ALL BASES (TO).** Consult with everyone involved in a decision.

"The Education Division's goal is to have a coherent program at all educational levels that touches all bases." (*Chemical and Engineering News*, Jan. 1995, p. 57)

**TOUCH BASE (TO).** Consult with casually (baseball). See also RUN BY.

"Instead of being bottled up in offices, the new vice presidents walk the hallways and touch base constantly with what is going on." (*HR Magazine*, Jan. 1995, p. 84)

**TOUGH NUT TO CRACK.** Difficult person or problem.

**TOUGH THING TO DO.** Very difficult.

**TOURIST TRAP.** A cheap, tasteless tourist attraction.

"Although detractors call such 'entertainment alleys' little more than GLITZY tourist traps, a handful of big-name, deep-pocketed restaurant companies see them as the future." (*Restaurants and Institutions*, May 1, 1995, p. 50)

**T-PLUS THREE.** Stock market settlement rule: trade day plus three days.

**TRACK RECORD.** Past performance.

"Research conducted in the U.S. in 1994 shows that a corporation's track record on citizenship and responsibility-related matters such as employee treatment, environmental protection, and community relations is now being considered in addition to price, quality, and service in corporate purchasing decisions." (*Marketing News*, Sept. 11, 1995, p. 8)

**TRAFFIC BUILDER.** Marketing promotion designed to generate more customers.

"Retailers say private label brings big profit numbers to the ailing non-foods section in supermarkets, and they point to it as an emerging traffic builder." (*Supermarket Business*, July 1995, p. 75)

**TRAVEL DAZZLE.** Efforts to impress the boss during a day he or she travels with you.

**TRIAL PERIOD.** Time allowed to test and try the product.

**TRICKLE-DOWN THEORY.** Economic idea that benefits to the wealthy eventually benefit poorer groups; associated with the Reagan administration.

"The trickle-down theory is supposedly the notion that the way to benefit the poor is to have the government provide benefits to the rich, which will then trickle down to the poor. However, there is no such theory." (*Forbes*, Jan. 30, 1995, p. 81)

**TRIM THE FAT (TO).** Reduce excess employees or costs; budget cutting.
"Companies are being forced to reevaluate their organization, consolidate, and trim the fat." (*Business Mexico*, March 1995, p. 46)

**TRIPLE WITCHING DAY.** The third Friday in March, June, September, and December, when three types of options expire on the same day.

**TROLLING.** Making COLD-CALLS soliciting new business (fishing).

**TROOPS.** Workers.
"Assistant Attorney General Anne K. Bingaman's antitrust troops are looking into whether, as rivals and PC makers allege, Microsoft Corp. is using anticompetitive tactics with their new software, Windows 95." (*Business Week*, July 10, 1995, p. 100)

**TRY TO TAME THE MARKET (TO).** Make money from investments.

**TUNNEL VISION.** Limited perception or understanding.
"Avoiding tunnel vision requires broadening one's view. The classic mistake is to fall in love with a specific technology." (*Datamation*, Feb. 15, 1995, p. 88)

**TURKEY.** A poorly performing investment, decision, or product line.
"Mexico's economy: A real turkey?" (*Economist*, Aug. 5, 1995, p. 68)

**TURKEY TROT.** A turkey trot is "the practice of transferring a marginal, incompetent, or problem employee from one department or job to another." (*Across the Board*, Nov./Dec. 1994, p. 52)

**TURN A SOW'S EAR INTO A SILK PURSE (TO).** Make a bad business profitable.

**TURN BACK THE CLOCK (TO).** Go back to earlier times.
"Uncertainty will continue, because the power struggle is not over between the reformers and those who want to turn back the clock." (*Business Week*, Jan. 30, 1995, p. 50)

**TURNING POINT.** The beginning of a new time or era.

**TURNKEY.** A project delivered ready for use.

"A retail customer had purchased a turnkey system from a major software house." (*Capacity Management Review*, June 1995, p. 1)

**TURN-OF-THE-MONTH (TOM) EFFECT.** Stock market phenomenon where prices tend to go up because investors receive cash to put into the market.

"Messrs. Hensel and Ziemba found that the turn-of-the-month period, defined as the last trading day of the month through the first four trading days of the next month, generated an average daily return six times that of the daily average for the rest of the days of the month." (*Wall Street Journal*, Nov. 11, 1995, p. B1)

**TURN ON (TO).** Cause excitement or pleasure; introduce people to something new.

**TWEAK (TO).** Manipulate .

"Tweak is a marvelous word. . . . At Columbia it tends to mean 'to manipulate figures so they come out the way you want them to.'" (*Institutional Investor*, Jan. 1994, p. 176)

**2-10 NET 30.** Two percent discount when a bill due in thirty days is paid in ten days.

"I knew I was beginning to understand business when I found myself telling a customer that my terms were 2–10 net thirty." (Rebecca Folsom, Sunshine Productions, 1995)

**TWADDLE.** Financial salesmanship.

"Twaddle is irrelevant, erroneous, or irresponsible financial information." (Bill Holland, KNSD-TV, Aug. 16, 1996)

**TWOFERS.** Two for the price of one.

**TYPE A.** Aggressive, compulsive (personality).

# U

**UNBRIDLED OPTIMISM.** Uncontrolled enthusiasm, feeling good. Owners of new businesses and inventors of new products frequently are blinded by unbridled optimism.

"Uncertainty and hesitation regarding the information superhighway began to affect the electric utility industry in 1994. The unbridled optimism of 12 months earlier seems to have been tempered by a new sense of economic realism." (*Electrical World*, Jan. 1995, p. 60)

**UNBUNDLE (TO).** Separate the costs of the various operations in a business.

**UNCLE SAM.** The United States government. During the War of 1812, a New York pork packer named "Uncle Sam" Wilson shipped so many barrels of pork to troops with his first two initials on each barrel that his name came to symbolize the U.S. government itself.

**UNDERCUT (TO).** Price lower than competitors.

"Dissident players, . . . think the new 6-year pact the basketball players' union and the NBA reached in mid-August would undercut players' ability to sell their services to the highest-bidding team." (*Business Week*, Sept. 4, 1995, p. 58)

**UNDER THE GUN.** Under pressure to deliver or perform.

**UNDER THE TABLE/COUNTER.** Secret, illegal. The phrase is associated with bribes passed under the table, the opposite being an ABOVE BOARD agreement.

"In places like Jakarta or Bangkok, you often have to pay under the table or else wait three days to clear the package, says Mr. Chan." (*Wall Street Journal*, Aug. 7, 1995, p. B6A)

**UNDERWRITERS LABORATORIES (UL).** Company that reviews the safety of electrical products.

**UNITED PARCEL SERVICE (UPS).** A large, privately held package delivery company headquartered in the United States.

**UNITED WAY.** Cooperative nonprofit organization that solicits donations from local businesses and distributes the funds to local charities.

**UNLOAD (TO).** Get rid of/dispose of. Managers try to unload unwanted products, divisions, or employees.

"That has led to accumulations of unsold inventory that the company has had to unload at discount prices." (*Wall Street Journal*, March 22, 1996, p. B14)

**UNQUALIFIED OPINION.** An independent auditor's opinion of a company's records.

**UP A TREE.** A difficult situation, predicament. Like a stranded animal, managers sometimes find themselves up a tree.

**UP FOR GRABS.** Available. In a dynamic, changing economy, new opportunities are up for grabs.

**UP FRONT.** In advance; honest, open.

"Expressive systems are designed to support exceptions from operating procedures, . . . none of which, by definition, can be specified up front." (*Sloan Management Review*, Winter 1995, p. 41)

**UP-FRONT MONEY.** Money paid in advance. When making sales to new customers or expensive customized products, businesses often require up-front money.

**UP TICK/UPSWING.** An increase in stock market prices, or the economy in general.

**UP TO PAR.** Meets standards. An analogy to golf, where par is considered the normal number of strokes to take on a hole.

"Included in the Golden Gate update will be access to the Internet that will include Usenet groups, FTP file servers and many popular mailing lists. But such improvements will only bring the World up to par with current on-line services." (*Adweek*, Feb. 6, 1995, p. IQ27)

**UP TO THE MINUTE.** The latest, most current.

**UPGRADE (TO).** Improve. In airline travel, to switch from economy to higher-class seating.

**UPSCALE.** Superior, better quality, often more expensive.

"[Ms.] Martin of Loews Hotels prefers to head to Paris, where her favorite hotel is the antique-filled Bristol, which she describes as upscale, small and friendly." (*Working Woman*, Oct. 1995, p. 81)

**USED CAR SALESMAN.** Fast-talking promoter.

"Nobody trusts a used car salesman, whose job—according to the stereotype—is to cover up defects and make the used look almost new." (*Safire's New Political Dictionary*, 1993, p. 837)

**USER-FRIENDLY.** Designed for easier use. The term is frequently used in discussions of computer software, but manufacturers are redesigning many products to be more user-friendly as a means to increase customer satisfaction.

# V

---

**VANILLA MODEL/PLAIN VANILLA.** Standard, ordinary. A product with few amenities is called a vanilla model. See also STRIPPED-DOWN.

"Many corporations, in fact, have stopped discussion of their risk management practices with outsiders, since they almost inevitably involve the use of some kind of derivative, even if it is only currency forwards or plain vanilla interest rate swaps." (*Global Finance*, June 1995, p. 60)

**VAPORWARE.** Products, usually referring to technology or software, that are ineffective. The term is a parody on Tupperware, a manufacturer of long-lasting plastic products.

"@dtech.96 will help you sort the solutions from the vaporware, and show you how to plan for the changes occurring in marketing communications and advertising." (*Adweek*, March 13, 1996, p. 19)

**VEG OUT (TO).** Relax, to "vegetate."

"Following the tests, Mr. Napoli likes to 'veg out' by the pool or have his body painted in mud." (*Wall Street Journal*, Jan. 19, 1996, p. B7)

**VEER OFF COURSE (TO).** Go the wrong way.

**VESTED/VESTING.** Having worked for a company the minimum amount of time necessary to qualify for various benefits.

"National City launched an employee stock option plan . . . which rewards employees for their dedication by offering those employed on May 17, 1995 . . . —once they are vested—to buy 150 National City common shares over the next 10 years for the price set on that date." (*Bank Marketing*, Aug. 1995, p. 29)

**VESTED INTEREST.** Personal financial involvement.

**VISIBLE SYMBOL.** Something one can see.

**VISION CONGRUENCIES.** Thinking the same way.

**VISION STATEMENT.** Management's prediction of the future.

"The next step is for the senior managers to meet and draft a vision statement." (*Supervisor*, March 1995, p. 24)

**VISION THING.** See VISION STATEMENT.

"It appears that vision may be the most sought-after executive characteristic of the 1990s. Even President George Bush talks about 'the vision thing.' Vision is not mystical, mysterious insight. Rather, it paints a picture of where and what the executive wants the organization to be." (*Executive Excellence*, Jan. 1990, p. 3)

**VOLDIS.** Abbreviation for "volume discounts." Many companies offer lower prices for large-volume orders.

**VOODOO ECONOMICS.** Critic's description of REAGANOMICS. The Reagan political platform included increased defense spending, decreased taxes, and a balanced budget. Critics suggested that these goals could only be simultaneously accomplished using voodoo.

" 'It's voodoo economics all over again,' Senate Minority Leader Thomas Daschle said in a statement Friday." (*Wall Street Journal*, Oct. 16, 1995, p. A3)

**VOTING STOCK.** Stock that includes the right to vote on the company's business.

**VOLUNTARY REDUCTION IN FORCE (VRIF).** Management's first method of DOWNSIZING. As part of downsizing in the 1990s, U.S. companies offer their employees incentives in order to get voluntary reductions in force.

**VULTURE FUND.** An investment fund which speculates in companies or real estate holdings that have declined significantly in value.

"MK is in the humbling position of being wholly at the mercy of its lenders, many of which now are vulture-fund BOTTOM FISHERS that have picked up MK debt in the secondary market for about 60 cents on the dollar." (*Wall Street Journal*, Feb. 29, 1996, p. R2)

# W

**WAGE FREEZE.** No raises for employees. During recessions many U.S. companies announce a wage freeze.

**WAIVER.** A release from a contract.

**WALK ON WATER (TO).** When one can do no wrong. An analogy to the biblical story about Jesus; the phrase is often used to describe someone who thinks highly of himself.

"KPMG's management consulting arm claims to have had an excellent response to its recruitment advertisement seeking consultants who could limbo dance or walk on water." (*Global Finance*, June 1995, p. 22)

**WALK THE PLANK (TO).** Take on a dangerous project or situation, one that could end one's career.

"So far, only Gonzalez's associates have been forced to walk the plank. Naturally, these scandals have not exactly bolstered Gonzalez's reputation with the voters of Spain." (*Global Finance*, June 1995, p. 49)

**WALKING PAPERS.** Notice of job dismissal. See also PINK SLIP.

**WALLPAPER.** Securities that have no value except as wallpaper.

**WALL STREET.** The financial district in lower Manhattan, New York City. Wall Street got its name in the seventeenth century, when settlers erected a wall to keep pigs out of their crops.

**WAR CHEST.** Financial resources of a company.
"Japan's industrial giants have historically used their cash troves as war chests. This has allowed exporters to slash prices abroad, grabbing more market share without worrying about profits." (*Business Week*, May 1, 1995, p. 37)

**WARM FUZZIES.** Verbal compliments.
"David Goodall, a Motorola compensation executive, tells managers 'to think beyond cash' about the 'warm fuzzies.'" (*Wall Street Journal*, Sept. 27, 1994, p. A1)

**WARRANT.** Option to purchase shares of stock in a company for a specified period of time. Many U.S. companies with less than INVESTMENT-GRADE financial ratings offer warrants with their debt securities.

**WASH.** Situation where one outcome cancels another, as in when an increase in sales to one customer offsets a loss of sales to another.

**WATCHDOG.** Person or group that scrutinizes the actions of business or government. See also NADER'S RAIDERS.
"The GENERAL ACCOUNTING OFFICE said yesterday the IRS* has delayed the start of a pilot program. The congressional watchdog agency said its review of Cyberfile plans found 'many of the management and technical weaknesses' that long have plagued IRS attempts to modernize its operations." (*Wall Street Journal*, March 27, 1996, p. A1)

**WATERING HOLE.** A bar.
"The pubs are Bruder's most successful strategy. He provides how-to-kits to investors interested in opening their own Irish watering hole." (*Fortune*, Nov. 28, 1994, p. 20)

**W-CUBED.** Whatever, wherever, and whenever you want it. To emphasize the importance of customer service, managers will claim their mantra is W-cubed.
"So instead of subscribing to some a la carte, 24-hour channel, you'll just get the show you want on demand, whenever you want it. It will be W-cubed, whatever, wherever, and whenever you want it." (*Wall Street Journal*, Feb. 16, 1995, p. A14)

**WEAR MANY HATS (TO).** Have many different responsibilities.

" 'You've got to wear a lot of hats as an adjuster,' he says. 'I've got to be a carpenter, I've got to be an attorney, I've got to be an agent. It's a salesman's job too,' he adds." (*Wall Street Journal*, Feb. 5, 1996, p. B1)

**WEARS OFF.** Does not work after a while.

**WEATHER THE STORM/TASK (TO).** Survive.

**WEED OUT (TO).** Pick out and eliminate.

"One effect of this trend will be to weed out even more people who do not produce high volume." (*Life Associates News*, May 1995, p. 122)

**WELFARE STATE.** Conservative Americans' perception that the United States is moving toward socialism.

"Senator Bob Dole has, over the years, compiled a mixed record of tax cuts and tax increases, though he has been accused by Newt Gingrich of being the 'tax collector for the welfare state.' " (*Wall Street Journal*, Feb. 16, 1996, p. A12)

**WETBACK.** An ILLEGAL ALIEN in the United States, usually describing someone who has crossed the Rio Grande from Mexico into the country.

"In 1995 the number of illegals apprehended fell by 75% to just under 250,000 and the Immigration and Naturalization Service declared: The so-called 'wetback' problem no longer exists. . . . The border has been secured.' " (*Wall Street Journal*, Nov. 9, 1995, p. A20)

**WHAT IS THE DROP DEAD?** When is the last date possible/deadline?

"Elements that should be included in a letter of intent are price and payment terms, description of assets or stock to be acquired, closing and 'drop dead' dates, a statement that the parties will enter a final agreement later in the process, and a no-shop clause." (*Small Business Reports*, May 1994, p. 44)

**WHAT LINE ARE YOU IN?** What is your work/business?

**WHEN PIGS FLY!** Never!

"James DeLong . . . flew to Dallas to recruit Southwest Airlines, the large successful low-fare carrier. They weren't successful, but Mr. De-Long was heartened when Southwest Chairman Herb Kelleher didn't give them the response he had in past meetings: 'When pigs fly.' " (*Wall Street Journal*, Feb. 6, 1996, p. A1)

**WHERE THE ACTION IS.** The center of activity. It is important for CORPORATE LADDER–climbing workers to be where the action is. An assignment which takes an employee away from the center of activity is called being SENT TO SIBERIA.

**WHIPSAWING.** Moving violently; organized labor's description of the practice by companies of creating plant-against-plant competition for survival. The threat of closings is used to extract concessions from workers.

"Political risk, even in star performers like Mexico, still can whipsaw individual issues." (*Forbes*, Dec. 5, 1994, p. 301)

**WHISTLE BLOWER.** A person who reports unethical activity to authorities. U.S. laws protect workers from retaliation by employers, but whistle blowers are often ostracized by management and fellow employees.

"Sparked by whistleblower Mark E. Whitacre, the former head of ADM's BioProducts unit, three grand juries are looking into alleged price-fixing by ADM of lysine, high fructose corn syrup and citric acid." (*Business Week*, Oct. 23, 1995, p. 34)

**WHITE ANGLO-SAXON PROTESTANTS (WASPs).** Caucasian-Americans of European descent, some WASPs perceive themselves as the aristocracy of America.

"Unlike the country's old money, bound by convention, WASP reflexes and diminishing resources, the rich today are defining a different style of monied life." (*Mediaweek*, Nov. 7, 1994, p. SS14)

**WHITE-COLLAR.** Executives, managers, professional employees.

"Now, electronically controlled machines are replacing white-collar workers throughout major corporations." (*Industry Week*, Sept. 4, 1995, p. 58)

**WHITE-COLLAR CRIME.** Crimes committed by professional workers.

"According to a recent Office of Technology Assessment (OTA) report, the idea that computers armed with artificial intelligence (AI) can curb the money laundering that accompanies drug trafficking, prostitution, and white-collar crime is fraught with technical, political, legal and cost obstacles." (*Computerworld*, Sept. 18, 1995, p. 12)

**WHITE FLAG.** Symbol of surrender.

**WHITE KNIGHT.** Good guy; in finance, a friendly buyout.

"In March, 1995 Intelligence Electronics moved swiftly to protect itself by purchasing its largest franchise, The Future Now. That was a preemptive blow to anyone trying to play the role of the white knight with a rescue plan or attempt to take away The Future Now." (*Computer Reseller News*, March 13, 1995, p. 15)

**WHITE-KNUCKLE.** Tense, stressful.

**WHITE SALE.** A special promotion of bedding products and towels.

"Both domestics and housewares are among the most price competitive categories at retail, and one finely-timed and well-focused white sale can make all the difference." (*Stores*, Aug. 1994, p. 46)

**WHITE-SHOE FIRM.** A closed, "country club–like" firm.

**WHITTLE AWAY (TO).** Slowly reduce/shrink. Like a craftsman carving a piece of wood, managers may choose to slowly rearrange or reduce a department or division.

**WHO-KNOWS-WHAT.** An unknown.

**WHOLE BATTERY.** Many, a lot of different impacts.

**WHOOPS.** Washington Public Power Supply System. WHOOPS became (in)famous in the 1980s for its inept management of multiple nuclear power plant development projects, resulting in default on its bonds, the largest default in municipal bond history in the United States.

**WIDGET.** Generic for a firm's product. A favorite term used in economics classes.

"A commentary discusses how Representative Newt Gingrich, like many technophiles, is always in danger of embracing the technocratic vision that built the regulatory state—the notion that government planners, like engineers designing widgets, can build the good society from the top down." (*Forbes*, April 10, 1995, p. 100)

**WILLY LOMANS.** Sales people. Willy Loman was the central character in Arthur Miller's play, *Death of a Salesman*.

" 'The dominant image of the American salesperson is still Willy Loman from Arthur Miller's play, Death of a Salesman: the sad-sack peddler pushing items of dubious value on unsuspecting people,' says Gene Siskel, film critic for the Chicago Tribune." (*Sales & Marketing Management*, Oct. 1993, p. 142)

**WINDOW DRESSING.** Practice of mutual fund managers of making their portfolio of investments look good for reporting to investors.

**WINDOW OF OPPORTUNITY**. Short period of time when one has the chance to take advantage of a situation.

"In the business world, you have windows of opportunity. If you miss the window you're out of business." (Mary Grace Allenchey, AT&T Company, 1996)

**WING IT (TO).** Do something without a set plan.

**WOODEN NICKELS.** See DON'T TAKE ANY WOODEN NICKELS.

**WOODSHED (TO BE TAKEN TO).** Be verbally chastised.

**WOODSTOCK GENERATION.** Anti–Vietnam War teenagers in the 1960s. The 1969 rock music festival in Woodstock, New York, symbolized this generation's challenge of existing values and policies.

**WORD-OF-MOUTH.** Information passed from person to person. In the United States, an estimated 80 percent of professional positions are filled through word-of-mouth.

**WORKLOAD COMPRESSION.** Office humor for a situation when there is a lot of work to be done in a short period of time.

**WORK-OUT (TO).** Sell by the end of the trading day at any price. See also BE FLAT. Also to restructure a problem loan so that the borrower will not default.

**WORK-OUTS.** Intense, structured conferences where managers respond to employee problem-solving proposals.

**WORK A CROWD (TO).** Impress people at a gathering by moving around the room meeting and greeting people.

"Endless Referrals discusses how to work a crowd, practical and sensible follow-up techniques and clever strategically designed promotional pieces." (*Managers Magazine*, April 1995, p. 4)

**WORKAROUND.** An ingenious, undocumented way to solve a problem.

"One workaround is to print a business letter on plain stock and then photocopy it onto the letterhead." (*MacWorld*, Dec. 1994, p.135)

**WORK LIKE A DOG (TO).** Work very hard.

"All sorts of advertisers now use the same theme: We know you work like a dog, so we work like dogs for you." (*Adweek*, May 22, 1995, p. 20)

**WORKPLACE SENSITIVITY.** Awareness of topics and language that are particularly offensive to minorities and ethnic groups.

**WORLD BANK.** See INTERNATIONAL BANK FOR RECONSTRUCTION AND DEVELOPMENT

**WREAK HAVOC.** Make a mess, do damage.

**WRINKLE (NEW).** An idea or feature that will be attractive to buyers.
" 'Miller's thinking appears to be, if you have a new wrinkle in (what remains a) very large segment, there's big potential volume to be gained,' says Benj Steinman." (*Wall Street Journal*, Feb. 1, 1996, p. B7)

**WRITE OFF.** Give up on; in accounting, to remove from a balance sheet because it no longer has value.
"Japan's Nippon Credit Bank lowered its earnings forecast for fiscal 1996 and said it will go INTO THE RED in order to write off 420 billion Yen of nonperforming loans." (*Wall Street Journal*, March 29, 1996, p. C1)

**WRITTEN ON ICE (SOMETHING).** A gift, loan, or agreement that will be forgiven or forgotten.

# X

**X OUT (TO).** Delete words from a contract. A phrase frequently used by lawyers.

**XERIOD.** A person who works for Xerox Corporation. Xerox employees refer to themselves as Xeroids, implying that they are like robots.
   "They were stymied by 'Xeroids'—veterans of the hugely successful electro-mechanical copier business who saw electronics as more threat than opportunity." (*Business Week*, Feb. 13, 1989, p. 92)

# Y

---

**YANKEE BOND.** A bond issued by non-U.S. entities trading in the U.S. stock market.

"In the corporate market a total of $450 million of corporate debt was priced, including a $250 million, two-part issue for Darden Restaurants and a $200 million Yankee bond issue for Corporation Andina de Fomento, a Caracas, Venezuela, banking company." (*Wall Street Journal*, Jan, 29, 1996, p. C1)

**YELLOW GOODS.** Products bought only rarely which offer high profit margins to retailers.

**YELLOW SHEETS.** U.S. National Quotation Bureau lists of over-the-counter corporate bonds.

**YELLOW UNION.** A company-controlled union with no real interest in representing the workers.

**YEAR-END CLOSE.** Business completed by the end of the year.

**YES MAN.** An employee whose main function is to endorse a supervisor's decisions. In many management environments, these people are easily identified by the deference they show to superiors and the condescending manner shown to subordinates. See also ASS-KISSER.

"The ubiquity of the yes man is especially puzzling to economists, who more than most people tend to believe that organizations act rationally to make the most of something, namely money." (*Fortune*, Nov. 28, 1994, p. 31)

**YOU BET.** An affirmation meaning surely or certainly. It is considered casual and less-than professional speech.

" 'Any new city, any new market poses a revenue risk,' said Mr. Kelly, 'but the Florida move does imply we are confident about our finances now and next year, you bet.' " (*Wall Street Journal*, July 14, 1995, p. C17)

**YO-YO.** To destabilize deliberately a business relationship by increasing or decreasing orders or frequently changing other arrangements; as in the toy, the business is kept on a string, going up and down.

**YO-YO STOCK.** A stock that fluctuates wildly with no apparent stable pattern.

"Textile industry sales usually follow a yo-yo path with a down year following a good one, but the industry broke tradition with its second consecutive good year in 1993." (*Textile World*, June 1994, p. 23)

**YUPPIE.** A "young urban professional person." A popular, uncomplimentary characterization of young American business people in the 1980s. It implied that these people were especially mercenary.

"Free-spending yuppies helped fuel the 1980s' retailing industry boom." (*Chain Store Age Executive*, Aug. 1993, p. 15A)

# Z

**ZERO-BASED BUDGETING.** A management policy which calls on all programs to justify every aspect of their funding at the start of each year. The idea behind this policy is that nothing is sacred and all expenditures must be continually justified.

"Zero-based budgeting is a means of rooting out waste by challenging each component of overhead on an annual basis." (*D&B Reports*, Sept./ Oct., 1991, p.48)

**ZERO-COUPON BONDS.** A bond that does not pay periodic interest but instead is sold at a discount from its face value. The value of the bond increases as the bond reaches maturity.

**ZERO POPULATION GROWTH (ZPG).** When a country's birth rate equals its death rate. In the 1970s ZPG was a popular political and social goal among environmentalists in the United States.

**ZERO-SUM GAME.** A management game theory in which advantages to one party are exactly equal to the disadvantages suffered by another. The term was popularized by Lester Thurow's 1985 book, *Zero-sum Solution*.

"The challenge is to turn reengineering from a zero-sum game, in which shareholders benefit from the pain suffered by employees, into a win-win solution for all constituencies." (*Chief Executive*, April 1995, p. 36)

**ZILCH.** Zero.
"Also Netscape has its own devotees on the Internet. They know plenty about computing, but zilch about investing." (*Wall Street Journal*, Aug. 10, 1995, p. A1)

**ZILLION.** A zillion is an exceedingly large, indeterminate number. See also JILLION.
"The idea that there are zillions of Chinese eagerly rushing out to buy anything from an offshore company at fat profits is pure bunk." (*Forbes*, Jan. 31, 1994, p. 140)

**ZINGER.** A quick and sharp response or retort.
"Mr. Moyers' moralizing has sometimes given him a sanctimonious air, but surprisingly, now that he has his own bully pulpit, it's rarely in sight. Instead, he has sent sharp, crisp zingers flying in all directions." (*Wall Street Journal*, March 13, 1995, p. A12)

**ZIP.** Zero. See also ZILCH.

**ZOMBIE BONDS.** Bonds that were thought to be valueless (dead) for which trading resumes. The term was first attributed to traders at Goldman Sachs, a large New York investment company.
"Highly speculative bonds called 'zombie bonds' have run up in recent weeks, though they pose a risk to investors." (*Wall Street Journal*, Feb. 27, 1995, p. C2)

# ACRONYMS

| | |
|---|---|
| **AA** | Affirmative action; Alcoholics Anonymous; Associate of arts (degree) |
| **ABA** | American Bankers Association |
| **ACRS** | Accelerated-cost-recovery system |
| **ADA** | Americans with Disabilities Act |
| **ADR** | American depository receipt |
| **AE** | Account executive |
| **AFDC** | Aid to families with dependent children |
| **AFL-CIO** | American Federation of Labor–Congress of Industrial Organizations |
| **AGI** | Adjusted gross income |
| **AID** | Agency for International Development |
| **AIDA** | Attention, interest, desire, action |
| **AIS** | Accounting information systems |
| **A.K.A.** | Also known as |
| **AMA** | American Medical Association; American Marketing Association; American Management Association |

| | |
|---|---|
| **AMEX** | American Stock Exchange; American Express credit card |
| **ANOVA** | Analysis of variance |
| **AON** | All-or-none order |
| **AP** | Associated Press |
| **APR** | Annual percentage rate |
| **ARM** | Adjustable rate mortgage |
| **ASAP** | As soon as possible |
| **ASQC** | American Society for Quality Control |
| **AT&T** | American Telephone and Telegraph |
| **ATM** | Automated teller machine |
| **AV** | Audiovisual |
| **BA** | Bachelor of arts (degree) |
| **B&B** | Bed and breakfast |
| **BBB** | Better Business Bureau |
| **BLM** | Bureau of Land Management |
| **BLS** | Bureau of Labor Statistics |
| **BS** | Bachelor of science (degree); Bull shit |
| **BTB** | Business-to-business |
| **CAD/CAM** | Computer-aided design/manufacturing |
| **CALPERS** | California Public Employees' Retirement System |
| **CATS** | Certificates of accrual on treasury securities |
| **CBOE** | Chicago Board of Options Exchange |
| **CBOT** | Chicago Board of Trade |
| **CBS** | Columbia Broadcasting System |
| **CC** | Copy correspondence |
| **CCC** | Civilian Conservation Corps |
| **CD** | Certificate of deposit |
| **CE** | Capital expenditures |
| **CEA** | Council of Economic Advisers |
| **CEO** | Chief executive officer |
| **CEU** | Continuing education unit |
| **CFC** | Chartered financial consultant |
| **CFO** | Chief financial officer |
| **CFS** | Chronic fatigue syndrome |

| | |
|---|---|
| **CIF** | Cost, insurance, and freight |
| **CMO** | Collateralized mortgage obligation |
| **COD** | Cash on delivery |
| **COE** | Corps of Engineers |
| **COLA** | Cost of living adjustment |
| **CPA** | Certified public accountant |
| **CPI** | Consumer Price Index |
| **CPM** | Cost per thousand |
| **CSMS** | Customer Satisfaction Measurement Survey |
| **CU** | Consumers Union |
| **CV** | Curriculum vita |
| **CYA** | Cover your ass(essment) |
| **DAP** | Developmental action plan |
| **D&B** | Dun and Bradstreet |
| **DIDMCA** | Depository Institutions Deregulatory and Money Control Act |
| **DINK** | Double-Income No Kid |
| **DJIA** | Dow Jones Industrial Average |
| **DM** | Deutsche Mark |
| **DMA** | Direct Marketing Association |
| **DOA** | Dead on arrival |
| **DOMA** | Die or move away |
| **DOL** | Department of Labor |
| **EBIT** | Earnings before interest and taxes |
| **ECU** | European currency unit |
| **EEOC** | Equal Employment Opportunity Commission |
| **EFTS** | Electronic Funds Transfer System |
| **EIS** | Environmental impact statement |
| **EM** | Electronic mail |
| **EP** | European plan; Extended play |
| **EPA** | Environmental Protection Agency |
| **EPS** | Earnings per share |
| **ERISA** | Employment Retirement Income Security Act |
| **ESOP** | Employee Self-Ownership Plan |
| **ETA** | Estimated time of arrival |

| | |
|---|---|
| **EU** | European Union |
| **FAQs** | Frequently asked questions |
| **FCC** | Federal Communications Commission |
| **FDIC** | Federal Deposit Insurance Corporation |
| **FEMA** | Federal Emergency Management Agency |
| **FHA** | Farmers Home Administration |
| **FHLB** | Federal Home Loan Bank |
| **FHLMC** | Federal Home Loan Mortgage Corporation, "Freddie Mac" |
| **FICA** | Federal Insurance Contribution Act |
| **FIFO** | First in, first out accounting system |
| **FNMA** | Federal National Mortgage Association, "Fannie Mae" |
| **FOB** | Free on board |
| **FOIA** | Freedom of Information Act |
| **FOMC** | Federal Open Market Committee |
| **FRB** | Federal Reserve Board, "Fed" |
| **FSLIC** | Federal Savings and Loan Insurance Corporation |
| **FTC** | Federal Trade Commission |
| **FUBAR** | Fouled up beyond all recognition |
| **FUD** | Fear, uncertainty, and doubt |
| **FY** | Fiscal year |
| **FYI** | For your information |
| **G-7** | Group of seven |
| **GAAP** | Generally accepted accounting principles |
| **GAO** | General Accounting Office |
| **GATT** | General Agreement on Tariffs and Trade |
| **GDP** | Gross domestic product |
| **GIC** | Guaranteed investment contract |
| **GM** | General manager; General Motors |
| **GNMA** | Government National Mortgage Association, "Ginnie Mae" |
| **GO bond** | General obligation bond |
| **GOP** | Grand Old Party (Republican Party) |
| **GS** | General service (rating) |
| **GTC** | Good till canceled |
| **HLM** | Honorary life member |

| | |
|---|---|
| **HMO** | Health maintenance organization |
| **HR** | Human resources; House of Representatives |
| **HUD** | Department of Housing and Urban Development |
| **HUT** | Households using television |
| **IBRD** | International Bank for Reconstruction and Development, World Bank |
| **ICC** | Interstate Commerce Commission |
| **ID** | Identification |
| **IMF** | International Monetary Fund, "the Fund" |
| **IMHO** | In my humble opinion |
| **IPO** | Initial public offering |
| **IRA** | Individual retirement account |
| **IRC** | Internal Revenue Code |
| **IRIF** | Involuntary reduction in force |
| **IRR** | Internal rate of return |
| **IRS** | Internal Revenue Service |
| **JC** | Junior college |
| **JD** | Juris Doctor (degree) |
| **JIT** | Just-in-time |
| **JTPA** | Job Training Partnership Act |
| **KISS** | Keep it simple, stupid |
| **KKR** | Kohlberg, Kravis, Roberts |
| **KO** | Knock out |
| **K&R (insurance)** | Kidnap and ransom insurance |
| **LAN** | Local area network |
| **LBO** | Leveraged buyout |
| **LDC** | Less developed country |
| **LIBOR** | London Inter-Bank Offered Rate |
| **LIFO** | Last in, first out |
| **LP** | Limited partnership |
| **MA** | Master of arts (degree) |
| **MAP** | Modified American plan |
| **MBA** | Master of business administration (degree) |
| **MBO** | Management by objectives |

| | |
|---|---|
| **MBWA** | Management by walking around |
| **MERC** | Chicago Mercantile Exchange (nickname) |
| **MFN** | Most favored nation |
| **MIS** | Management information system |
| **MIT** | Massachusetts Institute of Technology |
| **MITI** | Ministry of International Trade and Industry (Japan) |
| **MLS** | Multiple listing service |
| **MNC** | Multinational Corporation |
| **MO** | Modus operandi |
| **MS** | Master of science (degree) |
| **MSRP** | Manufacturer's suggested retail price |
| **NAFTA** | North American Free Trade Agreement |
| **NAPM** | National Association of Purchasing Management |
| **NASDAQ** | National Association of Securities Dealers Automated Quotations |
| **NAV** | Net asset value |
| **NBC** | National Broadcasting Corporation |
| **NC** | No charge |
| **NCUA** | National Credit Union Administration |
| **NICs** | Newly industrialized countries |
| **NIH** | National Institute of Health |
| **NIMBY** | Not in my backyard |
| **NLRB** | National Labor Relations Board |
| **NOW** | Negotiable order of withdrawal; National Organization of Women |
| **NPV** | Net present value |
| **NSF** | Not-sufficient funds |
| **NYSE** | New York Stock Exchange |
| **OAG** | Official Airline Guide |
| **OAS** | Organization of American States |
| **OASDI** | Old age, survivors, and disability insurance (Social Security) |
| **OASIS** | Ordering and shipping improvement system |
| **OB** | Or better; Out-of-bounds |
| **OE** | Operating expenses |
| **OECD** | Organization for Economic Cooperation and Development |
| **OIG** | Office of Inspector General |

| | |
|---|---|
| **OMB** | Office of Management Budget |
| **OPM** | Other people's money; Office of Personnel Management |
| **OSHA** | Occupational Safety and Health Administration |
| **OT** | Overtime |
| **OTC** | Over the counter |
| **PAC** | Political action committee |
| **PC** | Politically correct; Personal computer |
| **P/E** | Price/earnings ratio |
| **PI** | Performance improvement |
| **P&I** | Principal and interest |
| **PIK** | Payment in kind |
| **PIN** | Personal identification number |
| **P&L** | Profit and loss |
| **PLC** | Product life cycle |
| **PO** | Purchase order; Post Office; Piss off |
| **POP** | Point-of-purchase |
| **POS** | Point of sale |
| **PPI** | Producer Price Index |
| **PR or pr** | Public relations |
| **PS** | Postscript |
| **PSA** | Public service announcement |
| **PUR** | People using radio |
| **PVC** | Poly-vinyl chloride |
| **QA** | Quality assurance |
| **QT** | Quiet |
| **R&D** | Research and development |
| **REIT** | Real Estate Investment Trust |
| **RICO** | Racketeer Influenced and Corrupt Organization Act |
| **RIF** | Reduction in force |
| **RJR** | R. J. Reynolds Tobacco Company |
| **ROI** | Return on investment |
| **RPM** | Revolutions per minute |
| **RR** | Railroad |
| **RTC** | Resolution Trust Corporation |

| | |
|---|---|
| **RTW** | Right to work |
| **SBA** | Small Business Administration |
| **SDR** | Special drawing rights |
| **SEC** | Securities and Exchange Commission |
| **SIC** | Standard Industrial Classification |
| **SIPC** | Securities Investor Protection Corporation |
| **SKY** | Stock keeping units |
| **S&L** | Savings and Loan |
| **SLMA** | Student Loan Marketing Association |
| **SMSA** | Standard Metropolitan Statistical Area |
| **SNAFU** | Situation normal, all fouled up |
| **SOB** | Son of a bitch |
| **SOMO** | Sell one, make one |
| **SOP** | Standard operating procedure |
| **S&P** | Standard & Poor's |
| **SPC** | Statistical process control |
| **SRO** | Standing room only |
| **SSA** | Social Security Administration |
| **STD** | Short-term disability |
| **SWOT** | Strengths, weaknesses, opportunities, and threats |
| **T&A** | Tits and ass |
| **TBA** | To be announced |
| **TGIF** | Thank goodness it's Friday |
| **TI** | Texas Instruments Corporation |
| **TIAA** | Teachers Insurance and Annuity Association |
| **TIN** | Tax identification number |
| **TLC** | Tender loving care |
| **TM** | Trademark |
| **TOM** | Turn-of-the-month |
| **TQM** | Total quality management |
| **TSA** | Tax sheltered annuity |
| **UAW** | United Auto Workers |
| **UMW** | United Mine Workers |
| **UPC** | Uniform practice code |

| | |
|---|---|
| **UPS** | United Parcel Service |
| **USCC** | United States Chamber of Commerce |
| **USPS** | United States Postal Service |
| **VA** | Veterans Administration |
| **VALS** | Values and lifestyles |
| **VAT** | Value-added tax |
| **VIP** | Very important person |
| **VM** | Voice mail |
| **VP, VEEP** | Vice president |
| **VRIF** | Voluntary reduction in force |
| **WASPs** | White Anglo-Saxon Protestants |
| **WHOOPS** | Washington Public Power Supply System |
| **WPA** | Works Projects Administration |
| **WSJ** | *Wall Street Journal* |
| **WYSIWYG** | What you see is what you get |
| **X/XD** | Ex-dividend |
| **ZPG** | Zero population growth |

# BIBLIOGRAPHY

Bennet, Steven. *Guide to Management and Technology*. Amsterdam: Information Innovation, 1994.

Burke, David. *Biz Talk 1: American Business Slang & Jargon*. Los Angeles: Optima, 1993.

Chapman, Robert L. *New Dictionary of American Slang*. New York: Harper & Row, 1986.

Downes, John, and Jordan Elliot Goodman. *Dictionary of Finance and Investment Terms*, fourth ed. New York: Barrons, 1995.

Gozzi, Raymond, Jr. *New Words and a Changing American Culture*. Columbia, S.C.: University of South Carolina Press, 1990.

Green, Jonathon. *Dictionary of Jargon*. New York: Routledge & Kegan Paul, 1987.

Green, Tamara. *The Greek & Latin Roots of English*. New York: Ardsley House, 1990.

Makkai, Adam, ed. *Dictionary of American Idioms*, second ed. New York: Barrons, 1987.

Pritchett, Thomas K., Betty M. Pritchett, and Caroline M. Fisher. *Study Guide for Schoell-Guiltinan Marketing*, fifth ed. Boston: Allyn and Bacon, 1992.

Schaaf, Dick, and Margaret Kaeter. *BusinessSpeak*. New York: Warner Books, 1994.

Wentworh, Harold, and Stuart Berg Flexner. *Dictionary of American Slang*, second ed. New York: Thomas Crowell, 1975.

**About the Author**

W. DAVIS FOLSOM is Professor of Marketing and Economics in the School of Business at the University of South Carolina–Aiken. He is involved in both local and international consulting and research activities and is the coauthor of *Understanding NAFTA and Its International Business Implications* (1996) and *International Business Agreements in the People's Republic of China* (1996).

ISBN 0-313-29991-9

90000>

EAN

9 780313 299919

HARDCOVER BAR CODE